Ancient Greek Philosophy

losophy

From the Presocratics to the Hellenistic Philosophers

Thomas A. Blackson

WILEY-BLACKWELL

A John Wiley & Sons, Ltd., Publication

This edition first published 2011
© 2011 Thomas A. Blackson

Blackwell Publishing was acquired by John Wiley & Sons in February 2007. Blackwell's publishing program has been merged with Wiley's global Scientific, Technical, and Medical business to form Wiley-Blackwell.

Registered Office
John Wiley & Sons Ltd, The Atrium, Southern Gate, Chichester, West Sussex, PO19 8SQ, United Kingdom

Editorial Offices
350 Main Street, Malden, MA 02148-5020, USA
9600 Garsington Road, Oxford, OX4 2DQ, UK
The Atrium, Southern Gate, Chichester, West Sussex, PO19 8SQ, UK

For details of our global editorial offices, for customer services, and for information about how to apply for permission to reuse the copyright material in this book please see our website at www.wiley.com/wiley-blackwell.

The right of Thomas A. Blackson to be identified as the author of this work has been asserted in accordance with the UK Copyright, Designs and Patents Act 1988.

Wiley also publishes its books in a variety of electronic formats. Some content that appears in print may not be available in electronic books.

Designations used by companies to distinguish their products are often claimed as trademarks. All brand names and product names used in this book are trade names, service marks, trademarks or registered trademarks of their respective owners. The publisher is not associated with any product or vendor mentioned in this book. This publication is designed to provide accurate and authoritative information in regard to the subject matter covered. It is sold on the understanding that the publisher is not engaged in rendering professional services. If professional advice or other expert assistance is required, the services of a competent professional should be sought.

Library of Congress Cataloging-in-Publication Data
Blackson, Thomas A.
 Ancient Greek philosophy : from the Presocratics to the Hellenistic philosophers / Thomas A. Blackson.
     p. cm.
 Includes bibliographical references (p.   ) and index.
 ISBN 978-1-4443-3572-9 (hardcover : alk. paper) – ISBN 978-1-4443-3573-6 (pbk. : alk. paper)
 1. Philosophy, Ancient. I. Title.
 B171.B53 2011
 180–dc22   2010039900

A catalogue record for this book is available from the British Library.

This book is published in the following electronic formats: ePDFs 9781444396072; ePub 9781444396089.

Set in 10.5/13pt Minion by Thomson Digital, Noida, India

1 2011

In memory of my brother, Gary Lee Blackson
(4/21/59–11/9/01). He was wonderful.

In gratitude to my children, Wyatt Dashiell and Jarrett Lee.
May they find a better way than their father and his brother.

Contents

Preface

I wrote this book for students in the ancient philosophy course required for a philosophy major in most American universities. In the case of my students, it had become clear that they were not satisfied with the traditional anthologies. The same was true for the newer, topically organized anthologies. The ancient texts are difficult to understand, and the anthologies contain little explanation.

The situation got worse when I supplemented the anthologies with some of the standard scholarly works. These works are narrowly focused, either on a period within the history or on a specific text, and my students found such detailed analysis difficult if not impossible to comprehend because so much of it presupposed a general understanding of ancient philosophy.

In the beginning, I failed to see a solution. It is impossible to give the necessary explanation in lecture, and this would not be desirable even if it were possible. Students are not interested in spending all their time taking notes. Most of them want to listen and think about the material as it is presented, and many want to be part of a discussion. For this to work, they must have explanations to consult outside class. And when I first thought about the form these explanations might take, I failed to appreciate the full range of possibilities. I thought that every form would suffer from the problem Julia Annas ascribes to those surveys that run "through a selection of works of some great ancient thinkers in chronological order." In her anthology, she says that "we are now suspicious of these narratives" and that "a single authoritative narrative, particularly one that takes the student past a selection of Great Thinkers, is false to the spirit of ancient philosophy itself" because "[p]hilosophy in the ancient world was typically characterized by discussion and debate, and by an awareness of alternative points of view . . ."[1]

In thinking more about the problem, I realized that the surveys Annas has in mind represent only one attempt to provide the necessary explanation. Instead of surveying the ancient philosophical tradition, I realized that it would be better to focus on the development of certain key lines of thought within the tradition. This approach would avoid the problem that plagues the anthologies and the surveys Annas has in mind. These works have limited value because they do not show how the selected texts belong to, and are manifestations of, the various lines of thought that push the ancient philosophical tradition forward. A series of brief discussions that takes "the student past a selection of Great Thinkers" is unlikely to provide any insight into the history of philosophy.

It is true, as Annas notes, that ancient philosophy was "typically characterized by discussion and debate" and "an awareness of alternative points of view," but this does not entail that every form of what one might term a "single narrative" is unacceptable. Arguments in philosophy rarely occur in isolation, and the arguments in the ancient philosophical tradition are no exception. The ancients constructed their arguments within the context of certain relatively continuous lines of thought, and only against this background can the student begin to understand what these philosophers thought and hence why certain interpretations of the texts are more plausible than others.

Since Socrates is the central figure in so much of the ancient philosophical tradition, my focus in this book is on lines of thought that in one way or another pass through him. I do not provide exhaustive philosophical and historical analyses of the texts that form these lines of thought. Nor do I catalogue and discuss the strong and weak points of even the most important alternative interpretations. Such extended and detailed analysis is the province of the traditional scholarly works. Similarly, I make little or no attempt to explain how different focuses would emphasize different lines of thought within the ancient philosophical tradition. In my opinion, there should be narratives that emphasize lines of thought I do not emphasize. There should also be narratives that provide different interpretations of the texts I connect into lines of thought. These narratives, I believe, would go a long way toward making ancient philosophy a little easier to appreciate for the fascinating and beautiful subject it is.[2] I hope this book is a step in that direction, but I am aware that the task is enormous and that my talents in the history of philosophy are limited.

I do not assume my discussion eliminates the need to read the works of the ancient philosophers. On the contrary, I intend this book to be read in conjunction with extended selections from their writings. I include translations of some of the most fundamental texts in the lines of thought I feature in this book, but it is necessary to read the context in which these texts occur. The traditional anthologies are helpful in this regard, and nowadays many older translations are available on the internet. The *Perseus Digital Library* (http://www.perseus.tufts.edu/hopper/) is especially valuable. It provides both translations and Greek texts, as well as many other helpful resources. The *MIT Internet Classics Archive* (http://classics.mit.edu/) also provides translations, some of which, in the case of Aristotle for example, are not currently available in the *Perseus Digital Library*.

The format of my discussion in this book is familiar in all respects except for the notes. Rather than follow the more usual practice, I have divided the notes into footnotes and endnotes. The footnotes provide supplementary information directly relevant to the discussions in which they occur. The endnotes are primarily about the scholarly literature. This division within the notes preserves the integrity of the discussions and points the way to a more advanced study.[a]

Notes

1. *Voices of Ancient Philosophy. An Introductory Reader*, 2001, xv. Annas's anthology is one of the two newer, topically organized, anthologies. The other such anthology is Terence Irwin's *Classical Philosophy*, 1999. The two primary older anthologies are *Readings in Ancient Greek Philosophy. From Thales to Aristotle* (ed. S. Marc Cohen, Patricia Curd, and C. D. C. Reeve, 2000) and *Hellenistic Philosophy. Introductory Readings* (ed. Brad Inwood and L. P. Gerson, 1997).
2. For examples of narratives that emphasize different lines of thought and take different pedagogical approaches, see Terence Irwin's *Classical Thought*, 1989, Christopher Shields' *Classical Philosophy*, 1989, and David Roochnik's *Retrieving the Ancients*, 2004. Shields and Roochnik cover the Presocratics through Aristotle. Shields intends his book to provide the reader with the sort of "encounter" he might have had with Socrates (ix). He makes less effort to set out the overall structure of ancient Greek philosophical tradition, but the suggestion is that the tradition begins with Thales and *a priori* reasoning about things, continues with the insistence on, and defense of, this sort of reasoning in Socrates and Plato, and finishes in the classical period with Aristotle's trenchant engagement with the Presocratics and with Plato (5, 36, 59, 110). Roochnik intends his readers to see, among other things, that "Plato and Aristotle are worth retrieving today because of their profound appreciation and attempt to comprehend the meaning of life" (6). To bring this out, Roochnik surveys the ancients "dialectically," in the sense of Hegel. In contrast to Shields and Roochnik, Irwin covers the entire thousand-year tradition. He begins with Homer and ends with Augustine. His primary intention is to allow the reader to "watch the growth of philosophical thinking"

---

[a] For additional information in connection with this book and the undergraduate course in ancient philosophy I teach, see my university web page: http://tab.faculty.asu.edu/.

as it unfolds (3), but he places particular emphasis on the critical response to Homer by the Presocratic naturalists, the attempt by Socrates, Plato, and Aristotle to overcome problems inherent in this Presocratic response to Homer, the attempt in the Hellenistic philosophers to produce systems of philosophy, and the revival of Platonism and the rise of Christianity (2–3, 6, 19–20, 67). These approaches, with their different emphases and methodologies, show how extraordinarily rich the ancient philosophical tradition is.

Acknowledgments

When I began to study ancient philosophy, I had little idea how to proceed. Gary Matthews showed me the way, by both example and instruction. In particular, he helped me appreciate that the texts are indications of past thought and that a primary goal in the history of philosophy is to construct a point of view that sees these texts as natural expressions of this thought. I have employed this methodology in this book, but of course the methodology itself does not carry a specific point of view. For that, I have relied heavily on the work of the late Michael Frede.

In my judgment, Frede's work is the best place to look for insight into the most general lines of thought that run through and unify the ancient philosophical tradition. Throughout this book I have relied on Frede's interpretations to help me understand the history, but I wish to acknowledge two points where my debt is particularly large. The first concerns the ancient concept of rationality. In a series of papers, Frede isolated a line of thinking about this concept that stretches throughout the ancient philosophical tradition. I have followed his interpretation. The second point concerns Aristotle's metaphysics. Aristotle's discussion is one of the most difficult in ancient philosophy, and I would have been lost if it were not for Frede's now classic work on this subject.

In addition to my debt to Matthews and Frede, I am pleased to acknowledge several more specific debts. Alan Sidelle commented on both a very early and a very late version of the manuscript. This helped me correct many errors, and more importantly he has been my good friend since we were colleagues so long ago. Many of the students in my undergraduate history class helped me improve my discussion in various places, either by making particular suggestions or, more often, by asking good questions. My teaching assistants read various drafts of the book and made many helpful suggestions. I am grateful to all these students and assistants, but I am especially grateful to Chris Burrell, Ryan Lind, Josh Reynolds, Heidi Speck, David Sundahl, and Ian Vandeventer. My colleague, Michael White, helped me better understand various parts of ancient philosophy. I am indebted to Julia Annas and Mark McPherran for invitations to the Arizona Colloquium in Ancient Philosophy. Over the years, I learned a lot listening to the views presented and discussed there. I am grateful to my editors at Blackwell. Jeff Dean gave me a second chance and helped me through the first part of the process. Tiffany Mok, Sarah Dancy, and Rob Matthews helped me through the rest of the process. I am also indebted to the readers commissioned by Blackwell. Their reviews were detailed and insightful, and I believe they helped me greatly to improve many parts of this book.

Text Acknowledgments

The author and publisher gratefully acknowledge the permissions granted to reproduce excerpts from copyrighted material in this book:

Jacques Brunschwig and Geoffrey E. R. Lloyd, eds., *The Greek Pursuit of Knowledge*, translated under the direction of Catherine Porter, pp. 5–6, 8, 9, 10, Cambridge, MA: Harvard University Press. © 2000 by the President and Fellows of Harvard College. Reprinted by permission of the publisher.

Michael Frede, *Essays in Ancient Philosophy*. University of Minnesota Press, 1987. Reprinted by permission of the publisher.

Michael Frede, "The Stoic Conception of Reason," in *Hellenistic Philosophy*, vol. II, 1994, pp. 54, 55–56, and 60. Reprinted with the permission of The International Centre of Greek Philosophy and Culture.

Michael Frede and Gisela Striker, eds., *Rationality in Greek Thought*. Oxford University Press, 1996. Reprinted with the permission of Oxford University Press.

Brad Inwood and Lloyd P. Gerson, eds., *Hellenistic Philosophy. Introductory Readings*, 2nd edn. © Hackett Publishing Company, Inc., 1998. Reprinted by permission of Hackett Publishing Company, Inc. All rights reserved.

G.S. Kirk, J.E. Raven, and M. Schofield, *The Presocratic Philosophers. A Critical History With a Selection of Texts*, 2nd edn. © Cambridge University Press, 1983. Reprinted with the permission of Cambridge University Press.

A.A. Long and D.N. Sedley., eds., *The Hellenistic Philosophers*. Vol. I: *Translations of the Principal Sources, with Philosophical Commentary*. Cambridge University Press, 1987. Reprinted with the permission of Cambridge University Press.

Introduction

The history of ancient Greek philosophy is a sequence of events and an academic discipline. The discipline seeks to understand the events from 585 BC to AD 529.[a] These two dates are themselves conventional. Thales of Miletus foretold the solar eclipse of 585. The prediction was not a philosophical achievement, but it was an achievement. Moreover, the eclipse itself figured in a memorable story.[b] The prediction thus came to mark the ascent of Thales and the naturalists over the older school of thought represented by Hesiod and the theologists. Thales and his fellow Milesian naturalists seemed to possess a new way of thinking, a way that promised the practical benefits of a deeper and more thorough understanding of things,[c] and the ancient philosophical tradition was born in an attempt to understand and evaluate this intellectual revolution.

---

[a] This roughly thousand-year period of philosophy is traditionally subdivided into three parts. Jonathan Barnes describes them. "First, there were the salad years, from 585 until about 400 BC, when a sequence of green and genial individuals established the scope and determined the problems of philosophy, and began to develop its conceptual equipment and to fix its structure. Then came the period of the Schools – the period of Plato and Aristotle, of the Epicureans and the Stoics, and of the Sceptics – in which elaborate systems of thought were worked out and subjected to strenuous criticism. This second period ended about 100 BC. The long third period was marked in the main by scholarship and syncreticism: the later thinkers studied their predecessors' writings with assiduity; they produced commentaries and interpretations; and they attempted to extract a coherent and unified system of thought which would include all that was best in the early doctrines of the Schools" (*Early Greek Philosophy*, 1987, 9).

[b] The eclipse brought an end to the war between the Lydians and Medes (Herodotus, I.74).

[c] It was thought that human beings started out exposed to a hostile environment and that the traditional technologies had developed over time in an effort to create better and more secure lives. The technological development was slow, and it moved in fits and starts. Thales and his fellow Milesian inquirers seemed to promise a way of hastening the pace by bringing ever more areas of the natural world under human control. In this way, the Milesians were part of an enlightenment. They held out the promise that human beings could think about things in a new way to move beyond the traditional practices and hence flourish in ways that had not been generally possible.

Ancient Greek Philosophy: From The Presocratics to the Hellenistic Philosophers, First Edition.
Thomas A. Blackson.   © 2011 Thomas A. Blackson. Published 2011 by Blackwell Publishing Ltd.

By convention ancient philosophy ends in 529 when the Christian Emperor Justinian prohibited pagans from teaching in the schools, but my discussion ends with the initial segment of a skeptical movement that continued from the Hellenistic Age[d] into the third century AD. It began in 268 when Arcesilaus instituted a new focus within the Academy, the institution Plato founded in 387.[e] This new focus was an instance of a more general reaction to the prior classical tradition, the tradition of Plato and Aristotle. The Epicureans and the Stoics (the other schools prominent in the Hellenistic Age) were part of this same reaction.[f] These Hellenistic schools of philosophy differed in important ways from one another, but they were united in motivation: they opposed what they understood as the philosophical excesses of the classical tradition.

The Epicureans, Stoics, and Academic Skeptics were part of a short-lived burst of creativity. The motivation uniting these schools faded around 100 BC as the reaction against the classical tradition of Plato and Aristotle was slowly replaced by a resurgence of interest in non-skeptical forms of Platonism.[1] This renewed interest in Platonism grew much stronger over time, but it did not go completely unopposed. Some of the Academic Skeptics were upset by what they understood as a failure of leadership within their own institution. Hence, they broke from the Academy to promote skepticism, as they understood it, under the name of "Pyrrhonian Skepticism."[g] Pyrrhonian Skepticism persisted into the third century AD, and although the movement is an extremely important part of the reaction

---

[d] The Hellenistic Age is the period from the death of Alexander the Great in 323 to the end of Ptolemaic Egypt and the Roman Republic in 31 BC. These dates are not significant in the history of philosophy.

[e] Plato's nephew, Speusippus, became the head of the Academy when Plato died in 347. Plato himself arranged for this succession, but subsequently the head was elected. Xenocrates followed Speusippus. Polemo followed Xenocrates. Crates followed Polemo, and Arcesilaus followed Crates.

[f] Aristotle's school had no real presence in the period, although it would be influential after 31 BC in the Roman Imperial era. "[In 272, Aristotle's] old associate, and successor as head of the Peripatetic school, Theophrastus, was fifteen years dead. With him had died the last representative of Aristotle's own encyclopedic conception of philosophy. Many of the school's adherents had drifted away to Alexandria, and even its library had been shipped abroad by Theophrastus' heir. Aristotle's own most technical philosophical work (the school texts by which we know him today) was, it seems, relatively little circulated or discussed" (A. A. Long and D. N. Sedley, *The Hellenistic Philosophers*. Vol. 1: *Translations of the Principal Sources with Philosophical Commentary*, 1987, 2).

[g] Pyrrho of Elis (360–270) is the traditional founder of Pyrrhonian Skepticism. He left no writings, but his follower, Timon of Phlius, recorded some of Pyrrho's thoughts. When Timon died, the movement lapsed until Aenesidemus broke from the Academy to re-establish skepticism, as he understood it.

against the classical tradition, it falls outside the Period of Schools and so outside the frame for my discussion of ancient philosophy in this book.

Socrates and the Period of Schools

In the ancient philosophical tradition, as well as in philosophy as a whole, Socrates is the philosopher whose name has penetrated popular culture most deeply. He abandoned a conventional life to devote himself to ethical matters. He called what he did the "love of wisdom,"[h] and although in 399 he faced a death sentence from the city of Athens rather than abandon his practice, it remained unclear exactly what the love of wisdom was and hence why it was so important.

Socrates himself wrote nothing, but he had an outsized effect on many of the people he met. His followers were convinced that he glimpsed something fundamentally important about human beings and the path to happiness, and so they went to great lengths to understand the love of wisdom and its significance. Plato was one of the young men in Socrates' inner circle of associates, and he is now generally regarded as the most important philosopher in this tradition of thinking about Socrates. The tradition itself, however, continued long after Plato's death.

The details of Plato's understanding of Socrates and his love of wisdom are controversial, and perhaps always will be so, but there is more agreement on the general idea. Plato thought that what Socrates had glimpsed and had begun to understand was that human beings are psychological beings,[i] that rationality in human beings is a matter of proper psychological organiza-

---

[h] The noun and adjective "love of wisdom" (φιλοσοφία) and "lover of wisdom" (φιλόσοφος) occur rarely in the extant Greek literature until about the time of Socrates. The words transliterate as *philosophia* and *philosophos* and thus are etymological ancestors of the English words "philosophy" and "philosopher."

[i] The conception of human beings as psychological beings is familiar today, but it was not so readily available in antiquity. In the opening lines of Homer's *Iliad*, for example, the wrath of Achilles is said to send the souls of heroes to Hades and to leave the heroes themselves on the battlefield as food for dogs and birds. This shows that the human soul was not always understood as an integrated set of mental abilities in terms of which human beings do what they do. This understanding of the soul developed slowly and at least in part as a result of philosophical reflection. This reflection changed the conception of the soul, but in thinking about human beings and their actions, Socrates and the philosophers that followed him did not introduce a new term for the object of their reflections. They continued to use the word "soul" (ψυχή), which transliterates as *psyche* and thus is related to the word "psychology." Hence, from a historical perspective, the study of psychology starts out as a study of human beings whose existence is understood in a certain way.

tion, and that human beings with this psychological organization have a greater expectation for happiness than those who lack it. Socrates, in this way, as Plato understood him, was the most splendid example of the enlightened attitude that previously had manifested itself in the form of the Milesian intellectual revolution. Socrates held out the promise that by thinking about human beings in a certain way, it was possible to see a clearer route to happiness and the good life.

Human beings must transform themselves to follow this route, but this is possible, according to Plato, because the crucial knowledge required for the transformation is not acquired. Instead, it is an inborn and structural part of the human psyche or soul.[j] At the same time, Plato did not think that human beings can become rational without considerable effort. They typically enter adult life so confused by false beliefs about the good that their actions reinforce improper psychological organizations and hence bring misery rather than happiness. Justice, when properly understood, according to Plato, is the remedy for this destructive behavior. The rules of correct behavior in a just society ensure that, to the extent that is humanly possible, the parts of the soul become properly organized and hence that in individuals knowledge of the good determines action.

This remarkable line of thought was not without its critics. For the most part, however, the criticism remained within the broad philosophical framework Plato pioneered. Aristotle, who spent the better part of two decades as a student in the Academy, is Plato's first great critic. However, he is also the first great Platonist. The Hellenistic philosophers, Epicurus and the Epicureans, the Stoics, and the Academic Skeptics, were united in their opposition to what they perceived as the excesses of the classical tradition of Plato and Aristotle, but for the most part it was the excesses, not the general framework itself, that they opposed. In this way, although there are very real differences between the ancient Greek philosophers, ancient Greek philosophy is not simply a sequence of philosophers who lived in the period from 585 BC to AD 529. There are broad lines of thought that make these philosophers part of a single philosophical tradition.

---

[j] It is important to keep in mind that "[t]he original [Greek] word [that transliterates as] *psyche* avoids the overtones which the English translation 'soul' has acquired through centuries of use in a Christian context" (W. K. C. Guthrie, *A History of Greek Philosophy. The Fifth Century Enlightenment*. Part 2: *Socrates*, 1965, 147).

The History of Philosophy

It is important to understand the methodology that characterizes the study of this philosophical tradition. Philosophy itself aims to answer philosophical questions, but the history of philosophy does not, at least not primarily.[2] The goal in the history of philosophy is to answer certain questions about historical figures. The historian wants to know *what* these figures thought about certain issues, and he wants to understand *why* they thought in these ways. But since the thoughts in question are philosophical thoughts, a thorough acquaintance with philosophy and its methods is part of the history of philosophy. In the absence of this knowledge of philosophy, it is difficult if not impossible to identify what the ancient philosophers thought and to understand why they thought in these particular ways.

The primary evidence in the historical study of the ancient philosophical tradition is the extant writings of the ancient philosophers. Since these texts must now be read much later in time, this evidence leaves considerable leeway in deciding exactly what the ancients thought. The words on the page leave important questions unanswered. Additional problems follow from the fact that the ancients struggled to pioneer new theories about difficult subjects. For these reasons, we should not expect that it will always be clear exactly what the ancient philosophers thought. This is an unavoidable fact of life for the historian of philosophy, but it can be minimized to some extent by reconstructing the historical context in which the philosophers worked.[3]

Once the historical context is reconstructed, to the extent that this is possible, the historian employs a two-stage strategy to ascertain what the philosophers thought, and why they thought this. The first part consists of an examination of the texts themselves to determine whether the philosopher said things the historian can reconstruct as an argument. When the texts provide no such statements, as is often the case, it is necessary to turn to the second stage in the strategy. At this point, given that the texts themselves do not tell the story, the historian tries to construct an explanation on the basis of likely influences from the historical period in which the philosopher worked. In such cases, the only way to explain why the philosopher held a certain view is to place him within a historical context in which it would have been natural for him to form the view in question. This is not an easy task, not only because it presupposes extensive knowledge of the ancient world, but because "naturalness" is a familiar but difficult-to-apply concept.

In spite the inherent difficulty of the subject, the history of philosophy is a particularly rewarding discipline. The texts are almost always captivating, and many of the ancient philosophers had extraordinary lives. Socrates is the most famous example, as he was tried and executed by the city of Athens, but even the minor figures are interesting. Diogenes of Oenoanda,[k] who lived in the second century AD (and about whom little else is known), had a long wall erected and inscribed for the benefit of others. On the wall, in his introductory remarks, Diogenes says this:

> The majority of people suffer from a common disease, as in a plague, with their false notions about things, and their number is increasing (for in mutual emulation they catch the disease from another, like sheep); moreover, it is right to help generations to come ... and, besides, love of humanity prompts us to aid the foreigners who come here. Now since the remedies in this inscription reach a larger number of people, I wish to use this structure to advertise publicly the medicines that bring salvation. These medicines we have put fully to test; for we have dispelled the fears that grip us without justification, and, as for pains, those that are groundless we have completely excised, while those that are natural we have reduced to an absolute minimum.[4] (Fragment 3)

The remedy he recommends to the ages is not original to him. This particular understanding of rationality and human psychology, with its corresponding instructions for living a good life and finding happiness, derives from Epicurus, who lived in the fourth and third centuries BC. But the sentiment that motivates Diogenes to erect a public wall inscribed with philosophical medicine is immediately recognizable as wonderfully human. In this way, the wall with its inscription illustrates what to my mind is a general truth about the ancient philosophers. They are not always right, or even always understandable, but they belong to one of the nobler parts of human history.[5]

Notes

1. For a discussion of Platonism, see Terence Irwin, *Classical Thought*, 1989, 185–201. For an account of the Hellenistic schools after about 30 BC, see Michael Frede, "Epilogue," 1999b.
2. This is not to say that the history of philosophy cannot answer philosophical questions. Mary Louise Gill and Pierre Pellegrin make the point: "We believe that the history of ancient philosophy, properly understood *historically* in its own cultural and intellectual context, has much to contribute to our present understanding of philosophical problems. That is not because Ancient

---

[k] The city of Oenoanda is in modern-day south-west Turkey.

Philosophy is answering the very same questions as modern philosophers are asking. On the contrary, it is because the questions and answers we find in ancient philosophy may stimulate us to think again or to reconsider a well-worn issue from a new perspective" (*A Companion to Ancient Philosophy*, "Introduction," 2006, xxxvi.) Gill and Pellegrin rely on Michael Frede for the point: "[T]he historian of philosophy has more to rely on than contemporary philosophical views. His work, ideally, would have taught him new views that one could take, new reasons for or against old views; he may have discovered there was good reason for views which at first seemed unreasonable. All this work may have substantially changed his notions and his assumptions of what constitutes good reason and of what at least is reasonable. Hence, the historian of philosophy might very well be in a position to diagnose a development in the history of philosophy as an aberration, when, from the point of view of contemporary philosophy, this development seems entirely reasonable. ... [Moreover,] if one studies the philosophy of the past not just as a historian of philosophy, but in all its aspects, one has further resources to fall back on. It may be that at some junctures in the history of philosophy where the historian of philosophy believes he has to diagnose a failure, the failure may be the result of thoughts which themselves are to be explained in good part in terms of some other history. One may even be able to show that this other history interfered with the 'natural' development of philosophical thought at this point, however philosophically reasonable this development may now seem to us" ("Introduction: The study of ancient philosophy," 1987a, xxvii).

3. Jonathan Barnes makes this important point (and expresses pessimism about various academic disciplines): "You can't do anything at all in ancient philosophy unless you know a bit of Greek and Latin, and you can't do anything worthwhile in ancient philosophy unless you are a semi-decent classical scholar. But classical scholarship is a dying art ..." ("Bagpipe music," 2006, 17). In addition, Barnes highlights the connection between the history of philosophy and philosophy: "Ancient philosophy is part of the history of philosophy; and although the history of philosophy – despite what many historians like to say – is no more part of philosophy than the history of mathematics is a part of mathematics, nonetheless you can't do anything much in the history of the subject without having some sort of acquaintance with the subject itself. So if the ancient philosopher does not thereby philosophize – he must, so to speak, be a philosopher without doing philosophy. That being so, the general state of philosophy will influence the state of ancient philosophy. And the general state of philosophy is at present pretty dire" (18).

4. Except for the use of "structure" for στοά, this translation is Martin Ferguson Smith's, from *Diogenes of Oenoanda: The Epicurean Inscription*, 1993, 368.

5. The introductory sentences in Hero's treatise on artillery provide an opposing sentiment: "The largest and most important part of philosophical activity is that which is devoted to peace of mind. Those who want to attain wisdom have

carried out and, indeed, carry out to this very day a large number of investigations concerned with peace of mind. In fact, I believe that theoretical inquiry about this will never end. In the meantime, however, mechanics has progressed beyond the theoretical study of peace of mind, and it has taught all men, how, with the help of part of it – a very small part indeed – to live with peace of mind, I mean the part concerned with artillery." (This translation is Michael Frede's: "The sceptic's beliefs," 1987f, 199–200.) Hero was a Greek mathematician and engineer who lived in the first century AD.

Part I

The Presocratics

From 585 BC until Socrates (469–399 BC)
changed the focus

The enlightenment, the inquiry into nature, and reason and experience

By about 550 BC, the Persian Empire had expanded westward. Greek cities in Ionia on the eastern shore of the Aegean, including Miletus, came under Persian rule. Ideas moved with refugees in advance of the Persians, north along the coast, to the southern part of mainland Greece (the Peloponnese), and to Sicily and southern Italy. This transmission of ideas continued during the Persian Wars. In 492, the Persians invaded the northern part of the Greek peninsula. In 490, against all odds, the Greeks were victorious at Marathon. The Persians launched a second invasion in 480, but they were defeated again, this time at sea. In the aftermath, Athens, who played a leading role in defeating the Persians, set up a league of cities, the Delian League, to clear the Aegean of Persian power.

Philosophy traditionally begins in 585 BC, the year of the solar eclipse which Thales of Miletus foretold. Thales was one of the leaders in the new inquiry into nature. This inquiry was a particular expression of the more general enlightenment attitude that human beings could know the truth about things, if they would think for themselves, rather than rely uncritically on the traditional habits of thought and received wisdom. The attempt to understand the inquiry into nature, as well as the enlightenment tradition more generally, gave birth to a philosophical tradition. It was thought that there are two kinds of cognition in human beings, reason and experience, and that knowledge of what exists is an exercise of reason, not experience. Moreover, it was thought that the inquiry into nature, when properly understood, employs reason to evaluate and possibly correct the traditional conception of reality, which is formed in experience and hence does not constitute knowledge of what exists.

Time Line

The dates of the Presocratics are uncertain. Homer is traditionally dated to the eighth century and Hesiod to the eighth or early seventh century. Socrates lived from 469 to 399 BC.

625	575	525	475	425	375	325

Thales

Anaximander

Anaximenes

Pythagoras

Heraclitus

Parmenides

Anaxagoras

Empedocles

Leucippus?

Democritus

1

The Milesian Revolution

According to convention, philosophy begins in 585 BC. This is the year of
the solar eclipse Thales of Miletus foretold. This prediction was significant
because it was understood as an achievement of the enlightenment tradition
that had taken root in the ancient world.[a] Thales was the leading figure in
a new field known as the "inquiry into nature." This inquiry sparked a set of
intense reflections which gave birth to a philosophical tradition as intellectuals tried to understand the issues raised by the inquiry into nature, and the
enlightenment generally.

1.1 The Milesians Turn to Nature

Thales, Anaximander, and Anaximenes are the Milesian[b] *inquirers into
nature*. They were "naturalists." They did not construct explanations in

---

[a] In the period from 1250 to 1150 there was a collapse of settled conditions caused by the fall
of the Hittite Empire. Early in this "Dark Age," as part of the resulting movement of
populations, Greeks speaking the Ionic dialect settled in Asia Minor on the coast of the Aegean
Sea. This part of the coast came to be called "Ionia" and it was here, particularly in Miletus, the
dominant city, that the enlightenment took root. Beginning in about 700, Miletus was part of
a marked increase in trade and colonization throughout the eastern Mediterranean. This
brought increasing awareness of the surrounding kingdoms: Babylon, Egypt, and later, Persia.
The Greeks, however, were not overwhelmed by these cultures. Instead, they assimilated them
in a way that would give rise to a philosophical tradition.
[b] The description "Milesian" stems from their city of origin: Thales, Anaximander, and
Anaximenes were from the city of Miletus in Asia Minor on the coast of the Aegean Sea. The
lines of influence are not easy to reconstruct, but subsequent intellectual activity within the
Presocratic period seems to have spread out from Miletus. The use of the label "Presocratic"
originates with the German scholar Hermann Diels. His magisterial collection of evidence for
early Greek philosophy, first published in 1903, is entitled *Die Fragmente der Vorsokratiker*
(*The Fragments of the Presocratics*). This title, however, is unfortunate because it suggests that
these figures lived before Socrates. In fact he overlapped with some of them, and one at least,
the atomist Democritus, seems to have outlived him.

Ancient Greek Philosophy: From The Presocratics to the Hellenistic Philosophers, First Edition.
Thomas A. Blackson. © 2011 Thomas A. Blackson. Published 2011 by Blackwell Publishing Ltd.

terms of the gods, as was the practice of the older school represented by Hesiod and the "theologists." Instead, they explained things in terms of what they called a "nature."[c] Furthermore, rather than write in verse, as was the practice of the older school, they employed a new literary form to express their investigations. They wrote prose "inquiries," the results of their work on a variety of subjects. The investigation into the past in the *Histories* of Herodotus is perhaps now the most well-known "inquiry,"[1] but Thales and the Milesians were the first inquirers. They were inquirers into nature.

The new inquiry into nature was the most prominent example of the enlightenment attitude that had taken root in the eastern Mediterranean. It was thought that human beings could flourish, and get more and more parts of their lives under control, if they would think about things clearly and systematically, rather than rely so heavily on received wisdom and traditional ways of thinking about things. Thales and the Milesians directed this intellectual optimism to what now (in our debt to them) is said to be *naturally* occurring phenomena. They abandoned the older tradition represented by Hesiod and the theologists. In contrast, they thought that reality has a nature and that rain and other natural phenomena are manifestations of changes in this nature.[d]

The details of what the Milesians had in mind are difficult to determine because so little historically reliable evidence of their thought

---

[c] The Greek word is φύσις. It transliterates as *phusis* and is an etymological ancestor of the English word "physics." In this way, Thales and the Milesians are the first "physicists."

[d] This has led many scholars to claim that the Milesians gave birth to science. "[A] new thing came into the world with the early Ionian teachers – the thing we call science.... [T]hey first pointed the way which Europe has followed ever since, ... [and so] it is an adequate description of science to say that it is 'thinking about the world in the Greek way.' That is why science has never existed except among peoples who have come under the influence of Greece" (John Burnet, *Early Greek Philosophy*, 1920, v). "[Περὶ φύσεως ἱστορίαν ("inquiry into nature")] is the oldest name for what we call 'natural science'" (John Burnet, *Plato's* Phaedo, 1911, 99). "All the histories of Greek philosophy, from Aristotle's time to this day, begin with Thales of Miletus. It is generally agreed that with him something new, that we call Western science, appeared in the world ..." (Francis Cornford, *Before and After Socrates*, 1932, 5). "Western philosophy and science trace their beginnings to ... Miletus ..." (Richard McKirahan, *Philosophy Before Socrates*, 1994, 20).

has survived.ᵉ Indeed, a very substantial part of what is thought about these intellectuals depends on a report in Aristotle. He placed them within a longer history of philosophy, but he wrote this history not as history for its own sake, but as part of an introduction to a set of doctrines he presents in a work now entitled *Metaphysics*. In his report of what previous thinkers thought, Aristotle says that the "first lovers of wisdom," by whom he means Thales and the Milesians, thought that something material is the starting point of all things:

> Most of the first lovers of wisdom thought that principles in the form of matter were the only principles of all things; for the original source of all existing things, and that from which a thing first comes-into-being, and into which it is finally resolved (the substance persisting but changing in its qualities), this they declare is the element and first principle of existing things, and for this reason they consider that there is no absolute coming-to-be or passing away, on the ground that such a nature is always preserved ... for there must be some natural substance, either one or more than one, from which the other things come-into-being, while it is preserved. Over the number, however, and the form of this kind of principle, they do not all agree; but Thales, the founder of this school, says that it is water. (*Metaphysics* I.3.983b = DK 11 A 2, A 12²)

If Aristotle is right about Thales and the Milesian "school," the naturalists and the theologists provide their accounts against different background conceptions of reality.

Anaximenes provides an example. He offered a new and revolutionary answer to the question of why drops of water sometimes form in, and subsequently fall from, the sky:

> [Anaximenes says] that the underlying nature is one and infinite ..., for he identifies it as air; and it differs in substantial nature by rarity and density.

ᵉ This problem holds for the Presocratics generally. The evidence for what they wrote depends on discussions in the surviving works of subsequent authors, many of whom lived much later and had very different views of the world. "Our knowledge of the Presocratics, then, unlike our knowledge of Plato and Aristotle, is not gained directly from the books they wrote" (Jonathan Barnes, *Early Greek Philosophy*, 1987, 24). Furthermore, there was no tradition of writing history for the sake of history. "The modern concept of 'history of philosophy' did not exist in the Greco-Roman antiquity. Philosophers turned to their predecessors in order to throw light on the problems they themselves were dealing with or in order to reject competing views, not because they were interested in the historical development of human thinking" (Jorgen Mejer, "Ancient philosophy and the doxographical tradition," 2006, 23.) For these reasons, it is exceedingly difficult to have much confidence in any very detailed theory of what the Presocratics thought.

Being made finer it becomes fire; being made thicker it becomes wind, then cloud, and when (thickened still more) it becomes water, then earth, then stones, and the rest come into being from these. He too makes motion eternal and says that change also comes to be through it.[3] (DK 13 A 5; Simplicius,[f] *Commentary on Aristotle's* Physics)

The older theological answer to the question, the answer Hesiod gives in his poem *Works and Days*, takes the form of an explanation in terms of the mind of the god, Zeus. According to this account of the phenomenon, rain is a manifestation of Zeus' stormy mood:

1. Rain falls when Zeus the Storm King is stormy in mood.
2. Zeus the Storm King is stormy in mood.

———————

3. It is raining.

Anaximenes, by contrast, shows no interest in any such answer that makes reference to the traditional pantheon of gods. Instead, he adopts the style of explanation that defines the new school of Thales and the Milesian naturalists. Anaximenes tries to explain rain as a condensed

———————

[f] Simplicius (late-fourth to mid-fifth century AD) was one of the last of the Neoplatonists, and he is the only source for some of the texts of the Presocratic philosophers. Without Simplicus, some of these philosophers would be mere names. The details of his connection to the texts are complicated, but the primary points are these. The Neoplatonists for the most part thought of themselves as recovering the true philosophy which Plato had been the last to see at all clearly. The object was philosophical truth, not historical fact. To understand Aristotle, who was obviously influenced by Plato, but who also criticized Plato, the Neoplatonists settled for a middle ground that allowed them to treat Aristotle as an authority on logic and physics, but not on the higher realms of reality. Simplicius, in discussing Aristotle, quotes some of the earlier philosophers Aristotle mentions and discusses. For these quotations, Simplicius seems to have relied on summaries of Theophrastus' writings on the Presocratic philosophers. Theophrastus (370–285) succeeded Aristotle as head of the Lyceum, the school Aristotle had founded in 335. Theophrastus' own writings have almost entirely been lost, but they were summarized by Alexander of Aphrodisias. These summaries themselves have been lost, but some extracts are preserved in Simplicius' commentaries on Aristotle's works. Alexander of Aphrodisias (second to third century AD) was an Aristotelian commentator who aimed to articulate and defend Aristotle's philosophy. The Neoplatonist commentators knew and consulted Alexander's work in their attempt to incorporate Aristotle's work into their reconstruction of the true philosophy that Plato had been the last to glimpse.

state of air. Put more formally, his explanation of rain may be recast as follows:

1. Rain is a state of the nature of reality: rain is condensed air.
2. The air here is condensed now.

---

3. It is raining.

On this account, the condition in the world that makes the sentence "It is raining" true is a state of nature with a certain history. In opposition to the theologists, rather than conceive of the signs for the coming of rain as an indication of Zeus' mood, Anaximenes seems to have thought of these signs as an indication of a sequence of events ending in the condensation of air.[g]

The Milesians left no record of how they arrived at the conception of reality Aristotle takes to underlie their explanations, but perhaps it was natural for them to think that the older explanations in terms of the traditional pantheon of gods were inadequate because really the behavior of the gods is determined by local customs and tradition.[4] A more objective conception of reality was necessary. The question would be how to construct it, and a natural strategy would have been to revise the theological conception so that the pantheon is replaced by something independent of tradition. This might be accomplished by stripping the personal attributes from the notion of a responsible agent and applying the remaining idea of causation directly to reality.[h] Reality would have a "nature," and whether it rains, for example, would be up to reality, not

---

[g] Richard McKirahan stresses just how "revolutionary" this was. "[W]here Homer and Hesiod worked within traditional frameworks, the early Ionians rejected tradition as a source of knowledge . . . . It is hard to underrate . . . the intellectual courage it took to make this step . . . . [Thales and the Mileisans] rejected Homer's and Hesiod's authority and challenged a way of looking at the world that was universal both among the Greeks and among all the foreign peoples known to the Greeks at the time" (*Philosophy before Socrates*, 1994, 73).

[h] This change did not happen all at once. Anaxamander, for example, says that "the source of coming-to-be for existing things is that into which destruction, too, happens, 'according to necessity; for they pay the penalty and retribution to each other for their injustice, according to the assessment of Time'" (DK 12 B 1). In this fragment, he still seems to be thinking of the natural order in terms of agency. As Heraclitus would later observe, the steering principle in the universe "does not and does consent to be called by the name of Zeus" (DK 22 B 32).

because it has a mind and makes choices,[5] but because rain is a function of changes in the "nature" of reality.[6]

This new conception of reality must have occurred as part of a more general attempt to reach a more secure understanding of things once people noticed and were bothered by the different theological traditions and their conflicts with one another. Since it is now difficult to take the accounts of Hesiod and the theologists seriously, it is necessary to keep in mind that the Milesian solution was not an immediate success. Reality did not appear the way they claimed it is. This, in turn, raised the question of how they *knew* that reality has a nature and that naturally occurring phenomena are manifestations of changes in this nature. The theologists had relied on a traditional source to validate their stories. They relied on the Muses.[i] Hesiod relies on them in *Works and Days* and *Theogony*. This appeal to divine authority had traditionally gone unchallenged, but the new enlightenment attitude that had taken root in this part of the ancient world was making it increasingly difficult for intellectuals to have confidence in the traditional ways. Thales and the Milesians might have capitalized on this skepticism if they had offered arguments for their new inquiry into nature and its novel conception of reality, but this is something they apparently did not do.

This lack of justification prompted *philosophical* questions, both about the inquiry into nature and about the enlightenment assumption generally. To understand the case for the new inquiry into nature and its novel conception of reality, intellectuals began to ask epistemological and onto-logical questions. They asked questions about the kinds of cognition involved in knowledge, and they appealed to their answer to this question to help settle the original question of what really exists. In the surviving reports of what they wrote, Thales and the Milesian naturalists themselves do not explicitly engage in this philosophical project. Yet, it is clear as a matter of history that a deep and sustained interest in various philosophical questions soon emerged and took center stage as the intellectuals who followed the Milesians tried to understand both the inquiry into nature and the enlightenment assumptions. In this way, although Thales and the Milesians may have been more scientists than philosophers,[7] their inquiry into nature gave birth to a philosophical tradition.

---

[i] The Muses are characters of mythology. According to the myth, before Hera became his wife, Zeus took the form of a shepherd and consorted with Mnemosyne. She gave birth to nine daughters, the Muses. In the cultural tradition that created and was informed by this myth, all inspired knowledge was transmitted to human beings by the Muses. Hence it became a standard practice to invoke the Muses to confirm the content of what was about to be said. Hesiod begins his *Works and Days* this way: "Muses of the sacred spring . . . Who give glory in song, Come sing Zeus' praises . . ."

1.2 Parmenides

Parmenides of Elea[j] is a towering figure in the new philosophical tradition.[k] He took some of the first steps to understand the enlightenment contrast between thinking clearly on the one hand, and relying on habit and tradition on the other. He used his understanding to answer the question of what exists, the question to which the Milesians had given such a revolutionary answer.

In his poem, certain parts of which are difficult to understand, Parmenides distinguishes three *paths for inquiry* in the search for knowledge. He identifies the path to knowledge as "the path of Persuasion" that "attends Truth." This is the path corresponding to "it is":

And the goddess greeted me kindly, and took my right hand in hers, and addressed me with these words: Young man, you who come to my house in the company of immortal charioteers with the mares which bear you, greetings. No ill fate has sent you to travel this road – far indeed does it lie from the steps of men – but right and justice. It is proper that you should

---

[j] Elea was a Greek city in what is now southern Italy. This city is far removed from Miletus, which was located in what is now Turkey. The connection is not known, but the link from Parmenides to Thales and the Milesians may have run through Xenophanes. Xenophanes came from Colophon, near Miletus, and he may have moved to southern Italy. Parmenides himself, in his surviving work, does not mention any of his predecessors by name.

[k] Although Parmenides is one of the most important of the early philosophers, he is not the first philosopher in the ancient philosophical tradition. Xenophanes, who preceded Parmenides, said that "[n]o man knows, or ever will know, the truth about the gods and about everything I speak of; for even if one chanced to say a complete truth, yet oneself knows it not; but seeming is wrought over all things" (DK 21 B 34). In the light of this and similar remarks about the nature of knowledge, Edward Hussey calls Xenophanes "the first Greek philosopher": "The supporters of the theoretical approach in cosmology were forced henceforward to apply that same approach to higher-order questions about knowledge, about reasoning and reasonableness, about the epistemic status of the theoretical approach itself. The person whom our evidence shows unambiguously to have been concerned with these problems is Xenophanes of Colophon (active before and around 500 BCE). It is Xenophanes, then, who has the best claim to the title of 'the first Greek philosopher.'" (Edward Hussey, "The Beginnings of science and philosophy," 2006, 13.) Xenophanes, nevertheless, despite being first, had much less influence than Parmenides. "Parmenides had, through the medium of Plato, an unrivaled influence on the course of Western philosophy" (Jonathan Barnes, *Early Greek Philosophy*, 2006, 130).

learn all things, both the unshaken heart of well-rounded truth, and the opinions of mortals, in which there is no true reliance. (DK 28 B 1; Sextus Empiricus,[1] *Against the Professors* VII; Simplicius, *Commentary on Aristotle's* On the Heavens)

Come now, I will tell you (and you must carry my account away with you when you have heard it) the only ways of inquiry there are for knowing.[8] The one, that it is and that it is impossible for it not to be, is the path of Persuasion (for she attends upon Truth); the other, that it is not and that is needful that it is not, that I declare to you is an altogether indiscernible track; for you could know what is not ... (DK 28 B 2; Proclus,[m] *Commentary on Plato's* Timaeus; Simplicius, *Commentary on Aristotle's* Physics)

It is not at all clear what Parmenides means by "it is," but the main line of thought is reasonably straightforward. He thinks that "it is" corresponds to the path to knowledge but that the inquirers into nature have taken a different path. Their path is not the path of persuasion and hence their inquiries do not result in knowledge. Their path, to use Parmenides' word, is "backward-turning":

I hold you back [from this way of inquiry, that it is not, and next from the way] on which mortals wander knowing nothing, two-headed; for help-lessness guides the wandering thought in their breasts, and they are carried along, deaf and blind at once, dazed, undiscriminating hordes, who believe that to be and not to be are the same and not the same; and the path taken by them all is backward-turning. (DK 28 B 6; Simplicius, *Commentary on Aristotle's* Physics)

---

[1] Sextus Empiricus (second to third century AD) was an empiricist physician and philosopher in the Pyrrhonian skeptical school. Very little is known about him. Three of his philosophical works have survived. Two of these works are grouped together under the title *Adversus Mathematikos* (*M*), which translates as *Against the Professors*. This work is a comprehensive criticism of the ancient schools of thought and hence an important source of information about the ancient philosophical tradition. The other philosophical work is *Outlines of Pyrrhonism* (*PH*). In addition to his philosophical works he also wrote some medical works, which have not survived.

[m] Proclus (412–485) was a Neoplatonist and the last major Greek philosopher to work before the Christian Emperor Justinian forbade the pagans from teaching in the schools in 529 AD. Proclus' interest in early Greek philosophy is driven by his interest in Platonism. "Proclus is inclined to give a positive, though neoplatonically coloured account of those early Greek philosophers whom he believes to be important forerunners of a dogmatic Plato. His selection is restricted to individuals who figure in Plato's dialogues ..." (Jaap Mansfeld, "Sources," 1999, 37).

The "mortals," including Thales and the Milesians,[9] turn back from the path of persuasion when they draw conclusions for which "there is no true reliance" and hence which are not knowledge. Rather than stay on the path of "it is," they allow that "it is and is not" is true of things.

An example helps illustrate what Parmenides has in mind. Consider Anaximenes' inquiry into the nature of rain. The impressions to which he assents have "no true reliance." He says that air is the nature of reality and that drops of water come into and go out of existence as a state of air when it rains. For his knowledge of rain, Anaximenes relies on ordinary experience. He does not make the point explicitly, at least not in the extant fragments, but presumably he expects his readers to think that they know from experience *that* water droplets sometimes form in the sky and subsequently fall to the ground. What they do not know, and what he tries to explain, is *why* this happens. Anaximenes explains why this happens by saying that air is the nature of reality and that a droplet of water is air in a condensed state. In this way, as Parmenides understands the explanation, Anaximenes does not stay on the path defined by "it is." He allows that "it is and it is not" is true of water droplets: they come into and go out of existence in terms of air.

Parmenides himself was convinced that experience is misleading and that the inquirer should make judgments in terms of cognition he describes very vaguely as "reason." He insists that the inquirer should "judge by reason," not lapse into habits enforced by "much experience":

> For never shall this be forcibly maintained, that things that are not are, but you must hold back your thought from this way of inquiry, nor let habit, born from much experience, force you down this way, by making you use an aimless eye or an ear and a tongue full of meaningless sound: judge by reason the strife-encompassed refutation spoken by me. (DK 28 B 7; Plato, *Sophist*; Sextus Empiricus, *Against the Professors* VII)

Anaximenes, accordingly, does lapse into such habits. His conclusion about what exists depends partly on what Parmenides describes as "much experience." Anaximenes concludes that drops of water *come into* and subsequently *go out of existence*. In the language of the three paths of inquiry, Anaximenes says of rain that "it is and it is not."

Parmenides thought that neither drops of water nor anything else comes into or goes out of existence. He thought that the widespread belief to the contrary has its basis, not in "reason" and cognition that follow the path of persuasion (the path that issues in knowledge), but in the "habit born of much experience," a habit that manifests itself in the customary use of names. In truth, according to Parmenides, the things that names suggest are "real" are in fact just names:

> For there neither is nor will be anything else besides what is, since Fate fettered it to be whole and changeless. Therefore it has been named all the names which mortals have laid down, believing them to be true-coming-into-being and perishing, being and not being, changing place and altering bright color. (DK 28 B 8; Simplicius, *Commentary on Aristotle's* Physics)

The details in this passage are not easy to grasp, but the rough idea is that people use names on the false presupposition that they experience objects that come into and go out of existence. This use of names is what underwrites the mistaken "habit, born of much experience."[10]

Parmenides supposes that he himself, because he employs "reason," has the truth about existence. The poem, however, shows that he is keenly aware that to follow "it is" is to insist on a paradoxical conception of reality. This conception, as he says, is far from "the steps of men," but nevertheless Parmenides is convinced that the path of persuasion that attends truth, the path that ends with knowledge, begins with and strictly adheres to the consequences of the principle that "it is":

> There still remains just one account of a way, that it is. On this way there are verymany signs, being uncreated and imperishable it is, whole and of a single kind and unshaken and perfect. (D 28 B 8; Simplicius, *Commentary on Aristotle's* Physics)

Parmenides thinks that "reason" shows that reality is not how the inquirers into nature think it is. If they had taken the path to knowledge, they would conclude that nothing comes into or goes out of existence, and that reality is "whole and of a single kind and unshaken and perfect."

One premise in Parmenides' argument for this paradoxical conclusion is that whatever exists is both "uncreated and imperishable." The reasoning for the two conjuncts is symmetrical. In each case, it proceeds by *reductio ad absurdum*. It is assumed, in the first case, that something has come into existence. Given this assumption, it is supposed to follow that "it is not" is true of the thing in question at the times before it came into existence. This consequence, however, is supposed to be absurd. According to Parmenides, "it is not" cannot be true of anything. Otherwise, something would both exist and be nothing at all. Hence, he concludes that "coming to be is extinguished":

It never was nor will be, since it is now, all together, one, continuous. For what birth will you seek for it? How and whence did it grow? I shall not allow you to say nor to think from not being: for it is not to be said nor thought that it is not; and what need would have driven it later rather than earlier, beginning from nothing, to grow? Thus it must either be completely or not all. Nor will the force of conviction allow anything besides it to come to be ever from not being. Therefore Justice has never loosed her fetters to allow it to come to be or to perish, but holds it fast. And the decision about these things lies in this: it is or it is not. But it has in fact been decided, as is necessary, to leave the one way unthought and nameless (for it is no true way), but that the other is and is genuine. And how could what is be in the future? How could it come to be? For if it came into being, it is not: nor is it if it is ever going to be in the future. Thus coming to be is extinguished and perishing unheard of. (DK 28 B 8; Simplicius, *Commentary on Aristotle's* Physics)

Parmenides realized that people believe they experience objects that come into and go out of existence, but he was convinced that such thinking is confused. It is the unfortunate judgments of "mortals." These confused mortals ("knowing nothing wander, two-headed," as he unflatteringly describes them) wrongly persist in the common but false thought that reality consists in objects that come into existence, change in various ways, and go out of existence.

This argument against the "mortals" is central for understanding Parmenides and his importance. His work is an early and seminal effort to identify the kind of cognition involved in knowledge of the structure of reality. He does not identify judgment in accordance with "reason" or with "much experience," with a determinate set of cognitive procedures. He seems instead to understand the contrast imprecisely, but he does provide an example. The argument against coming into and going out of existence is an example of judgment in accordance with "reason."

In this way, Parmenides' work figures in a line of thought that runs through much of the ancient philosophical tradition. Subsequent philosophers, beginning with his successors in the Presocratic period, see Parmenides' project as central for philosophy. To get beyond traditional thinking, and hence to gain control over more of the world, they thought it was necessary to distinguish the way things *appear* from the way things *are* (and would appear from an objective point of view). For Parmenides, and the philosophical tradition that depends on him, this distinction turns on the difference between two kinds of cognition: "experience" and "reason."

1.3   A Defense of the Inquiry into Nature

Empedocles, Anaxagoras, Leucippus, and Democritus[n] figure in the last of
the three parts into which the Presocratic period naturally subdivides. These
Presocratics are united by their attempt to work out in more detail
Parmenides' analysis of the enlightenment contrast between clear and
traditional thinking as a matter of "reason" versus "experience." They
appeal to the result of this work to answer the question of what exists and to
defend the inquiry into nature.

On the question of what exists, these Presocratics suppose that the nature
of reality consists in a *plurality* of objects. These objects come together and
come apart. Empedocles says that four things come together and separate
according to what he terms "Love" and "Strife":

> A twofold tale I shall tell: at one time they grew to be one alone out of
> many, at another again they grew apart to be many out of one. Double is
> the birth of mortal things and double is their failing; for the one is brought
> to birth and destroyed by the coming together of all things, the other is
> nurtured and flies apart when they grow apart again. And these never cease
> their continual interchanging, now through Love all coming together into
> one, now again each carried apart by the hatred of Strife. (DK 31 B 17;
> Simplicius, *Commentary on Aristotle's* Physics)

> Come now, I shall tell you first what in the beginning the sun and all those
> others which we now see became distinct – earth and swelling sea and moist
> air and Titan sky. (DK 31 B 38; Clement, *Miscellanies*[o])

Empedocles' language now sounds particularly archaic, but there are more
modern-sounding examples. Democritus thinks that atoms and void are the
nature of reality:

> Democritus believes that the nature of the eternal things is small sub-
> stances unlimited in multitude. As a place for these he hypothesizes
> something else, unlimited in size, and he calls the place by the names of

---

[n] These Presocratics are mixed geographically. Empedocles came from Acragas in southern
Italy, but the others were from the east. Anaxagoras came from Clazomenae, and Democritus
came from Abdera. Clazomenae is north of Miletus, and Abdera is further north and east.
Leucippus is an obscure figure whose life is unknown.

[o] Clement of Alexandria (second to third century AD) was an early Christian theologian. In his
Miscellanies, he allows a place for philosophy but emphasizes the superiority of faith over
philosophy.

"void," "nothing," .... He holds that the substances are so small that they escape our senses. They have all kinds of forms and shapes and differences in size. Out of these as elements he generates and combines visible and perceptible bodies. The substances contend with one another and move in the void on account of their dissimilarity and the other differences I mentioned, and as they move they strike against one another and become entangled in a way that makes them be in contact and close to one another.[11] (DK 68 A 37; Simplicius, *Commentary on Aristotle's* On the Heavens)

But what does Democritus say? – That substances infinite in quantity, indivisible and indestuctible, and also qualityless and impassive, are carried about scattered in the void. When they approach one another or collide or are entangled, the aggregates appear as water or fire or plants or men, but all things really are what he calls these indivisible forms and nothing else. For there is no generation from what does not exist, while from the things that exist nothing can be generated in virtue of the fact that, because of their hardness, the atoms neither are affected nor change.[12] (Plutarch, *Against Colotes*, 1110f–1111a)[P]

Democritus supposes that atoms move through the limitless void and that groups of these atoms sometimes hold together or separate upon becoming entangled or disentangled.

Although these Presocratics recognized certain forms of change, they remained in agreement with Parmenides about the impossibility of coming into and going out of existence. So, for example, according to Anaxagoras, when something is said to come into or go out of existence what *really* happens is that certain "things that are" become mixed together or separated apart:

The Greeks are wrong to recognize coming into being and perishing; for nothing comes into being nor perishes, but is rather compounded or dissolved from things that are. So they would be right to say coming into being is composition and perishing dissolution. (DK 59 B 17; Simplicius, *Commentary on Aristotle's* Physics)

To say that something comes into or goes out of existence is to say something false. As Anaxagoras puts the point, the "Greeks are wrong to recognize coming into being and perishing."

[P] Plutarch (46–c. 122) was a Greek biographer and essayist. Colotes was a student of Epicurus.

This rejection of coming into and going out of existence was not thought to entail that ordinary assertions must be rejected completely. Nothing really comes into or goes out of existence, but these Presocratics thought that this way of talking, although "not far-reaching," was part of a "custom" acceptable for everyday purposes. Empedocles makes the point:

> Another thing I will tell you: of all mortal things none has birth, nor any end in accursed death, but only mingling and interchange of what is mingled – birth is the name given to these by men (DK 31 B 8). And when they are mixed in the form of a man or of plants or of birds, then they say that this comes into being; but when they are separated, they call this wretched fate: they do not name them as is right, but I myself comply with their custom (DK 31 B 9). Fools – for they have no far-reaching thoughts, since they think that what before did not exist comes into being, or that a thing dies and is completely destroyed (DK 31 B 11). (These three fragments are from Plutarch's *Against Colotes*)

In "wretched fate," or death, nothing has really gone out of existence. Death is not a matter of going out of existence. Rather, according to Empedocles, what really happens in what is called "death" is that certain objects become arranged differently. This fact about reality is obscured by the customary practice of referring to this sort of rearrangement among objects by saying that the dead man "is no longer," and by thinking of death as a way of going out of existence.

The atomists make a similar point about "custom." Democritus supposes that the ordinary belief in sweetness stems from the customary way to talk about features of the atoms and void. When experience issues in the judgment that something is sweet, the judgment is supposed to be false because "in truth" there are only "atoms and void" in a certain arrangement:

> He says that ". . . in reality we know nothing about anything; but for each of us there is a reshaping-belief," and further that ". . . to know in reality what each thing is in character is baffling" (DK 68 B 7, 8). Democritus sometimes does away with what appears to the senses, and says that none of these appears according to truth but only according to opinion: the truth in real things is that there are atoms and void. "By custom, sweet," he says, "by custom, bitter; by custom, hot; by custom, cold; by custom, color; but in truth, atoms and void" (DK 68 B 9). He says there are two kinds of knowing, one through the senses and the other through the intellect. Of these he calls the one through the intellect "legitimate,"

attesting its trustworthiness for the judgment of truth, and that through the senses he names "bastard," denying it inerrancy in the discrimination of what is true. To quote his actual words: "Of knowledge there are two forms, one legitimate and the other bastard. To the bastard belong all this group: sight, hearing, smell, taste, touch. The other is legitimate and is separate from this" (DK 78 B 11). (These fragments are from Sextus Empiricus, *Against the Professors* VII)

People in everyday life use their tongues to detect certain arrangements of atoms and void, and it is their custom to express their judgment by saying that some object is, or is not, sweet. They think that sweetness is a property of objects and that they can detect its presence, but, in fact, according to Democritus, there really are no objects that have the property of being sweet.

This ontology is far more radical than it may first appear. In reality, as it is usually conceived, objects come into existence, persist through change, and eventually go out of existence. According to Empedocles and Democritus, there are *no such objects*. The only objects are ones that exist eternally. They do not come into or go out of existence. They become arranged in various ways, but nothing comes into or goes out of existence because arrangements of objects are not themselves objects and hence are not objects that come into or go out of existence.[13]

To explain why reality appears otherwise, Democritus seems to have tried to build on the prior suggestion in Pamenides that "much experience" can make false propositions appear true. The atomists thought that sense experience is a "bastard" form of judgment. Things appear as they do because these appearances are generated by beliefs formed and retained in this illegitimate form of judgment. Such judgments are perfectly good for getting along in most circumstances in ordinary life, but this "bastard" form of judgment *does not produce "legitimate" knowledge*. According to Democritus, judgment in terms of "reason" is somehow "separate" from judgment in terms of sense experience. This "separate" judgment provides "legitimate" knowledge of what exists.[14]

The atomist epistemology is some improvement over Parmenides' suggestive remarks, but clearly serious problems remain. First of all, Democritus has not identified his two forms of judgment with a precise set of cognitive procedures. He characterizes judgment in terms of "reason" by negation: he says only that it is not judgment in terms of sense experience. Secondly, one may well wonder whether "reason" can be more legitimate than "experience" since "reason" would seem to depend on such experience for information. Democritus himself makes the point:

> Wretched mind, do you take your assurances from us and then overthrow us?
> Our overthrow is your downfall. (DK 68 B 125; Galen, *Outline of medical empiricism*)[q]

Throwing down the senses is a fall for "reason" because any persuasive argument to undermine judgment produced in sense experience must be based on more reliable judgments. Yet, in the absence of a precise characterization of reason, it is not clear that such judgments are more reliable. Indeed, the suggestion in the passage is that they are not more reliable. This worry threatens to undermine the atomist thesis that in reality only atoms and the void exist.

In spite of these problems, it is possible to see how this epistemology is supposed to provide a defense of the enlightenment tradition in general and of the inquiry into nature in particular. The Milesians may have followed a "backward-turning" method of inquiry, as Parmenides argued. Nothing essential, however, is supposed to be wrong with the inquiry into nature itself. Traditional judgments about what exists are false, just as Parmenides thought, but it is supposed to be unnecessary to reject the ordinary forms of speech used to make these judgments. The inquiry into nature is supposed to describe reality, not by supposing that objects in the traditional conception of reality exist in terms of some underlying nature, such as water, as the first inquirers into nature may have thought, but by supposing that the traditional way to talk about objects as coming into and going out of existence is a confused way to describe the various arrangements of objects that constitute the nature of

---

[q] Galen (c. 129–200) is a physician, second in fame in antiquity only to Hippocrates (c. 460–370), the father of the art of medicine. But like Sextus Empiricus, Galen also was a philosopher. Galen's *Outline of Medical Empiricism* concerns a philosophical debate among Hellenistic doctors over knowledge in connection with medicine: "This debate, which arose towards the middle of the third century BC, concerns first of all the nature of medical knowledge. But though the debate also addresses questions which are due to the specific nature of medical knowledge, what is at issue for the most part is the nature of expert or scientific knowledge quite generally, even if this issue is discussed almost exclusively in terms of medicine. It was in this debate that, for the first time, a sharp and clear contrast was developed between rationalism and empiricism. In fact the very terms *empiricist* and *rationalist* have their origins in this debate" (Michael Frede, "Introduction" in *Galen. Three Treatises on the Nature of Science*, 1985, ix).

reality.[r] This insight into existence and the structure of reality is supposed to be known in the cognition that constitutes the judgments of "reason," not the habits "born from much experience," habits that impede human understanding and progress.

Notes

1. The Greek noun ἱστορία ("inquiry") transliterates into English as *historia*, but it was not originally restricted to investigations into the past. John Burnet and Charles Kahn explain the etymology: "The restriction of the term to what we call 'history' is due to the fact that Herodotus followed his predecessors in calling his work ἱστορίη, and his predecessors belong to Miletus, where all science went by that term. The term 'Natural History' partly preserves the ancient sense of the word, a circumstance due to the title of Aristotle's Περὶ τὰ ζῷα ἱστορίαι (*Historiai Animalium*)" (John Burnet, *Plato's* Phaedo, 1911, 99–100). "Greek prose was at first employed primarily for the publication of Ionian ἱστορίη: for presenting the results for systematic 'inquiry' or 'research' on a variety of subjects from astronomy to biology, including historical research in connection with the description of lands and people (as in the travel book of Hecataeus, a Milesian contemporary of Heraclitus). The old Ionic term ἱστορίη soon became fixed in its narrow application to 'history' in our sense, because it was this type of investigation that first gave birth to major works of prose literature: the *Histories* of Herodotus and Thucydides" (Charles Kahn, *The Art and Thought of Heraclitus*, 1979, 96).

2. The abbreviation "DK" refers to *Die Fragmente der Vorsokratiker* by H. Diels and W. Kranz (1952), which is a standard edition of the ancient writings about the Presocratics. To each Presocratic, DK assign a numbered chapter divided into testimony (A) and quotation (B). So, for example, 'DK 11 A 2' refers to the second entry in the testimony in the chapter devoted to Thales. In this way, for the first time, virtually all the material on the Presocratics was collected together

---

[r] "[T]here is a real world in which we are contained, and appearances result from our interaction with the rest of it. We cannot accept those appearances uncritically, but must try to understand what our own constitution contributes to them. To do this we try to develop an idea of the world with ourselves in it, an account of both ourselves and the world that includes an explanation of why it initially appears to us as it does" (Thomas Nagel, *The View from Nowhere*, 1986, 68). Cf. Brad Inwood, *The Poem of Empedocles*: "Empedocles concludes that no mortal thing, that is, none of the compounded objects of our ordinary experience, ever really comes into being in . . . the strictest sense possible, which would mean that they came to be from nothing. Reference to birth and death, coming-to-be and passing-away, is a natural human failing, the crystallization in conventional language of the limited perceptions of men . . . . What really happens in such cases is a mixture and 'interchange' of basic entities" (2001, 34).

in a source book. It became the standard work for research and went through several editions, four in Diels' lifetime and two posthumously directed by Kranz. It is somewhat dated now, but it still provides the standard reference.

3. Except when otherwise noted, my translations diverge little if at all from those in *The Presocratic Philosophers* by G. S. Kirk, J. E. Raven, and M. Schofield (1983).

4. This is the generally accepted explanation for the break with the older school of thought. For a recent statement, see Richard McKirahan, *Philosophy before Socrates*, 1994, 74. "[The Greeks] faced two … [prestigious] civilizations, the Egyptian and the Mesopotamian, each with its own pantheon, mythology, and views on the origin of the world. In this unusual if not historically unique situation, it is understandable that a few highly intelligent and reflective people should have come to question their own religious tradition and the others as well, inventing and developing ways of examining beliefs for their plausibility and intelligibility. It is also understandable that this examination should have led to dissatisfaction with all known religions, mythologies, and world systems, and to a desire to replace them with more satisfactory accounts…." Cf. Xenophanes, DK 21 B 5: "If cattle and horses or lions had hands, or were able to draw with their hands and do the works that men can do, horses would draw the forms of gods like horses, and cattle like cattle and they would make their bodies such that they each had themselves."

5. One of the important consequences of the Milesian revolution, important especially in the development of physical science, is the introduction of geometric models for the heavens and the motions of celestial bodies. These models replace the older ones in terms of mind. Charles Kahn makes this point: "Now the important thing is not that the early models were so crude – that is only to be expected. What was important was that a geometric model for celestial motions had been proposed, with explanatory intent. At the technical level, it is this model that essentially defines the new philosophical view of the natural world as a κόσμος, a system governed by regularity and order. And it is this same model that brings into existence scientific astronomy in a new sense: a structured theory capable of explaining (or trying to explain) the observed phenomena of the heavens. In this sense the cosmology of Anaximander and Parmenides is closer in principle to that of Ptolemy and Copernicus than it is to Hesiod or to any of the predecessors – unless one finds a geometric model in Babylon" ("The origins of Greek science and philosophy," 1991, 3–4).

6. "In the earliest Greek literature the word αἴτιος is used in reference to responsibility, usually with the added connotation of blame. The extension of the notion of responsibility to all the objects and events of experience marks the beginning of the study of causation. The early Greek philosophers, so far as we know, did not speak specifically of causes; yet their systems may be considered as attempts to place the ultimate responsibility for the nature of things" (Philip DeLacy, "The problem of causation in Plato's philosophy," 1939, 97–98). Cf. William Heidel, *The Heroic Age of Science*, 1933, 6: "What is undoubtedly true of primitive man is that, while he can not strictly be said to

regard the world as composed or controlled by persons, because 'person' conveys a more clearly defined idea than he himself has framed, he looks upon all that occurs about and within him as the result of agencies akin to himself. The means he employs in the effort to control nature are essentially the same as those which he finds effective in dealing with his fellows. According to the stage which he attains in the organization of his world, his procedure may be described as magic or religion; but it is practically impossible, even at the highest stage yet reached by man, to divest the concept of causation, which underlies every effort at explaining the world, of its primal associations of nature. And when one speaks of processes of nature the analogy which from the first held the interest of man is no less apparent."

7. "There does not seem to be anything philosophical about Thales' views, at least the way we understand philosophy ..." (Michael Frede, "Aristotle's account of the origins of philosophy," 2004, 28). "No doubt, *as we use the terms today*, the Milesians were scientists ('physicists' and 'physiologers,' as Aristotle called them, those who studied *physis*, 'nature'), not philosophers. That is to say, the kinds of issues with which they were concerned are what we today would all agree to be scientific issues, problems to be dealt with by the specialists we call *scientists*" (Merrill Ring, *Beginning with the Pre-Socratics*, 2000, 32). "Many people have turned expectantly to the beginnings of Greek philosophy, only to find that the first philosopher they meet, Thales in the sixth century BC, held, apparently, that 'everything is water.' Anyone teaching ancient philosophy has to cope with the bafflement that this discovery tends to produce. It is an odd beginning to a philosophical tradition. Yet *something* happens in the sixth century, later to acquire the name *philosophia* or love of wisdom, which we can recognize as philosophical. What exactly is it? It is in keeping with what we have seen of the varied and disputatious nature of ancient philosophy that this question is quite hard to answer" (Julia Annas, *Ancient Philosophy. A Very Short Introduction*, 2000, 94). Part of the reason for this difference of opinion among scholars is tied to a lack of agreement about the nature of philosophy itself. Edward Hussey makes the point: "In general, any particular understanding of 'early Greek science and philosophy' inevitably involves some general conception of *science* and of *philosophy*. It is hardly surprising, given the contestability of any such conceptions, that many different kinds of answer to these two questions are to be found in recent scholarship" (Edward Hussey, "The beginnings of science and philosophy," 2006, 17).

8. A more usual translation of νοῆσαι here is "to be thought of," or "thinking," but I follow Charles Kahn by translating the word as "knowing." The primary question with which Parmenides concerns himself in the poem is what sort of thinking or cognition results in the grasp of truth, and this makes "knowing" the right translation, not the more general "thinking." Kahn himself puts the point as follows: "The problem which Parmenides raises *from the beginning of his poem* is ... the problem of knowledge, more exactly, the problem of the search for

knowledge, the choice between alternative ways for thought and cognition to travel on in pursuit of Truth" ("The thesis of Parmenides," 1968, 703).

9. Charles Kahn stresses the importance of this point: "Most historians have followed Plato and Aristotle in seeing Parmenides against the background of earlier Greek cosmology. Thus they interpret his doctrine of the one Being as a response to, and criticism of, the various Ionian monisms which sought to explain the natural universe on the basis of a single cosmic principle: air, water, fire, the unlimited. . . . For my part, I am convinced that there is a very intimate connection between Parmenides' argument and the doctrines of his Ionian predecessors, and I doubt whether we can understand him properly if this historical continuity is lost sight of" ("The thesis of Parmenides," 1968, 702).

10. Despite the obscurity of the texts, this general interpretation is standard. Cf. Charles Kahn: "Language and ontology in Plato's *Cratylus*," 1973, 154: "In considering the νόμος-φύσις antithesis in connection with the theory of names, it should be borne in mind that the philosophically relevant sense of νόμος goes back to Parmenides, and is fairly constant in the post-Eleatic tradition down to Democritus. The point is not only that names are 'conventional' and man-made, but that they express a false theory of reality. That is very clear in Parmenides . . . ."

11. Richard D. McKirahan, Jr., *Philosophy Before Socrates*, 1994, 305.

12. Jonathan Barnes, *Early Greek Philosophy*, 1987, 252.

13. Christopher Shields makes the point: "[Democritus] understands his atomism to render great stretches of sensory data non-objective and merely conventional. He says directly that in reality there are *only* atoms and the void; whatever else exists does so only by convention, as a sort of convenient fiction" (*Classical Philosophy*, 2003, 22). "There are in fact change and plurality; but all change is merely alteration and not generation; and all plurality is a plurality of atoms swirling in the void. We do perceive the world; but our perceptions yield only bastard judgments which cut us off from all that exists in reality, atoms in the void" (*Classical Philosophy*, 2003, 24). Cf. David Roochnik, *Retrieving the Ancients*: "Ordinary experience suggests that the book you are holding in your hand is a real object in and of itself. As a result, if someone asked you, 'what is it that you are holding?,' you would quickly answer, 'a book.' . . . But according to Democritus, you would be wrong. What you hold in your hands is not really a book at all. Instead, it is a collection of atoms moving through the void that happened to clump together and will soon separate" (2004, 51).

14. Michael Frede puts this point in historical context: "[H]ow does it come about that, if reality is the way Parmenides describes it, we nevertheless perceive it the way we do? It was Democritus who took up this problem, and, in taking it up, had to face the question of the relative roles of thought and perception in cognition. He thus, instead of having a vague and indefinite notion of some cognitive power of thought, came nearer to having a notion of reason by trying to determine more precisely the relative role of thought in cognition. Unfortunately Democritus' thought is preserved highly selectively, and there is not

much evidence concerning his views on the soul. But given that he thought of philosophy as providing therapy for the afflictions of the soul, it would seem that he, too, had a substantive notion of the soul integrating perception, thought, belief, and desire in some systematic way. And so we, finally, come at least fairly close to a notion of reason, as we find it from Socrates onward" ("Introduction" in *Rationality in Greek Thought*, 1996a, 21–22). Cf. Charles Kahn, "Democritus and the origins of moral psychology," 1985, 23: "The ordinary, pre-theoretical notion of reason is ... [given] by the opposition between acting reasonably or foolishly, with foresight or without. This practical notion of rationality is then given an entirely new content by the philosophers (beginning with Heraclitus and Parmenides) who develop a notion of mind or intelligence as a theoretical capacity to understand the nature of things. It is this notion which Democritus has identified by the contrast with sense perception. And once he has done so, the concept of mind or reason is in a state of creative fermentation and confusion. It will have to be clarified by a systematic account of the parts or faculties of the psyche, in which the epistemic and prudential roles of reason are somehow distinguished and reconciled. That will be the work of Plato and Aristotle."

Further Reading for Part I

1. *Early Greek Philosophy*, Jonathan Barnes, 1987
   This is a collection of "English translations of all the surviving philosophical fragments of the Presocratic thinkers" (31). It includes translations of extracts from the doxographies in which many of the fragments occur. There is also an insightful introduction and synopsis.
2. *The Presocratic Philosophers* (in two volumes), Jonathan Barnes, 1979
   This discussion is more philosophical than historical. The primary aim is to assess the Presocratics, to determine "whether they spoke truly" and "whether their sayings rested on sound arguments" (vol. I, ix). The Sophists are included among the Presocratics. The notes and bibliography are especially valuable.
3. *A History of Greek Philosophy*, W. K. C. Guthrie, 1971
   Guthrie published six volumes before his death. The first two volumes are *The Earlier Presocratics and Pythagoreans* and *The Presocratic Tradition from Parmenides to Democritus*. As Jonathan Barnes observes in his bibliography, "English readers will find a treasury of humane scholarship" in these volumes (1979, vol. II, 319).
4. *The Presocratics*, Edward Hussey, 1972
   This is a general introduction to "the history of ancient Greek thought between approximately 600 and 400 BC" (vii). The discussion is both historical and philosophical.
5. *The Presocratic Philosophers*, G. S. Kirk, J. E. Raven, and M. Schofield, 1983
   This book is the now orthodox scholarly discussion of the "chief Presocratic 'physicists' and their forerunners, whose main preoccupation was with the nature (*physis*) and coherence of things as a whole" (xi). It contains texts both in translation and in Greek. As the authors note, the commentary is "for those who have more than a casual interest in the history of early Greek thought" (xi).
6. *Philosophy Before Socrates*, Richard D. McKirahan, Jr., 1994
   This is an introduction with both translations of the texts and extensive commentary. It is a source book, like *The Presocratic Philosophers*, but the discussion is more accessible. In addition, McKirahan includes a discussion of the fifth-century sophists and of the *nomos-physis* debate.

Part II

Socrates

*Lover of wisdom, executed by the city
of Athens in 399 BC*

Enlightenment thinking about human beings and the good life

The Peloponnesian War is the dominant political and social event in the background of the Platonic dialogues. In 480, the Persians mounted a second invasion of Greece. They were defeated, due in large measure to the Athenian general Themistocles, who led the Greek fleet to victory over the Persian navy. The events were dramatic. The Athenians withdrew from Athens, took to their fleet, and allowed Athens itself to be burned. They then trapped the Persian fleet and completely destroyed it. This crushing defeat was the beginning of the end for the Persian expansion, and Athens played an ever more prominent role in the region. The Persian threat was soon eliminated, but Athens continued to insist on a leading role. She rebuilt herself and became the rich and beautiful center of Greek civilization. This caused considerable friction between Athens and the other Peloponnesian states, especially Sparta. In 432, Sparta convinced the Greek states aggrieved with Athens to go to war against her. The war would devastate Athens, which would eventually be reduced to complete subjection. The long and terrible war, with its many atrocities,[a] marked the end of the so-called "Golden Age," the time of Themistocles, the statesman Pericles, and others whose leadership seemed to propel the Athenians to greatness. Plato writes about Socrates after his execution and in the aftermath of the Peloponnesian War. His motives are not always completely clear, but it is natural to understand parts of some of the dialogues as an indictment of the ways that led to Athens' demise, and as an exploration of a possible solution in the new way of thinking about human beings and their good that Socrates had begun to work out.

---

[a] One of the worst occurred when the city of Skione in Northern Greece allied itself with Sparta. In punishment, Athens killed all the men and sold the women and children into slavery.

Time Line

500	475	450	425	400	375

Protagoras

Gorgias

Peloponnesian War (431–404)

Socrates (469–399)

Plato (429–347)

The Academy (387)

2

The Good Life

Happiness, ethics, and the love of wisdom

Socrates focused the enlightenment attitude on human beings and their good. He wrote nothing, but the early dialogues suggest that he thought that human beings are psychological beings, that the expectation for happiness and the good life is a matter of having the right psychology, that this psychology underlies the life of practical wisdom about ethical matters, and that human beings become practically wise through the "love of wisdom." Socrates seems to have done little to explain or defend this new conception of human beings and their good, but he faced a death sentence from the city of Athens rather than abandon his love of wisdom. This inspired Plato to write about Socrates in an effort to understand his conception of human beings and their good.

The distinction between reason and experience from the Presocratic period figures prominently in the portrait Plato develops. In the early dialogues, Socrates again and again searches for a definition in connection with some ethical matter. This emphasis on reason, as opposed to experience, contrasts with the more common idea that the expertise involved in living a good life is a matter of living through situations of the sort human beings encounter as they live their lives. It is commonly thought that this experience is the key to seeing what should be done in various situations. The emphasis on reason is also prominent in the theory of desire which Plato has Socrates develop in his discussion with the Sophist, Protagoras. According to this theory, all desire stems from a certain sort of judgment and hence is a matter of reason. This contrasts with the more usual view according to which some action stems from desires that are not themselves a matter of judgment.

Ancient Greek Philosophy: From The Presocratics to the Hellenistic Philosophers, First Edition.
Thomas A. Blackson. © 2011 Thomas A. Blackson. Published 2011 by Blackwell Publishing Ltd.

Socrates is the best-known figure in philosophy, but little is known about him. What he thought must be inferred from the writings of others, since he himself wrote nothing. Plato,[a] who was in Socrates' circle of friends, is the primary source of this evidence. He features a character "Socrates" in many of his dialogues, and hence it is natural to think that in the early dialogues,[b] and perhaps also in some of the later ones, Plato has this character say the sorts of things the historical figure said. This assumption seems to have led Aristotle, in his remarks on the history of philosophy, to pinpoint Socrates' place in the tradition as follows: "Socrates was busying himself about ethical matters, neglecting the world of nature as a whole, and by seeking the universal in these ethical matters, he fixed thought for the first time on definitions" (*Metaphysics* I.6.987b1–4).[1]

---

[a] Plato was an Athenian aristocrat. He was born in 427 when Socrates was 42 years old and Athens was at the apex of its military and political power. Plato probably became friends with Socrates at an early age. Charmides, who was Plato's mother's brother, was both one of Socrates' close associates and partly responsible for Socrates' poor reputation among ordinary Athenians. During the political turmoil in the last years of the Peloponnesian War, Charmides and others ruthlessly subverted the democracy. Socrates dissented from this immoral behavior, but he was nevertheless put to death on trumped-up charges when the democracy was restored. This seems to have completely disillusioned Plato. He gave up any ambitions he naturally might have otherwise had for a political career. Instead, he founded the Academy in 387 and remained its head until his death in 347. Athens had by then lost much of its power and would soon lose the rest when Philip of Macedon, the father of Alexander the Great, would defeat the Athenians in the battle. This Macedonian victory resulted in the loss of independence for Athens and the other Greek cities.

[b] The early dialogues are the first in a tripartite chronological division into which scholars generally (but not universally) suppose the Platonic dialogues subdivide. The evidence for this division depends on the historical context, the content of the dialogues themselves, certain passages in Aristotle in which he talks about Socrates and Plato, and linguistic studies of Plato's style of composition. In alphabetical order, the early dialogues are the *Apology*, *Charmides*, *Crito*, *Euthyphro*, *Euthydemus*, *Gorgias*, *Hippias Major*, *Hippias Minor*, *Ion*, *Laches*, *Lysis*, and *Protagoras*. The middle dialogues are the *Cratylus*, *Meno*, *Phaedo*, *Phaedrus*, *Republic*, and *Symposium*. The late dialogues are the *Critias*, *Laws*, *Parmenides*, *Philebus*, *Sophist*, *Statesman*, *Theaetetus*, and *Timaeus*. There is controversy over the dates of particular dialogues, but this tripartite division is widely accepted as roughly correct. David Sedley expresses the current consensus: "[a]lthough there have in recent years been voicings of discontent about [the traditional ordering], the ball is still firmly in the court of anyone who wishes to undermine it" (*The Midwife of Platonism. Text and Subtext of Plato's Theaetetus*, 2004, 2). (For an important argument against the tripartite division and in favor of two thematic groupings prior to a grouping of six late dialogues, see John Cooper's "Introduction," 1997, xii–xvii.)

Aristotle's summary is part of a now standard interpretation of Socrates, and it provides a useful framework for organizing Plato's portrait of Socrates in the early dialogues. Socrates represents a break from the focus on nature in the Presocratics.[c] He was interested in ethical matters, and he abandoned a conventional life to pursue this interest. Moreover, Socrates stuck to his pursuit even though it cost him his life. He was executed by the city of Athens in 399.

This devotion in the face of death was both stunning and perplexing. The details of his pursuit were so undefined it was difficult to understand how the pursuit was supposed to work and hence why anyone should value it so highly. Socrates was legendary for his upright behavior.[d] Hence, it was tempting to think he was "busying himself about ethical

---

[c] Aristophanes' *Clouds* (423) suggests that Socrates was initially interested in the inquiry into nature. The resulting portrait had great comic effect, but it may not have been rooted in truth. In any case, if Socrates ever was interested in nature, he seems to have later abandoned this interest for questioning of the general sort Plato illustrates in his early dialogues with the character Socrates. In the *Apology*, which purports to be a description of the events at Socrates' trial, and which scholars sometimes assume is Plato's most faithful representation of the historical figure, Plato has Socrates tell the story of how his friend, Chaerephon, went to Delphi to ask whether anyone was wiser than Socrates. The answer was that no one was wiser. When he was told the answer, Socrates said that there must be a hidden meaning because the obvious one seemed false. Hence, he set about interrogating those with a reputation for wisdom so that he might discover what the oracle really had in mind (20e–21a). Many of the sons of the prominent Athenians of the day gathered around Socrates to hear him question those with a reputation for wisdom.

[d] For example, in 424, the eighth year of the Peloponnesian War, the Athenians were defeated at Delium. Laches, one of the Athenian generals, says that this disaster would have been avoided if the others had been as brave as Socrates (*Laches* 181b). Again, at Amphipolis in 422, the Athenians were defeated, and a general, Cleon, perished in the rout. Alcibiades says that Socrates was much more collected than Laches (*Laches* 221b). In Potidea, in 430, Alcibiades was wounded behind enemy lines. Socrates rescued him, and Alcibiades says that Socrates should have received the decoration that Alcibiades himself received (*Laches* 219e–220e.) In his trial, as Plato portrays it, Socrates twice alludes to his bravery in the face of mob rule. The first is in connection with the illegal attempt to try the generals who failed to pick up the survivors at the battle of Arginusae in 406, the last Athenian victory in the Peloponnesian War. A storm had prevented the rescue, but a democratic mob lobbied for a trial nonetheless. The second is in connection with The Thirty, an oligarchy set up in 404 to draft a new constitution after the final defeat of Athens in the Peloponnesian War. They waged a terror campaign against their Athenian enemies, and they ordered Socrates to take part in an illegal execution. Socrates refused, thereby putting his own life at considerable risk (*Apology* 32a–32e).

matters" because he wanted to make himself and his life good.[e] Yet, the way he busied himself with ethical matters, which he called the "love of wisdom," seemed much more like a theoretical enterprise than a practical one, since his focus was on definitions of the ethical virtues.[2] Moreover, even if the love of wisdom somehow did result in practical wisdom in ethical matters and hence in a life in accordance with ethical virtue,[f] it remains puzzling why this life should be singled out as the good life.

Plato, in his dialogues, makes a concerted effort to understand the love of wisdom and its significance. His aim is not to report conversations he

---

[e] The quest for the good life was a traditional pursuit among the Athenians, and it remains clearly recognizable and no less important today. For example, in the opening of the *Laches*, Lysimachus and Melesias seek advice on the proper education of their sons. They are ashamed that they themselves have not done nearly as well as their famous fathers (Aristides and Thucydides), and they seek advice about how to educate their children so that they will do better (179c–180a). It is clear, in this exchange, that Lysimachus and Melesias want to equip their children with what they need to lead good lives. The problem is that they themselves do not know what this is. Socrates, later in the conversation, rephrases the request in terms of virtue and the soul. He asks Laches, an Athenian general who is partner to the discussion, whether Lysimachus and Melesias are "asking our advice as to how virtue may be added to the souls of their sons to make them better?" (190b). Socrates had stressed previously that "it is by knowledge that one must make decisions, if one is to make them well" (184e), and in the ensuing investigation of the virtue the children need, Socrates takes up the more restricted question of whether they have a "sufficient knowledge of a part" (190c), namely courage, the part Laches and Nicias – the other Athenian general in the conversation – might be expected to understand. The generals cannot defend their accounts of courage, and like the early dialogues that search for definitions generally, the *Laches* ends without a clear answer to the original request. (Cf. Susan Sauvé Meyer, *Ancient Ethics*, 2008b, 22: "A modern reader of Plato might be unconvinced that these interrogations succeed in establishing that the refuted interlocutors lack knowledge of how to live well. Might not a person know how to live, and exhibit such knowledge in his or her life, but be unable to articulate it in a general formula? ... Plato's intended readership, however, would never make such an objection. That audience, which is at least a generation later than the dramatic date [of the dialogue, knows how things have played out]. ... The dialogue *Laches* is set in the early years of the thirty-year [Peloponnesian] war, when Athenian power still prevails and the Athenians are optimistic of victory. Nicias and Laches enjoy high public repute at the time, which is why the elderly fathers consult with them about how their sons might achieve excellence. The dialogue is written, however, after the bitter and humiliating defeat of Athens, and after Nicias, in particular, has been disgraced by foolish decisions that led to the defeat of the Athenian expedition against Syracuse in 413.")

[f] A person is typically said to have *wisdom* or to be *wise* if he is not confused about things that typically confuse others. Practical wisdom is wisdom about practical matters, about *what to do* in the situations one encounters as one lives one's life.

remembers, although he may do this to some extent.[g] Rather, his aim is to understand Socrates. Plato is convinced that Socrates was a great benefit to Athens and should not have been executed. Hence, for his readers and for himself, Plato tries to work out the details that Socrates left implicit. This begins with a picture of Socrates in the early dialogues, and it continues through the middle dialogues, culminating initially in the *Republic*, which is perhaps the greatest of the middle dialogues. The result is the first extended investigation into psychology, reason and rationality, ethics, and the good life.

2.1 Definitions

To understand Socrates and his place in the ancient philosophical tradition, it is necessary to understand what he did in pursuing the love of wisdom. If one looks to the early Platonic dialogues for an indication of what the historical figure thought, then Aristotle's description captures the most salient feature of Socrates' pursuit.[h] Plato

---

[g] To the modern reader, the dialogues can seem like records of historical conversations. This can encourage one to think that Plato is simply imitating conversations he remembers, in the way an apprentice imitates his master by trying to recreate a product the master has already produced, but there is another way to understand the dialogues. It may be that from the beginning, even in the *Apology*, which is sometimes thought to be the early dialogue to provide the strongest evidence for what Socrates thought, Plato is trying to bring out both what is important and what is problematic about Socrates. (In "Whatever became of the Socratic Elenchus? Philosophical analysis in Plato," Gareth B. Matthews (2009) calls this the "reassessment model." He favors it over the "apprenticeship model," which is a term he introduces in this paper.) It is impossible to choose between these two ways of reading the dialogues by looking to what Socrates wrote, since he wrote nothing, but many scholars warn against reading the dialogues as historical transcripts and make the general point that Plato is trying to understand Socrates. For example, Susan Sauvé Meyer says that the "dialogues are not accurate reports of conversations between Socrates and the characters depicted ... [but] are dramatic creations in which Plato uses the figure of Socrates to work through the ethical issues of the day" (*Ancient Ethics*, 2008b, 7). If this is true, there is no straightforward inference from what the character Socrates says in a dialogue to what the historical Socrates thought. Michael Frede summarizes the point and the current consensus among scholars: "It is notoriously difficult to say anything historically reliable about Socrates" ("Introduction" in *Rationality in Greek Thought*, 1996a, 6–7).

[h] A number of Socrates' followers wrote about him to celebrate his memory. These portraits do not paint a completely consistent picture of what the historical figure thought, and hence the details of what Socrates thought remains uncertain. "[W]hat little remains of the 'Socratic dialogues' written by others shows considerable variation in the doctrines and personality attributed to Socrates. The Socratic dialogues of Plato, Aeschines, and Antisthenes and the teachings of the Socratic Aristippus inspired such different ethical traditions that, in later Greek philosophy, Socrates is revered as a figurehead by schools that espouse rival doctrines" (Susan Sauvé Meyer, *Ancient Ethics*, 2008b, 7).

has the character Socrates search for an account, or a "definition,"[i] in connection with an ethical matter. This search occurs in more or less the same way. For various reasons, given the dramatic context of each of these dialogues, one of the interlocutors is portrayed as appearing to have a certain amount of expertise about some ethical matter. This portrayal allows Socrates to pursue his interest in definitions as a natural way to question this appearance of expertise. He asks his "What is it?" question, where this question is a request for a definition in connection with the matter in which the interlocutors appear to have expertise. The conversation thus takes an adversarial turn, but this too is natural because Plato's Athenian audience suspects, or even knows, that the interlocutors have no expertise.[j]

Socrates, however, does not press his search for a definition without some introduction. To clarify his intention in making the request, he first asks a preliminary question. Where *X*-ness is the matter under discussion, Socrates asks his interlocutor the following question:

(Q1) What is that by which all *X*–things are *X*?

---

[i] It is traditional to describe Socrates' search as a search for "definitions," and I follow this conventional practice. It should be remembered, however, that the search is a search for answers to the "What is it?" question, where this question is about piety, courage, and the other things Socrates uses his question to ask about.

[j] In the *Euthyphro*, Socrates discusses piety with a self-styled religious expert, Euthyphro. He claims special knowledge of piety, but the Athenians would not have been convinced and in fact would have been poisoned against him. He prosecutes his father for murder on behalf of the deceased, who was himself a murderer. Ordinary Athenians would have thought the prosecution a violation of filial piety, yet Euthyphro himself says that he engages in the prosecution in the name of piety. In the *Laches*, Socrates discusses courage with two generals made famous in connection with the Peloponnesian War, Laches and Nicias. The dialogue is set in the early years of the war, but Plato's Athenian audience knows that the war ends badly and that Nicias in particular dies in disgrace, captured and executed after his fleet was destroyed due to his indecision. In the *Charmides*, Socrates discusses temperance with Charmides and Critias. Charmides is Plato's uncle, on his mother's side. In the dialogue he is a teenager, a much-admired and to all appearances a temperate and, more generally, excellent youth from an important aristocratic family. Critias is Charmides' first cousin and guardian. But Plato's Athenian audience knows that Charmides and Critas became notorious tyrants. Critias was the leader and Charmides was a member of "The Thirty," wealthy aristocrats appointed in 404 by Sparta to draft a new constitution after the Athenian defeat in the Peloponnesian War. Instead, they brutally seized power and waged terror against their enemies. Both were killed when The Thirty were overthrown and the democracy restored. In the *Hippias Major*, Socrates discusses the fine with the sophist and polymath, Hippias. Hippias worked as a diplomat (281a) and as a paid public speaker (282b–e). Plato portrays him as a "pitchman" who says nothing very definite but says it in a manner that pleases the ignorant but offends those who are interested in truth and can think clearly.

Socrates hopes his interlocutor will say that

(A1) *X*-things are *X* by the "form" or "idea" of *X*-ness.[3]

Socrates proceeds in this indirect way because he wants his interlocutors to understand that his "What is *X*-ness?" question is a request for a correct specification of *being X* or of *what it is to be X*.[4] This is his point in his remarks in the *Euthyphro*[k] in the following passage:

> I did not ask you about some one or two of the many pious things. I asked you about the form itself that makes all pious things pious. You agreed that all pious things are pious because of one idea or form. Tell me what this itself is, so by looking to it, and using it as a paradigm,[1] I may say whether an action of yours or another's is pious or not. (6d–e[5])

Socrates reminds Euthyphro that in answer to the "What is piety?" question, he does not wish to be told what piety is in certain situations; rather, he wants to be told what piety is in every situation. This answer would specify what Socrates calls the "form" or "idea" of piety.

In the dialogues, after his interlocutors provide him with the desired (A1) response to the preliminary (Q1) question, Socrates then asks for a specification of the form mentioned in the (A1) response. He asks for this specification with a question of the following kind:

(Q2) What is *X*-ness?

He hopes his interlocutors will provide him with an answer such as:

(A2) *X*-ness is *G*-ness,

an answer the interlocutor can defend against subsequent questions. If the interlocutor can defend the answer, he will have defended his belief that the form of *X*-ness is *G*-ness.

---

[k] This dialogue is the first in the tetralogy of dialogues devoted to Socrates' life and death. It shows Socrates before his trial. The *Euthyphro* is followed by the *Apology, Crito*, and *Phaedo*. The *Crito* takes place in the time between Socrates' trial and the day of his execution. The *Phaedo* takes place on the day of his execution.

[1] Socrates is not asking for an example. The Greek noun here stems from a verb that means *indicate* or *point out*, and so Socrates expects the definition will point out or indicate what piety is.

The *Hippias Major* provides an example. In the guise of a doggedly persistent questioner – a questioner who no doubt really represents Socrates himself – Socrates presses his search for a definition in his conversation with his interlocutor, Hippias:

> He would say, is it not by justice that the just are just? Answer as if he were the questioner.
>
> It is by justice.
>
> And is justice something?
>
> Certainly.
>
> And by wisdom the wise are wise, and by the good good things are good?
>
> Of course.
>
> And by these being something? Obviously it cannot be that they are not.
>
> Indeed, they are something.
>
> Then are not all fine things fine by the fine?
>
> Yes.
>
> And by that being something?
>
> Yes.
>
> Then tell me, he would say, what is that, the fine? (287c–d)

Socrates uses the preliminary (Q1) question to help Hippias see, first of all, that X-things are X by being X and, secondly, that being X is the thing in need of definition. Once Hippias appears to understand, Socrates uses his (Q2) question to press for the definition.

It is difficult to know why exactly the historical Socrates started asking for definitions, if indeed this is something the historical Socrates actually did,[m]

---

[m] If the historical Socrates was interested in definitions, which is plausible but far from certain in the light of the available evidence, then presumably his practice crystallized in the interrogations that ensued in his attempt to understand the meaning of the oracle's answer to Chaerephon. Socrates, however, must have already been known for some sort of wisdom, perhaps because he talked about subjects that were hard to know about. Otherwise, it is not easy to see why Chaerephon went to Delphi in the first place. How Socrates got this reputation is not clear, but John Burnet offers an intriguing explanation: he says that the reputation rested on Socrates' novel doctrine of the soul: "The jests of Aristophanes made it plain that Socrates was known as a man who spoke strangely of the soul before 423 BC, and this takes us back to a time when Plato was not five years old, so that there can be no question of him as the author of the view he ascribes to Socrates. We may fairly conclude, I think, that the 'wisdom' which so impressed the boy Alcibiades and the impulsive Chaerephon, was just this" ("The Socratic doctrine of the soul," 1968, 161).

but the early Platonic dialogues suggest that he abandoned a conventional life so that he could persist in this unusual practice because, among other things, he thought that holding in mind a correct answer to this question is necessary to avoid confusion about related matters.[6] This, for example, seems to be the character Socrates' stated reason for asking the "What is justice?" question in Book I of the *Republic*:

> I have not done well. The fault, though, is mine, not yours. I behaved like a glutton, grabbing for every dish that passes and tasting it before properly considering the one before. So instead of finding the answer to the question of what justice is, I let that pass and turned to the new question of whether justice is a vice and ignorance, or a virtue and wisdom. Next the question of whether injustice is more profitable[n] than justice came before me, and, once again, I could not stop myself from abandoning the previous investigation and engaging in this one. Consequently, the outcome of the discussion for me is that I know nothing, because if I do not know what justice is, I do not know whether justice is a virtue, or whether a just human being is happy. (I.354a–c)

In this passage, he explains that his investigation has been unsuccessful because he has not followed the proper method of inquiry. He says that he is not clear on whether justice is wisdom and virtue, and whether the just man is happy, because he has not understood what justice is.

This interpretation of Socrates' search for definitions places him firmly within the tradition of the Milesian revolution. Thales and the Milesian naturalists were early participants in a period of enlightenment in Greek history. They exhibited the general attitude that the traditional beliefs and practices were no longer adequate and that instead of blindly following tradition, the inquirer should think about the matter for himself to reach a better understanding of things. Anaximenes provides an example. He wanted to know *what rain and other such phenomena are* because he thought this knowledge would provide him with a clearer understanding of the weather and hence eliminate his dependence on any false beliefs in the traditional understanding of these phenomena.

---

[n] The comparative adjective for "more profitable" is a compound formed from the words *free* and *end*. The end to be freed is usually identified by context. In this case, the context indicates that end is the good life. So in asking whether injustice is more profitable than justice, the question is about which of them can be expected to result in the good life.

Socrates was interested in ethical matters, but he too seems to have exhibited the same enlightenment attitude and was part of this same intellectual optimism that had taken root in the ancient Greek world.[7] Socrates did not blindly follow tradition. He did not simply accept the traditional thinking about ethical matters, thinking that conceived of expertise in ethical matters as consisting of long, and often hard, experience in the sorts of difficult situations human beings encounter as they live out their lives. Quite to the contrary, Socrates thought he could think for himself to reach a better understanding of ethical matters. The form he thought this thinking should take is uncertain since he wrote nothing, but Plato suggests that the search for definitions was part of Socrates' attempt to reach a better understanding. Socrates seems to have thought that definitions of the ethical virtues would provide a clearer understanding of *what the virtues are* and thus eliminate his dependence on false beliefs that have become part of the received wisdom.

Because Socrates stands within the enlightenment tradition that runs back to the Milesian inquirers into nature, it is natural to understand his emphasis on definitions in terms of the view in Parmenides, and subsequently in Democritus and the atomists, that "reason" (and not "experience") is the cognition involved in knowledge. For these Presocratics, this knowledge is about what exists and is about the structure of reality generally. Socrates seems not to have been interested in this sort of knowledge. He was interested in ethical matters and what the virtues are, but he did not attribute any particular ontological status to the definitions of these virtues. However, definitions would seem to be the sorts of things human beings know through the exercise of reason. Experience may be causally necessary for this knowledge, but the experience itself does not appear to be part of the justification for the knowledge. So in thinking more about Socrates, it is useful to keep these issues in mind and to expect that Plato himself will try to understand Socrates and the love of wisdom against a historical background that includes the inquiry into nature and the emphasis on "reason" in Parmenides and his successors.[o]

---

[o] In fact, this does happen in the *Phaedo*, where Plato has Socrates set out his intellectual autobiography. This passage, and its importance for understanding how Plato understood Socrates, is taken up in Chapter 5.

Socrates questions Euthyphro

The *Euthyphro* is one of Plato's portraits of Socrates in the pursuit of wisdom. The dialogue is from the early period of dialogues. The location is a public building where certain official duties were discharged. The conversation begins with an exchange of initial pleasantries, and Euthyphro lets it be known that he is bringing a suit against his father to satisfy the demands of piety.[P] Socrates is surprised and says to Euthyphro that he must be "far advanced in wisdom" to undertake such a case, as prosecuting one's father on any charge should not be taken lightly. Euthyphro is quick to boast that he does indeed have "accurate knowledge" of piety, and Socrates is not about to let Euthyphro's boast go untested. He asks Euthyphro what piety is.

Euthyphro fancies himself as an expert and is only too happy to reply to Socrates. He says that what he is doing right now is pious. Socrates explains that this reply is not an answer to the question he has asked, that he wants to know what piety is in general. Euthyphro seems to understand, but it quickly becomes apparent that he is no expert on piety. He makes several attempts to provide a correct definition of piety, but he is unable to defend any of these answers without contradicting himself in questioning. He soon decides he has more important business to attend, and the dialogue ends with Socrates expressing extreme disappointment because Euthyphro (in his rush to attend to other business) will not help him acquire wisdom about divine matters.[q]

A more detailed look at the Dialogue

In trying to answer Socrates, Euthyphro begins with the natural idea that piety somehow involves the gods. Once he understands the sort of

---

[P] Euthyphro farmed with his father on Naxos, one of the many Greek colonies where Athenians had property. In a drunken rage, one of the laborers killed a slave who belonged to the estate. The father had the laborer bound and left in a ditch, while a messenger was sent to Athens for instructions. The laborer died of exposure before the messenger returned. R. E. Allen explains the connection with piety: "In Athens, homicide differed from impiety in that it was not a crime against the City, and therefore not prosecuted under a *graphe*, or public indictment; it was treated as a private wrong actionable by *dike*, or civil suit. Yet murder was unusual, in that suit was initiated before the King, a religious magistrate, because murder implied the contagion of pollution and was therefore affected with a public interest" (Euthyphro, Apology, Crito, Meno, Gorgias, Menexenus. *The Dialogues of Plato*, 1984, 133).
[q] No interlocutor in the early dialogues ever successfully defends any of his answers to Socrates' "What is it?" question. These dialogues all end in perplexity.

answer Socrates wants, he suggests that "what is dear to the gods is pious, what it not is impious." Socrates, in his usual way, asks further questions. First of all, he asks Euthyphro whether the gods disagree with one another about what is "just, fine, ugly, good, and bad." Euthyphro replies that they do, and Socrates asks whether, in this case, some of the very same things are both loved and hated by the gods. Euthyphro concurs, and Socrates asks whether it follows, given Euthyphro's proposed definition, that some things are both pious and impious. Euthyphro admits the point and agrees that it is absurd. He sees that he has contradicted himself, and now he must either withdraw his definition or withdraw one of his answers.

In an effort to be helpful, Socrates suggests to Euthyphro that maybe he had spoken incorrectly initially and had really meant that "what all the gods hate is impious, and what they all love is pious." Euthyphro accepts the suggestion. Hence, to test Euthyphro with respect to this new definition, Socrates asks the following disjunctive question: (Q) "Are pious things loved by the gods because they are pious, or are pious things pious because they are loved by the gods?" After some explanation of the two alternatives, Euthyphro decides the first one is correct. Given this decision, Euthyphro, once again, has contradicted himself. He had previously answered the "What is piety?" question by saying piety is what the gods love, but now, in answer to Socrates' question (Q), Euthyphro has said the gods love pious actions because these actions are pious.

The contradiction may not be immediately apparent, but the point is not hard to appreciate once the consequences of the alternatives in (Q) are made clear. In asking his question (Q), Socrates is asking Euthyphro which is right, whether the gods love pious actions because they recognize these actions are pious, or, alternatively, whether pious actions are pious because the gods love these actions. In the case of this second alternative, the question is whether an action is pious because of the fact that the gods love it. If this were the case, then piety would be a matter of a certain subjective response by the gods. An action would be pious because the gods love it.

Once Euthyphro grants that the gods love pious actions because these actions are pious, he must, on pain of contradiction, give up his proposed definition of piety as what the gods love. If to be pious is to be loved by the gods, as is given in the definition he has proposed, then the gods do not love pious actions because these actions are pious. To say the gods love pious actions because these actions are pious is to say that piety is prior to the gods' love. The gods form the attitude of love toward certain actions because they have recognized that these actions are pious.

Euthyphro apparently finds Socrates' reasoning persuasive, but he seems not to understand the issues involved. He says he is thoroughly confused and can no longer say what he had "in mind about piety," because, as he goes on to complain, "somehow whatever I put forward refuses to stay put" (11b). Euthyphro had thought piety must be what the gods love, but by answering Socrates' "What is piety?" question in terms of a subjective response among the gods, as opposed to an objective feature of objects, he has now identified piety with a shared attitude in the gods. This identification undermines the expected explanation for why the gods love what they love. One would naturally think that they love certain actions because they believe these actions are pious. Given Euthyphro's definition, this sort of explanation is unavailable. Given that piety is defined as what the gods love, to say that the gods love pious actions because these actions are pious is to say nothing more than that the gods love pious actions because they love them.

Euthyphro is on the verge of quitting the conversation, but Socrates intervenes and pushes the discussion forward. He asks whether piety might be a part of justice. Euthyphro, desperate to show he really is an expert, quickly accepts the suggestion and says that "the pious is the part of the just concerned with the care of the gods, while that concerned with the care of men is the remaining part of justice" (12e). In the testing and examining that follows, Socrates focuses his questioning on the meaning of taking "care" in connection with the gods. Euthyphro tries but cannot see his way through this inquiry. Socrates, however, is not willing to let the matter drop. To help Euthyphro move forward in their search, he offers some tantalizing words of encouragement:

> You could tell me much more briefly, if you wished, what I asked you, but you are not in a hurry to teach me, Euthyphro, that is obvious. You were on the verge of teaching me but stopped short. If you had continued, I would have learned from you what piety is. (14b–c)

In these remarks, Socrates seems to hint at the answer to the "What is piety?" question. What Euthyphro was "on the verge of teaching," Socrates seems to suggest, is that to "care" in connection with the gods is to do what is *appropriate* in matters involving them. Piety, in this case, is what is appropriate with respect to the gods, whatever this is in the particular situation.[r]

Euthyphro, however, is unable to see the point (if indeed this really is the hint Socrates has in mind), and the conversation quickly comes to a close. Socrates is eager to stay the course, but Euthyphro has soon had enough. He is pressed for time. Socrates is left hanging and disappointed:

> What are you doing, leaving now! I had hoped I would learn the pious and the impious from you, and so escape Meletus'[s] indictment by demonstrating to him that I had acquired wisdom in divine matters, that my ignorance would no longer make me careless and innovative about these things, and that now I would be better for the rest of my life. (15e–16a)

Socrates hoped to acquire "wisdom" about divine matters. Euthyphro represented himself as an expert on such matters and thus, in light of the hint, as someone who knows that piety is what is appropriate in connection

---

[r] There is a similar but more developed suggestion along these lines in the *Protagoras*. At 329c–d, after Protagoras has tried to explain why virtue can be taught, Socrates asks him whether "virtue is one thing, with justice and temperance and piety its parts, or are the things I have just mentioned really that same thing?" Socrates himself seems to think that virtue is one thing because it is wisdom. To understand what he had in mind, consider the courageous and the cowardly. They move to or away from the fearful things they think it is appropriate to move to or away from. The difference is that the courageous are right about what is appropriate. "Given the notion of wisdom Socrates has developed, it is obvious that courage is just wisdom, and that fear will not prevent the wise person from doing what is courageous. Being wise, one will know what is bad. One will not be oblivious to the dangers of the situation. Otherwise one would be just rash or stupid. But one will also know that what appears frightful, and thus is shunned by cowards, in fact, on balance, is not. What appears frightful, in the light of one's corrective knowledge, will be seen at worst to be less awful than what would result from the opposite course of action. One will know that the really terrible thing, the thing really to be afraid of, would be to fail to do what the situation demands. Thus cowardice turns out to be ignorance, a failure to calculate properly what is to be feared and what is not" (Michael Frede, "Introduction" in *Plato*, Protagoras, 1992, xxxi). Note, however, that Frede, in his interpretation, makes wisdom consist in more than an understanding of what the virtues are. It also includes an understanding of good and bad.

[s] Meletus is one of Socrates' accusers in the *Apology*. Diogenes Laertius (early third century AD) preserves the indictment in II.40 of his *Lives and Opinions of the Philosophers*: "This indictment and affidavit is sworn by Meletus, the son of Meletus of Pitthos, against Socrates, the son of Sophroniscus of Alopece: Socrates is guilty of refusing to recognize the gods recognized by the city, and of introducing other new divinities. He is also guilty of corrupting the youth. The penalty demanded is death" (R. D. Hicks, *Diogenes Laertius. Lives of Eminent Philosophers*, 1972, 171).

with matters involving the gods. Socrates had hoped to acquire this wisdom from Euthyphro so that he would henceforth cease to be "careless and innovative about these things" and, consequently, would be "better" for the rest of his life, but Euthyphro has other business and does not stay to defend an answer to the "What is piety?" question.

Some questions about the search for definitions

There is much in the *Euthyphro* that deserves a closer look, perhaps especially the question of objectivity in the discussion of the second definition, but from the point of view of understanding what Socrates does and what he hopes to accomplish, two questions are pressing. The first arises in connection with the passage where Socrates seems to hint that piety is that which is appropriate in connection with the gods. If this definition of piety is correct, and if Socrates wants practical wisdom about ethical matters, then the definition alone provides no real guidance. A person who wants to act piously must know which of the available actions is appropriate.

The second question is about the method generally. The procedure Socrates uses (in his love of wisdom) to discover the definition of piety is itself puzzling, since it is not at all clear how being forced into contradiction is supposed to be related to knowledge of what piety is. The idea seems to be that once Euthyphro has eliminated the inconsistency among his beliefs, he will be left with knowledge of the definition. The elimination of inconsistency itself, however, does not confer justification, so it is unclear why Socrates' method should result in knowledge.

The proper understanding of the second issue is not obvious, but maybe the idea is that false belief, never the absence of knowledge, is the obstacle in need of removal. The idea, in this case, would be that once Euthyphro has eliminated his false beliefs he will be left with knowledge of the correct definition. It is not immediately clear why he should be left with this knowledge, but notice that this assumption presupposes that the knowledge itself cannot be lost in the elimination of inconsistency. This is not the weaker assumption that, in the course of many conversations, some beliefs repeatedly survive elimination. This weaker assumption does not entail that the surviving beliefs are knowledge, since survival alone shows only that the interlocutor is more confident in the surviving beliefs than in the ones he eliminates to preserve consistency. Socrates, on the contrary, seems to make the extraordinary assumption that everyone has the knowledge, that this knowledge is obscured by false belief, that this obscurity, but not the knowledge, is removed by eliminating inconsistency, and that inconsistency is removed by being forced into contradiction.[t]

All this makes Socrates a very perplexing figure, but by looking to the *Apology* (the dialogue in which the character defends himself against the charge he acknowledges with the magistrate when he meets Euthyphro), it is possible to gain a deeper understanding of what the historical figure might have had in mind. The character calls himself a "lover of wisdom" and his practice the "love of wisdom,"[8] and he indicates that his interest in virtue is an interest in "wisdom and truth" and that he believes this wisdom is good for the "soul." This additional information does not eliminate all the problematic aspects of the search for definitions, but it does put in place a significant piece of the puzzle. The interest in definitions is theoretical, but Socrates' ultimate interest is practical. He is interested in the expertise involved in living a good life and finding happiness, and he believes that this expertise includes knowledge of what the virtues are.

2.2   The Love of Wisdom

The *Apology* follows the *Euthyphro* as the second in the tetralogy of dialogues devoted to Socrates' life and death, and in this dialogue Plato portrays the sort of activity in which Socrates engaged Euthyphro and other interlocutors as something he himself called the "love of wisdom." This unusual practice of loving wisdom, which appeared subversive, was at least partly responsible for the charges brought against Socrates, but he would not abandon his practice, even if his steadfast adherence meant giving up his life, as in fact it did. At his trial in the *Apology*, he explains why the love of wisdom is so utterly important and why he persists in loving wisdom even in the face of death. He says, in his defense, that he is convinced that the Athenians have experienced "no greater good" than the questioning and testing in which he engages them in the pursuit of wisdom:

> As long as I have breath and am able, I shall not stop but continue with
> my love of wisdom, to exhort you in my customary manner, and to ask

---

[t] In the *Meno*, as will become clear in a subsequent chapter, Plato considers a defense of this assumption. He entertains the possibility that some knowledge is innate and hence a structural part of the human soul.

any one of you I happen to meet, why on earth do you, a citizen of the utterly powerful and wise city of Athens, care so much about accumulating money and honor and reputation, and so little about wisdom and truth and that your soul is as good as possible? Are you not ashamed of this behavior? And if he says he does care, I shall not let him go, but I shall question him, examine him and test him, and if I do not think he has virtue when he says he does, I shall reproach him because he attaches little importance to the most important things and greater importance to the less important things. I shall do this to anyone I happen to meet, young and old, citizen and stranger, and more so for the citizens because you are more nearly related to me. This is what the god commands, and I think there is no greater good in this city than my service to the god. I go about every day doing nothing but persuading young and old to care not for your body and for money but to the excellence of your soul. I tell you that money does not bring virtue and excellence, but from virtue come money and everything else good for men."[u] (29d–30b)

Socrates castigates the jury for their way of life. He says they should be ashamed that they do not care for "wisdom," and "that the soul is as good as possible." Furthermore, he suggests that their failure is the reason for his unpopularity. He says that he "questions and tests" those who say they do care about the most important things and that he "reproaches" them because their answers show that they do not care and that they have not taken proper care of their souls.

To his audience, Socrates' remarks must have been both striking and perplexing. First of all, the compound word "love of wisdom," together with its cognates, although not unknown, would have been relatively unfamiliar. They occur rarely in the extant Greek literature prior to Plato's dialogues.[9] The two most prominent occurrences are in Heraclitus and Herodotus. In these authors, a "lover of wisdom" is someone who arranges his life around an uncommon intellectual pursuit. Heraclitus says "men who *love wisdom* must be inquirers into many things" (DK 22 B 35), and his point is that acquiring wisdom is

---

[u] In the *Euthydemus*, there is an indication of what Socrates has in him in saying that human goods come from virtue. After the sophists Euthydemus and Dionysodorus affirm that they are "the men of today who can best exhort a man to the love of wisdom and the practice of virtue" (274e–275a), Socrates gives a demonstration of the kind of exhortation he has in mind. In the course of this demonstration, he argues that money and other things usually thought to be good depend on wisdom for their proper use and hence that the love of wisdom is necessary for the good life and happiness (278e–282d).

not simply learning,[v] but requires figuring out things people do not ordinarily bother to figure out. Herodotus uses the word similarly. He has King Croesus say the following to Solon:[w] "My Athenian guest, we have heard a lot about you because of your wisdom and of your wanderings, how as one who *loves wisdom* you have traveled much of the world for the sake of seeing it, so now I desire to ask you who is the most fortunate man you have seen?" (I. 30). In these remarks, Solon does not travel for typical reasons. He does not travel to engage in business or politics. He travels the world to learn about other customs and ways of life.[10]

This conception of a lover of wisdom fits Socrates, not just the character, but evidently the historical figure as well. He too seems to have arranged his life around an uncommon intellectual pursuit. He seems to have neglected his affairs, ordinarily understood, so that he could spend virtually all of his time in the sort of testing and questioning the character mentions in the *Apology*[x] and which Plato tries to understand in the dialogues generally. Socrates' doggedness is particularly evident in the closing remarks in the *Euthyphro*. In contrast to Euthyphro, who is in a hurry and must leave to attend to other matters, Socrates elevates the love of wisdom above all other business:

> From the beginning we must again ask what piety is. I will not give up before I learn this. And do not treat me lightly, but focus your intellect and tell me the truth. You know, if anyone does, and so I must hold you, like Proteus,[y] until

---

[v] To make the point, Heraclitus says that "learning many things does not teach understanding; if it did, it would have taught Hesiod and Pythagoras, and again Xenophanes and Hecataeus" (DK 22 B 40).

[w] Croesus (*c.* 560–546) ruled the Asia Minor kingdom of Lydia. He extended his kingdom and made himself extremely rich, but he provoked the Persians and eventually lost everything. Cyrus, King of the Persian empire, conquered Lydia and deposed Croesus. Solon (*c.* 638–558) was a famous Athenian lawmaker. In 594, he rewrote the constitution as a compromise between democracy and oligarchic aristocracy.

[x] In the *Apology*, Socrates says that to many "it does not seem like human nature" (31b) for him to have neglected his affairs and spent so much time in the sorts of conversations that have landed him in court.

[y] In saying that he wishes to hold onto Euthyphro as if he were Proteus, who is a character of Greek myth, Socrates suggests that Euthyphro has knowledge that would help a person make his way through life successfully. Plato's Athenian audience would know the reference. In the *Odyssey* at 4.38, Homer represents Proteus as the old man of the sea, servant of Poseidon, who knows the depth of every sea and thus can direct seafarers safely to their destinations.

you tell me. After all, if you did not have clear knowledge of piety and impiety, you certainly never would have thought to prosecute your father on behalf of a hired servant. In front of the gods you would be afraid that you were acting wrongly in carrying out this prosecution, and you would be ashamed in front of men. But now I know very well that you yourself think you have this knowledge of piety. So tell me, and do not keep hidden what you think.

Some other time, Socrates. I am in a hurry now. (15c–e)

Euthyphro had tried not to disappoint Socrates, but he could not make any of his answers to the "What is piety?" question hold their ground. He says, earlier in the dialogue, that whatever he puts forward in the conversation "refuses to stay put." Socrates, because he holds wisdom so very dear, stands ready to continue the search. Euthyphro, however, by the end of the dialogue, has had enough. He quits the conversation so that he can attend to other matters.

Secondly, Socrates' audience would have been struck by what he says about the "soul." He tells the jury, in no uncertain terms, that "wisdom and truth" are good for the soul and that the care of the soul is the most important thing to which one can devote himself. This is at odds with the older, Homeric conception of the soul. In the opening lines of Homer's *Iliad*, the wrath of Achilles is said to send many souls of heroes to Hades but to leave them, the heroes themselves, as food for dogs and birds. The soul, in these lines, is something a human being loses at the moment of death, but it is not something in the living that underlies feeling and thinking. At the time, this was generally thought to be the blood around the heart.[z] The soul, as it was popularly conceived, had little to do with feeling and thinking in the living. It was thought necessary for life, but the good life would not have been thought to be a matter of the goodness of the soul. Nor would it have been thought that the soul could be made better by the acquisition of "wisdom and truth."

By the fifth century, the time Socrates was active, it was more common for "soul" to be used in connection with the personality, but it still would have been striking to say that human beings are psychological beings, that the good life is a matter of the goodness of the soul, and that the goodness of the soul is completely a matter of "wisdom and truth." Socrates seems to have thought that soul consists either wholly or primarily in the cognition belonging to

---

[z] "We still speak of a 'touching' spectacle or an appeal that 'reaches' the heart, though we have forgotten the primitive psychology on which the phrases are found" (John Burnet, "The Socratic doctrine of the soul," 1968, 153.)

reason[aa] and that proper psychological functioning constitutes an expert form of rationality. He did not offer a theory to explain the range of psychological functioning possible in human beings. Rather, to identify proper psychological functioning, Socrates seems to have proceeded indirectly. He identified the particular functioning of the soul in which human goodness resides as the psychological functioning that embodies practical wisdom about ethical matters. He thought that this expertise is the aim of the love of wisdom and that love of wisdom transforms the soul in the process of instilling this expertise.

This interpretation, like all interpretations of the historical Socrates, cannot be demonstrated with much confidence, but it is a straightforward way to present his exhortation to care for the soul by engaging in the love of wisdom. Furthermore, it is consistent with Plato's portrayal in the early dialogues. The suggestion, in these dialogues, is that the love of wisdom transforms the soul so that it functions in a way that can be expected to result in a good life. This functioning must be identified, and Socrates identifies it as the expertise in the life of virtue. Now the problem of becoming good is tractable. It is necessary to become virtuous. To become virtuous, in turn, it is necessary to have practical wisdom about ethical matters. Traditionally it would have been thought that this wisdom is a matter of experience, but Socrates is part of the enlightenment tradition that put a premium on thinking for oneself as opposed to relying uncritically on custom and the habits of experience. As Plato understands him, Socrates thought that practical wisdom about ethical matters consists in the elimination of inconsistency in belief about the definitions of the virtues.

[aa] Michael Frede provides a statement of this important point (1996a): "[H]istorically the decisive step was taken by Socrates in conceiving of human beings as being run by a mind or reason. And the evidence strongly suggests that Socrates did not take a notion of reason which had been there all along and assume, more or less plausibly, that reason as thus conceived, or as somewhat differently conceived, could fulfill the role he envisaged for it, but that he postulated an entity whose precise nature and function was then a matter of considerable philosophical debate . . . . [W]hat Socrates actually did was take a substantial notion of the soul and then try to understand the soul thus substantially conceived of as a mind or reason. By 'a substantial notion of the soul' I [mean] . . . a notion according to which the soul accounts not only for a human being's being alive, but for its doing whatever it does, and which perhaps, though not necessarily, is rather like what we could call the self. This was not a common conception, it seems, even in Socrates' time, but it was widespread and familiar enough under the influence of nontraditional religious beliefs, reflected, for instance, in Pythagoreanism. And it seems to have been such a substantial notion of the soul which Socrates took and interpreted as consisting in a mind or reason" ("Introduction," in *Rationality in Greek Thought*, 1992b, 19).

It is important to notice that this view is extraordinary, even aside from the supposed role of definitions. A human being, in so far as he is rational, aims to change things in the world so that he likes his situation. The more effective he is in this endeavor the happier he is. Given this much, which seems like so much common sense, the difficult thing to know is what is desirable and how to bring it about. If a human being is rational he will act in ways he believes are best, given the alternatives as he understands them. He may or may not be correct, since it is not obvious what is most desirable. Nor is it obvious how to bring it about. Socrates, on the present interpretation, makes an extraordinary suggestion about how to proceed. He identifies what is desirable in the situation as what is appropriate in connection with ethical matters. Hence, a human being, to make his circumstances as good as possible for himself, should conform to the demands of virtue in the various situations he encounters as he lives out his life. Socrates, in this way, identifies the good life and happiness with the life of virtue.[bb] This is contrary to the more ordinary thought that happiness and virtue need not coincide and hence that what virtue demands in a given situation need not be the same as what is most desirable for the agent. In a case in which they fail to coincide, for the human being who understands his situation, it would seem rational for him to act contrary to the demands of virtue. Socrates denies the possibility, but it is far from clear that he is correct.[11]

2.3 Intellectualism

In the *Protagoras*, which is an inquiry into whether the expertise involved in living a life of ethical virtue can be taught, there is an indication of a solution to one of the puzzles this interpretation of Socrates raises. Since

---

[bb] It is because of this understanding of ethics and the good life that Socrates is sometimes said to be the founder of a certain philosophical tradition in ethical theory. "Socrates' importance for the history of ethics is indisputable. Socrates succeeded in defining the task of Greek moral theory as the reconciliation, the identification even, of the two themes we have discussed here: the topics of virtue and happiness, morality and the good life. It was really Socrates, not Plato, who did what Aristotle in a poem said of Plato: that 'he alone or first of mortals showed, by his life and the force of his arguments, that a man becomes good and happy at the same time' (Aristotle, fr. 673 Rose). We must be struck here with Kant, who has to invoke an omnipotent God in order to reconcile virtue with happiness. It is because of his success in uniting these two central themes of the Greek moral tradition that Socrates can properly be regarded as the founder of classical Greek moral theory" (Charles Kahn, "Pre-Platonic Ethics," 1998, 47–48).

the method he employs in the love of wisdom is the elimination of inconsistency, the idea seems to be that conversations of a certain sort make a human being good because they transform the human psychology so that it embodies practical wisdom about ethical matters. The *Protagoras* gives some indication of how Socrates could have thought this. The character suggests that all action is determined by belief[12] and hence that the life of virtue is a matter of wisdom, wisdom Socrates may have thought his conversations can produce.

This suggestion occurs in the context of a long and complex discussion of the relative strength of knowledge and wisdom among the sources of motivation in human beings. The discussion begins with Socrates asking Protagoras his opinion about the matter. Socrates asks him whether he agrees with the many in thinking that knowledge is not always "strong" and that in fact what rules a person is often something else. Protagoras tells Socrates that he himself stands against the many on this question of motivation. Socrates commends him for his stance:

> Protagoras, what do you think about knowledge? Are you part of the majority? They think that it is not powerful, neither a leader nor a ruler, that while knowledge is often present, what rules a man is something else, anger, pleasure, pain, love, or fear. They think as a matter of experience that his knowledge is dragged around by these things, as a slave. Is that your view, or does it seem to you that knowledge is a fine thing and a ruler, and if someone were to know what is good and bad, nothing would force him to act otherwise, and that wisdom and thoughtfulness would save him?

> Not only does it seem to me as you say, Socrates, but it would be shameful for me above all others to say that wisdom and knowledge are anything but the most controlling in the dealings of men.

> Yes, but you realize that the many think otherwise. They hold that most men are unwilling to do what is best, even if they know what it is and can do it, because they are overcome by pleasure or pain and so are ruled by one of the things I was just mentioning. (352a–e)

Socrates says to Protagoras in this passage that, although "wisdom and knowledge are the most controlling," the many are not convinced. They think a person can know what is best but nevertheless fail do it because he is overcome by something other than knowledge.

Thus, according to the many, a human being might know what is best in the circumstance but be overcome and hence choose something else instead. This understanding of human beings presupposes a distinction between how the soul should work and how it sometimes does in fact work. In the exercise of reason, a human being seeks to change the world in order to improve his situation. He evaluates the world, chooses goals, adopts plans, and takes action. Sometimes, in the course of executing a given course of action, a new possibility becomes salient. If this possibility is judged better than the current one, a new plan should be formed and set into motion. The "many," however, in opposition to Socrates, suppose that the new goal can replace the current one, not because it is judged better, but because there is an overpowering desire for the new goal. This desire interrupts the proper functioning of the soul. It causes the execution of the current plan to be suspended, and it triggers the pursuit of the new goal. This is not rational. It is not supposed to happen, but the many think that the human soul does sometimes function in this way.

To determine whether the many can hold on to their view, Socrates begins with an analogy to show that the knowledge characteristic of an "art," or expertise, can help secure "well-being" because this knowledge can help prevent the formation of false belief. He imagines a situation in which "well-being" depends, not on riches, honor, or any of the things usually thought necessary, but rather on "doing and choosing large things and avoiding and not doing the small ones." Socrates concludes that in this situation "our salvation in life" would be an art and its underlying knowledge. Belief formed strictly in response to apparent size alters with changes in one's distance and angle to the object, but a person skilled in the art of measurement is able to prevent such misleading impressions from resulting in false beliefs. By contrast, an unskilled person assents to these impressions and hence risks choosing something he thinks is large but in fact is small. Only with the art can he avoid assenting to these misleading impressions. "[T]he art of measurement," according to Socrates, were we to possess it, "would make the appearances lose their power by showing us the truth, would put our soul at peace, holding steadfast in truth, and would save our life" (356c–357c).

Now that Socrates has argued that the knowledge underlying an expertise can help a person choose the best of the available alternatives in the situation, he argues for the more surprising proposition that every choice of something other than the best of the available alternatives is squarely the fault of a false belief. Socrates insists that no human being chooses to do anything unless he believes the action he chooses is the best of the available alternatives in the situation at hand:

> No one who knows or thinks there is something better than what he is doing, something possible, will continue doing what he had been doing when he could be doing what is better. To give in to oneself is ignorance. To control oneself is wisdom.

They agreed.

And do you say that ignorance is to have a false belief and to be deceived about important matters?

They all agreed with this too.

So no one goes willingly toward the bad or what he believes is bad. Nor is it in human nature, so it seems, to seek what one thinks is bad rather than what one thinks is good. When a man is forced to choose between one of two bad things, he chooses the lesser if he can.

About all these things they all agreed.

Well, then, is there something you call dread or fear? And I am speaking particularly to you, Prodicus.^cc It seems to me that whether you call it fear or dread, it is an expectation of something bad.

Protagoras and Hippias thought this was true of dread and fear. Prodicus, however, thought it was true of dread but not fear.

It does not make a difference, Prodicus. This is the point. If what I have said is true, would anyone willingly go toward what he dreads, when he can go toward what he does not dread? Or is this impossible? For it was agreed that what one fears one holds to be bad and that no one goes toward that which he thinks is bad or chooses this willingly. (358b–e)

Socrates does not deny that human beings are sometimes irrational. He denies the understanding of the human soul according to which desire is ever the "ruling" or "controlling" factor.

Hence, in opposition to the many, Socrates understands desire in the human soul as controlled by belief about the good. A human being decides what to do by making a judgment about the expected value of a course of action. He considers the possibilities in the circumstance, and he chooses one he judges best. When he is "overcome," he abandons his original intention because he has new information about what is best. As Socrates conceives of human beings, all action stems ultimately from

---

^cc Prodicus was a sophist interested in the precise use of words, among other things. "Prodicus came from the island of Ceos in the Cyclades which had also been the birthplace of the poet Simonides. He was probably born before 460 BC and was still alive at the time of the death of Socrates in 399 BC. He went on many embassies for Ceos to Athens, and on one occasion spoke before the Council. Like Gorgias he gave epideictic speeches and also private teaching for which he earned a great deal of money, and he visited many cities, not Athens alone. ... Prodicus was above all famous for his work on language ..." (G. K. Kerferd, *The Sophistic Movement*, 1981, 45–46). (Epideitic oratory is public speech at formal events in which, typically, something is praised or blamed in a showy display of rhetorical skill.)

beliefs or judgments. It is true, according to Socrates, that human beings have desires, but in human beings desire is not independent of belief. In human beings, there are beliefs and the exercise of reason in terms of these beliefs to control their actions. Desire arises once a plan or goal is adopted, and goals and plans are adopted on the basis of a belief about their value.

Some questions about the love of wisdom

This intellectualist theory of desire helps explain why Socrates emphasizes "wisdom and truth" in connection with the good life, but the love of wisdom does not look to have the very substantial results Socrates seems to have claimed for it. For the sake of argument, one may suppose that the elimination of inconsistency results in knowledge of the definitions of the virtues. Yet, even with this assumption, the knowledge underlying the love of wisdom is not, or at least not obviously, the knowledge that underlies the expertise involved in living a good life and in being happy.[13]

The problem is easier to appreciate given the further assumption, which itself is extremely plausible, that Socrates believed that the virtues are defined in terms of what is appropriate in the matter. In this case, even if a given person knows and is not confused about the fact that piety is that which is appropriate in matters involving the gods, this knowledge alone does not tell the person what is, or is not, appropriate in a particular situation he faces. Thus, contrary to what Socrates seems to suggest, knowledge of the definitions of the virtues alone is not sufficient for living a good life. This knowledge does not necessarily result in any particular sort of life at all.

Maybe, for the sake of argument, it should be supposed that, in addition to knowledge of the definitions of the virtues, the elimination of inconsistency somehow results in whatever knowledge is involved in determining what is appropriate in various situations. This assumption makes the expertise produced in the love of wisdom like the "measuring art" that Socrates, in his example, says would be "our salvation in life." Given the assumption, the lover of wisdom knows how to "measure" the appropriateness of the alternatives in the situations he encounters.

Yet, even with this additional assumption, it does not follow that the love of wisdom has the results Socrates claims for it. A human being with practical wisdom about ethical matters is not confused about what is appropriate in the situations he encounters, but he must choose the appropriate alternative if he is to live a life of virtue, as opposed to knowing what is appropriate but choosing a different course of action. Further, even if he does choose correctly, it is unclear why this life is singled out as the good life, the life in which happiness is found most of all.

The right thing to say on Socrates' behalf is not at all obvious, but, in light of the discussion of motivation in the *Protagoras*, perhaps part of the idea is that the lover of wisdom knows that what is appropriate in ethical matters is the best thing he can do in the circumstances and hence is what contributes most of all to his happiness. In this case, given that practical wisdom about ethical matters includes this knowledge of the good, and given that all desire in the human psychology is a matter of belief about the good, then maybe such practical wisdom really is the expertise in the best exercise of reason. Socrates, however, as at least as Plato portrays him, offers no argument to show that the appropriate in ethical matters is connected to the good for human beings. Furthermore, his focus in the love of wisdom is on what the ethical virtues are, not on what the good is.

Socrates, in this way, is an enigma, but he is an enigma Plato works to understand throughout most of the dialogues. Plato sets out answers, but this does not happen all at once. Nor is it always clear just what the answers are supposed to be. In the *Protagoras* and the *Gorgias*, which are the subject of the next chapter, Plato is engaged in this project. He tries, in these dialogues, to put Socrates and the love of wisdom, with its emphasis on "reason," into sharper focus by contrasting the Socratic understanding of the good life with a competing understanding associated with the Sophists, which Plato understands to rely on "experience." This competing understanding has no concern with knowledge of the good. So, in the end, it is not a serious challenge to Socrates and his love of wisdom. But the conversations in these dialogues are important for what they show about how Plato understands the love of wisdom and the human soul. This is especially true with respect to an intriguing conversation that takes place toward the end of the *Gorgias*, where Socrates, for the first time, discusses the good, both in general and in connection with human beings.

Notes

1. Charles Kahn has challenged the importance of Aristotle's testimony for understanding what the historical Socrates thought. "I conclude," he writes, "that neither Aristotle nor Xenophon is in a position to tell us anything about

the philosophy of Socrates that he has not learned from Plato's dialogues" (*Plato and the Socratic Dialogue*, 1996, 87). This, of course, is plausible enough; however, Kahn also advances a more controversial thesis: he rejects Aristotle's claim that Socrates "fixed thought for the first time on definitions." To the question of whether we should "regard the what-is-*X*? question of the *Laches*, *Euthyphro*, and *Meno* as a Platonic innovation?," Kahn says that "the answer . . . must be 'Yes'" (93). His argument is an important challenge to the more traditional interpretation of Socrates.

2. Variations on this point are common in the secondary literature. Cf. Terence Irwin, *Classical Thought*, 1989, 73: "We may be surprised that Socrates chooses to cross-examine a person's life and moral outlook simply by asking him to define virtue; this seems too abstract and theoretical a question to show that our ordinary morality is 'upside down.'"

3. In early Greek literature, the word 'form' occurs in connection with the human figure to denote visual form as opposed to size and physique. This meaning is evident in the passage in Homer in which a figure comes to Agamemnon in a dream. Agamemnon says it "was most like Nestor in form and in stature and in build" (*Iliad*, II.58). In these remarks, he uses the word 'form' for the characteristic look he associates with Nestor. Nestor's appearance will vary over time, depending on what he is doing and what has recently occurred, for instance whether he is now smiling, seated, or has let his hair grow; but despite these differences, Agamemnon supposes that Nestor has a characteristic look. This look makes him recognizable even though strictly speaking he appears differently at different times.

4. Alexander Mourelatos stresses the historical significance of this sort of turn in the conversation. See his "The concept of the universal in some pre-Platonic cosmologists," 2006, 57.

5. John Burnet's *Platonis Opera* is the standard edition of the Platonic corpus. The references to lines in a work in the Platonic corpus, for example, *Hippias Major* 287c1–d3, are to the three-volume edition that Henri Estienne (*c.* 1528/31–1598) produced in 1578. These pages in this edition are commonly called "Stepanus pages" because "Stephanus" is the Latinized form of "Estienne." The first number in each reference refers to a page, the letter to a paragraph, and the second number to a line in the paragraph. The current standard set of translations is *Plato, Complete Works*. The *Clarendon Plato Series* from Oxford University Press also provides very good translations, as well as philosophical commentary. In constructing my translations, I have looked to the current standard set, those in the *Clarendon* series, and the older translations available in the *Perseus Digital Library* and the *MIT Internet Classics Archive*. My translations, however, aim for understanding, not literalness. I compress or eliminate what I regard as extraneous detail. This makes the texts much more readable, but the result is often more paraphrase than translation.

6. This is a standard interpretation. Cf. Terence Irwin, *Classical Thought*, 1989, 72: "Socrates assumes that to settle some practical and urgent moral questions we

need knowledge of the virtues, and that we should test claims to such knowledge by seeking definitions of the virtues. The *Laches* begins with a discussion of the sort of training that makes someone a brave soldier (a question of obvious importance for an Athenian citizen, who could expect to be called for military service). Socrates suggests that if they are to decide on the appropriate way to cultivate bravery, they ought to know what bravery is; and to see if they know, he asks for a definition. In the *Euthyphro* a moral dispute raises the problem. Euthyphro is prosecuting his father for impiety; but popular feeling regards prosecution of one's father as a scandalously impious action. Euthyphro despises popular feeling and is confident that the sort of thing he is doing is perfectly pious and required by religious duty. His confidence leads Socrates to ask him what piety is."

7. Many commentators have stressed that Socrates is a child of the Greek enlightenment. Michael Frede is a recent and influential example. He states the point within a more general discussion of the ancient empirical and rationalist traditions: "What made it easier for the educated doctor to ac- knowledge the fact that his art was severely limited and stood in need of reforms was a view characteristic of the enlightenment of the later fifth century. On this view, the various arts and crafts had evolved in the course of the history of humankind to enable human beings who originally had been exposed rather helplessly to a hostile environment to gain a secure life, and if one just systematically turned one's reason to it, instead of mindlessly following traditional belief and practice, ever further areas of life would be brought under rational control, and human beings would flourish. Socratic ethics is perhaps the most splendid and extreme reflection of this attitude. Thus, medicine was naturally conceived of as an art that had arisen rather late, but that could be set on the road of firm progress, if one merely put one's mind to it instead of following the traditional practices and beliefs as the ordinary doctors did" ("Philosophy and medicine in antiquity," 1987h, 233).

8. It is common to have Socrates call himself a "philosopher" and his practice "philosophy," but this can be misleading. Charles Kahn issues the right sort of warning in his review of a much discussed book by Christopher Bobonich. "Equally anachronistic is B[obnich]'s introduction of the distinction between philosophers and non-philosophers as if it were a conceptual given. Plato in the *Phaedo* is creating his own notion of philosophy, as a quasi-religious lifestyle. B. does not mention the pre-Platonic use of *philosophia* to mean something like 'high culture' or 'intellectual activity,' or the contemporary effort by Isocrates to apply this term to his own educational enterprise. It is because the meaning of *philosophia* is in dispute that the *Phaedo* must refer throughout to those 'who correctly philosophize.' In the *Apology* Socrates interprets philosophy in terms of his own practice of asking fundamental questions about popular values, and he claims that the unquestioned life (i.e. the life of 'non-philosophers') is not worth living. And since in the *Apology arete* [virtue] is understood as care of one's soul, it there is closely identified with the practice of philosophy. In the

Phaedo Plato redefines this Socratic lifestyle by reference to his own moral psychology and metaphysics: philosophy now becomes the purification of the soul from the body on the basis of knowledge, and ultimately on knowledge of the Forms" ("From *Republic* to *Laws*. A discussion of Christopher Bobonich, *Plato's Utopia Recast*," 2004, 345–346).

9. Pierre Hadot makes this point: "It is almost certain that Presocratic philosophers of the seventh and sixth centuries BC, such as Xenophanes and Parmenides, knew neither the adjective *philosophos* nor the verb *philosophein* ('to do philosophy'), much less the noun *philosophia*. Moreover, despite certain ancient but very controversial evidence to the contrary, this was probably also the case for Pythagoras and Heraclitus. In all likelihood, these words did not appear until the fifth century, the 'Age of Pericles,' when Athens shone by virtue of both its political dominance and its intellectual influence. This was the time of Sophocles, Euripides, and the Sophists, but it was also when the historian Herodotus, a native of Asia Minor, came to live in the famous city in the course of his numerous travels. It is perhaps in Herodotus' work that we find the first mention of 'philosophical' activity. Herodotus tells of the legendary meeting between Solon (an Athenian legislator of the seventh–sixth centuries, and one of the so-called Seven Sages) with Croesus, king of Lydia" (*What is Ancient Philosophy?*, trans. Michael Chase, 2002, 15–16).

10. Michael Frede explains the meaning of the passage in Herodotus. "Herodotus does not mean to say that Crosesus addressed Solon as a philosopher. The idea rather is that Solon wants to get to know different parts of the world, different nations, the way they think about things, the way they are organised, and the laws they are governed by, in the first instance just to have a better understanding of things, rather than in pursuit of the solution to a practical issue. But, the way Herodotus tells the story, it is Croesus, a barbarian, who finds it remarkable that somebody would engage in this pursuit of wisdom for no identifiable practical purpose" ("Aristotle's account of the origins of philosophy," 2004, 23). Frede also points out that Thucydides, in his well-known use of the verb, echoes the use in Herodotus. Thucydides, in the "Funeral Oration," has Pericles say that "we love wisdom without softness" (II.40.1). The idea in these remarks, as Frede understands them, is that "the Athenians cherish and pursue wisdom to a remarkable degree without, though, thereby getting soft and ineffectual, that is to say without losing sight of, and interest in, what needs to be done, one's affairs, one's own affairs, but in particular the affairs of the city. . . . [They] take a remarkable interest in general questions, go to great length discussing and arguing about them, though these questions are of no immediate relevance to their current affairs, private or public, indeed may have no bearing on them at all. They are interested in these questions for their own sake. But this does not make them in the least ineffective when it comes to practical matters" (21).

11. Terence Irwin offers a defense of the Socratic understanding of ethics and happiness. "If he can show that virtue ensures the satisfaction of the virtuous

agent's desires, he will have shown (he may suppose) that virtue is sufficient for happiness. A virtuous person clearly cannot expect to satisfy all the desires that an ordinary non-virtuous person might have. The ordinary person strongly desires not to face the sort of death that Socrates has to face, and so such a person will suppose that Socrates suffers some serious harm. Socrates can reply, however, that he is unreservedly committed to being virtuous, and so he has no desires to do anything that conflicts with his commitments to virtue. Once he discovers that in some circumstances wealth or safety, or even self-preservation, conflicts with the requirements of virtue, he has no desire to pursue any of these recognized goods in these circumstances. Although non-virtuous people in Socrates' situation might suffer frustration of their desires, Socrates does not suffer the frustration of any of his desires; but it is his desires for himself, not the desires others would have for themselves if they were in his situation, that determine whether he is happy. He claims that since he wants to be as virtuous as he can be and has no desire for anything that conflicts with being virtuous, he suffers no loss of happiness, and hence no harm, if he loses any of the supposed 'goods' that the virtuous person has to forgo. Socrates might also fairly claim that the virtuous person is less liable to frustrated desire than a non-virtuous person, since a non-virtuous person is liable to failures that do not affect a virtuous person. If I desire honor or wealth or political success as a means to happiness, it is not up to me whether I achieve them; even if I act wisely, I may be unlucky, and so I may have my desires frustrated. Socrates claims that this frustration does not face him if he sets out to be as virtuous as he can; for his aim is in his power to achieve, and he is not liable to be disappointed by external circumstances" (*Plato's Ethics*, 1995, 74–75).

12. "Here in the *Protagoras*, Socrates seems to argue as if the soul just were reason, and the passions were reasoned beliefs or judgments of some kind, and as if, therefore, we were entirely guided or motivated by beliefs of one kind or another. On this picture of the soul, it is easy to see why Socrates thinks that nobody acts against his knowledge or even his beliefs: nothing apart from beliefs could motivate such an action" (Frede, "Introduction," in *Plato, Protagoras*, xxx). "[Socrates'] extreme intellectualism seems to have been based on a conception of the soul as a mind or a reason, such that our desires turn out to be beliefs of a certain kind" (Frede, "The philosopher," 2000, 8). This, however, is not the only understanding of Socratic psychology. C. C. W. Taylor, for example, in his introduction to the historical figure, takes Socrates to suppose there is a fixed desire for the good that becomes focused by beliefs about the current circumstance: "Socrates maintains (*Meno* 77c, 78b) that everyone desires good things, which in context has to be interpreted as the strong thesis that the desire for the good is a standing motive, which requires to be focused in one direction or another via a conception of the overall good. Given that focus, desire is locked onto the target which is picked out by the conception, without the possibility of interference by conflicting desires. Hence all that is required for correct conduct is the correct focus, which has to be a

correct conception of the agent's overall good" (*Socrates. A Very Short Intro-duction*, 1998b, 62–63). For a detailed and interesting defense of this sort of interpretation of Socrates, see Terry Penner's "Desire and power in Socrates: the argument of *Gorgias* 466a–478e that orators and tyrants have no power in the city" (1991), and Penner's article with Christopher Rowe (1994), "The desire for good: Is the *Meno* consistent with the *Gorgias*?"

13. In the first volume of his magisterial study of the history of ethics, Terence Irwin succinctly states the sort of puzzle Socrates presents: "Socrates commits himself to three main paradoxes: (1) Knowledge of what is good for me is sufficient for action. (2) The virtues that promote my good are the moral virtues. (3) These virtues are sufficient for happiness. All of these Socratic paradoxes conflict with the prevalent outlook of modern moral philosophy" (*The Development of Ethics. A Historical and Critical Study*. Vol. 1: *From Socrates to the Reformation*, 2007, 14).

3

Against the Sophists

The problem with the flattering persuasion the Sophists taught

The Sophists filled a void in the traditional education, which had developed as Athens became a center of political power. The skillful use of rhetorical persuasion in the courts and elsewhere appeared as the key to success and hence to the good life and to happiness. The Sophists did not disavow this impression. They taught rhetoric, as well as other subjects which were not part of the traditional education, for high fees. This put them on a collision course with Socrates, who thought that the love of wisdom, not rhetorical persuasion, is the key to the good life and happiness.

In opposition to the Sophists, Socrates suggests that the good life is not the same as getting what one wants because what one wants may not be good. Skill in rhetorical persuasion may be useful for getting what one wants, but since it does not include knowledge of the good, Socrates concludes that the art of rhetoric is not the expertise involved in living a good life and finding happiness. In fact, according to Socrates, skill in rhetorical persuasion is likely to be more harmful than good. He says that knowledge of the good is a matter of reason, not experience, and that in the life the Sophists advocate, the use of rhetorical persuasion for the satisfaction of desire is a matter of experience. It is a practice and routine that works without reason, that can enslave reason, and hence can make one's life worse because it can cause a human being to accept goals he would not desire and pursue if he were rational and in possession of a properly functioning psychology.

Socrates' understanding of the good life was unorthodox. He thought that rationality in human beings was a matter of proper psychological functioning, that the best exercise of reason presupposes knowledge and takes the form of an expertise, that this expertise is practical wisdom about ethical matters, and hence that the life of ethical virtue is the good life for human beings.

A more common understanding of the good life entered the ancient philosophical tradition in association with the Sophists. They were itinerant teachers, primarily of rhetoric but also of other subjects. They were drawn to Athens, and they quickly found themselves in demand. In imperial Athens,

Ancient Greek Philosophy: From The Presocratics to the Hellenistic Philosophers, First Edition.
Thomas A. Blackson.   © 2011 Thomas A. Blackson. Published 2011 by Blackwell Publishing Ltd.

skill in rhetoric was increasingly thought to help a person get what he wants and hence to live a good life. Rhetorical training, however, was not part of the traditional education.

3.1 The Sophists Come to Athens

In the latter half of the fifth century, Pericles was the dominant political leader in Athens. Athenian imperial power was at its height, and the democracy reached its fullest development. Athens was extending her preeminent position among the confederation of Greek cities by rebuilding, on a grander scale, what the Persians had destroyed. The Assembly and the courts were the most important governing bodies. All adult male citizens were permitted to attend the assembly. Juries consisted of groups of such citizens, and the numbers were large.[1] The ability to make persuasive speeches was thus an important key to success in these bodies and in the new Athens.

The traditional education did not provide the tools necessary for such success. It centered primarily on memorizing the poets, but those armed with the maxims taken from this poetry were no match for those who were good at making speeches. Rhetorical skill was necessary to sway the Assembly as well as to plead cases in court, and those who were successful in the Assembly and in the courts could rise to positions of political and economic prominence.

To satisfy the need for rhetorical skill, the Sophists taught rhetoric for a fee.[a] The title "Sophist" meant "sage" or "wise man," and although the word

---

[a] Many of them came to Athens in connection with some political matter and, once in Athens, made large sums of money by giving displays in persuasive speaking. (In the *Hippias Major*, at 282d–e, Hippias tells Socrates that he has no idea how fine this business can be and that Socrates would be amazed if knew how much money he had made.) Protagoras had a close association with Pericles. In 444, Pericles chose him to write the laws for the new colony of Thurii in southern Italy. The *Protagoras* (which is named after the Sophist) takes place in the house of Callias just before the Peloponnesian War. Callias, whose mother was Pericles' first wife, was part of one of the richest families in Athens. In the *Apology*, he is said to have spent more money on sophists than everyone else put together (20a). Gorgias was from Leontini, a Greek colony in Sicily. In 427, he was the head of an embassy sent to Athens to request protection from Syracuse, which was allied with Sparta. He addressed the Assembly and was admired for his skill in speaking. Prodicus came as an ambassador from Ceos. In the *Hippias Major*, it is said that he "was popular with his speech in the council" (282c). Hippias came from Elis. He too was an ambassador. He says that "whenever Elis has business with another city, they come to me first when they choose an ambassador" because "they think I am the one best able to judge and report messages from the various cities" (*Hippias Major* 281a–b).

now has a decidedly negative connotation, this was not so originally.[b] Moreover, in at least one respect it was clear that the Sophists provided a valuable service. Democracy thrives on the public discussion of issues, and the Sophistical movement helped the many to become aware of the need for skill in analysis. The Sophists trained their students to present their ideas more forcefully. Studying with the Sophists was important and became fashionable for the younger members of wealthy families.

Furthermore, if studying with the Sophists did have a downside, it was not initially clear what it was. There were then, as now, the usual issues with a liberal education. Young men from aristocratic families were led in destructive argument against the traditional political and ethical views that seemed to provide a special place for members of their class. Moreover, as the fees for this training were high, these families found themselves in the position of paying huge sums to have their sons take a critical attitude toward their traditional way of life. This no doubt caused a certain amount of resentment. In addition, because the Sophists seemed to encourage the idea that success required special training, they undermined the democratic assumption that every citizen is equally competent to judge the affairs of the "City." This too presumably caused resentment.[c]

---

[b] The negative connotation is due in large measure to Plato's strong condemnation in his defense of Socrates. "Not one barrier but two stand in the way of anyone who seeks to arrive at a proper understanding of the sophistic movement at Athens in the fifth century BC. No writings survive from any of the sophists and we have to depend on inconsiderable fragments and often obscure or unreliable summaries of their doctrines. What is worse, for much of our information we are dependent upon Plato's profoundly hostile treatment of them, presented with all the power of his literary genius and driven home with a philosophical impact that is little short of overwhelming" (G. B. Kerferd, *The Sophistic Movement*, 1981, 1). "Most of what we can learn about the sophists, apart from the surviving work of Gorgias, stems from Plato, and nothing mattered to Plato more than defending Socrates from the widespread belief that he was, to many intents and purposes, a sophist" (A. A. Long, "The scope of early Greek philosophy," 1999b, 6).

[c] The Greek noun for "education" is from the adjective for "suited to the child." Education was thought to transform the child into a rational adult who has the skills and information necessary for living a good life. The real question and dispute was about the content of this education, and any answer to this question presupposes an understanding of how human beings function and what the human good is. To many in the new Athens, training in the art of rhetorical persuasion seemed like a necessary part of the content of a good education. The Sophists capitalized on this idea. They sold lessons in the art of rhetorical persuasion. "What the sophists were able to offer was in no sense a contribution to the education of the masses.

Plato's immediate Athenian audience, who lived in the fourth century,[2] knew all too well that things had gone terribly for Athens, but the underlying cause of this downfall was far from obvious. Many of course thought they knew who to blame. There were the generals Nicias and Laches, whose mistakes led to military defeat. There were Critias and Charmides, Plato's relatives and Socrates' companions, who used the power of the state for their own immoral ends. There was Socrates himself, with his incessant questioning, and who was executed for the influence he was thought to have had on many of the young men who played key roles in Athenian politics.

Plato, however, saw things differently. He thought that the problem lay in the failure of education, with its misunderstanding of the soul and the way it works, and that the Sophistical movement in Athens was the most visible manifestation of this failure. The Athenians themselves were nostalgic for the leadership of Pericles and the legends of the Golden Age, but the dialogues suggest that Plato thought that Pericles and the others engaged in the practice the Sophists managed to package and sell. This practice was the problem. It corrupted the young, not Socrates. It ruined the soul, which to function properly requires the vigilance Socrates urged.

3.2   The Sophist Sells Teachings for the Soul

Protagoras came from Abdera in Thrace on the north coast of the Aegean Sea. He visited Athens many times. He was friends with the legendary statesman Pericles, who had him help draft the laws for the new colony at

---

They offered an expensive product invaluable to those seeking a career in politics and public life generally, namely a kind of selective secondary education, intended to follow on after the basic instruction received at school in language and literature. . . . As the earlier school education was normally completed at the point at which a boy passed from being a child (*Pais*) to becoming a youth or young man (*Meirakion*) . . ., and since becoming a *Meirakion* was equated with the age of puberty, traditionally assigned to the fourteenth year . . . we can say, if we wish, in modern terms that the sophists provided a selective education at the age of fourteen-plus. This education, though it varied in content, seems always to have been to a considerable extent career-oriented. . . . As its main purpose remained to prepare men for a career in politics, it should cause no surprise that an essential part of the education offered was training in the art of persuasive speaking" (G. B. Kerferd, *The Sophistic Movement*, 1981, 17).

Thurii.[d] Plato, by contrast, thought less well of Protagoras (and of Pericles too) for his role in Athenian politics.[e] In the *Protagoras*, Plato portrays Protagoras as for the most part little more than a clever speaker with no expertise in ethics or politics.

What the Sophist does for his students

The *Protagoras* opens with Socrates telling an unnamed friend how earlier that morning Hippocrates[f] came to his door in a headlong rush to study with the great Sophist, Protagoras. Hippocrates was not really sure what he hoped to gain from his study, other than "a general education suitable for a gentleman." Nor did he know what Protagoras professed to teach. His best reply to Socrates' pointed questioning on these topics is that a Sophist is "someone who has understanding of wise things" and who "is an expert at making people clever speakers."

Socrates does not share Hippocrates' enthusiasm. He suggests that Protagoras is a salesman, not a teacher, and that he sells products that *appear* beneficial to the unwary:

> Is a sophist a merchant who sells provisions to nourish the soul? That is how he seems to me.
>
> What nourishes the soul, Socrates?
>
> Teachings, I would say. And be careful or he might deceive us as merchants who sell food do. Good or bad is not something they know – they just recommend everything. Nor do the buyers know, unless one is a

---

[d] In a battle for local dominance in southern Italy, Croton attacked Sybaris, destroying the city and killing virtually all of its inhabitants. The survivors appealed to Sparta and Athens to help them rebuild their city. Sparta declined, but Athens agreed and invited volunteers from Athens and the Peloponnese to join the new city. There were several notable volunteers, including the Sophists and brothers Euthydemus and Dionysodorus. In the *Euthydemus*, they are presented as professional teachers of wisdom and virtue (271b–c, 273d–274b).

[e] Susan Sauvé Meyer makes the general point: "[In the *Gorgias*, Socrates] alleges that Pericles, Themistocles, and Cimon were charlatans rather than true statesman. Their conduct of the city's affairs manifested . . . the greatest ignorance. The only revered figures who are omitted from this indictment are the grandfathers from the *Laches*: Thucydides, who opposed Pericles' policy of imperial expansion, and Aristides, who was a hero of the Persian wars which liberated Athens from Persian aggression. By contrast, he claims, those who lead Athens in the pursuit of wealth and empire were adept not at protecting and benefitting the city, but at flattering the population and catering to its appetites (*Gorg.* 515c–517c). These so-called 'statesman' were adept at the flattering persuasion taught by Gorgias (463a–465e), rather than the political knowledge sought by Socrates" (*Ancient Ethics*, 2008b, 24).

[f] Hippocrates of Athens was a member of a wealthy family. Little else is known about him.

trainer or a doctor. The same is true of those who take their teachings from town to town and hawk them to anyone who wants them. They recommend all their products, but it may be that some of them do not know which are good or bad for the soul. And the same is true of those who buy from them, unless one of them happens to be a doctor who specializes in the soul. (313c–e)

These products are advertised as a set of tools helpful in living a good life, but Socrates suggests that Protagoras himself has no interest in whether his products really are such tools. To Socrates, Protagoras is just a salesman and, like salesmen generally, interested only in the sale.

Despite his very serious worries about the value of a Sophistical education,[3] Socrates eventually agrees to take Hippocrates to see Protagoras. Once there,[g] and before handing Hippocrates over to Protagoras, Socrates asks Protagoras to explain what he will do for Hippocrates if Hippocrates becomes his student. After some prodding, Protagoras says that he teaches his students to be successful in domestic matters and in political debate and action:

Good judgment about one's affairs is the thing I teach, how to manage the household, and in the city, how to have the greatest influence in political life in speech and action.

Do I understand you properly? You seem to be talking about the art of living in a city and to be promising to make men good citizens.

That is exactly right, Socrates. (318e–319a)

Socrates does not let this assertion pass untested. If Protagoras gives his students the power to have successful lives within the city, then, on the assumption that successful lives are good lives, Protagoras is a suitable teacher for Hippocrates after all. Protagoras promises to teach his students to be successful by being "good citizens," and Socrates seems to think that Protagoras must mean that he teaches his students how to live in accordance with ethical virtue.

Socrates doubts that Protagoras can teach virtue. He says he would have thought no one can teach this, for otherwise, contrary to the actual course of events, Pericles and other Athenian gentlemen would have taught their

---

[g] Protagoras was being hosted in Athens by Callias, who belonged to one of the richest families in Athens. In addition to Protagoras, many other prominent figures of the day are present. The date is before the Peloponnesian War, and many of these figures will play prominent roles in shaping the future of Athens. For some discussion of the point, see Michael Frede's "Introduction," in *Plato, Protagoras*, 1992, xi–xii.

sons,[h] but the reader also gets the impression there is a deeper issue. Socrates challenges Protagoras, not so much because he believes a person cannot be taught to live a life of virtue, but because he wants to know what would be taught.

Protagoras casts his proof in the form of a "myth." He says, in explanation, that it is more pleasant to proceed in terms of a story involving the gods than it is to proceed by reasoning and in terms of an "argument." Socrates, presumably, thinks that clarity, not pleasantness, should determine the form of the proof, but he allows Protagoras to proceed nevertheless.

According to the myth, the gods gave politics to human beings so that the initially scattered groups could unite in political communities and hence effectively compete with the wild beasts for survival. The small groups were unable to defend themselves against the beasts, and so fear soon drove these groups together into larger communities, but the features necessary for the survival of these larger communities did not exist because human beings, in their original state, did not have the attitudes necessary for group living. The mutual antagonism among the people, antagonism based in greed and other individualistic desires, thus drove the larger communities apart, leaving the smaller groups once again at the mercy of the beasts, and finally Zeus had to intervene to save humankind from destruction. He directed Hermes, who was the messenger of the gods to human beings, to implant in human beings "shame and justice, so within cities there would be the ties of friendship to unite the people" (322c) and hence they would stay together in a city.

Because the democrats and aristocrats were (for different reasons) suspicious of the Sophists, Protagoras seems to have designed his myth to accommodate both groups. He says that shame is in all human beings more or less equally at birth. This pleased the democrats. The myth, however, is also anti-democratic. Protagoras associates justice with the traditional

[h] Socrates mentions Alcibiades and Clinias. Their father had been killed in battle. The statesman, Pericles, became their guardian and hence took primary responsibility for their rearing. (The boys' mother, Deinomache, was Pericles' first cousin.) Little is known of what became of Clinias, but Alcibiades became notorious for his outrageous behavior. The story is complicated, but some of the main points are the following. Alcibiades betrayed the Athenians in a way that was partially responsible for the military defeat of the Sicilian expedition, an expedition the Athenians undertook in the hope of extending their empire. After this betrayal, Alcibiades defected to Sparta and once again worked against the Athenians. In Sparta, he soon ran into trouble and fled to the Persian court. He was eventually recalled to Athens and returned to command, but soon he was disgraced in defeat and was forced again to leave Athens in exile.

morality. A person with shame tends to accept his place in society and have a regard for the rights traditionally accorded to others. In Protagoras' myth, the word translated as "shame" in the phrase "shame and justice" means "*respect* for the feeling or opinion of others."[4] This idea pleased the aristocrats.

Now that he has ingratiated himself with the two major groups in Athens, Protagoras argues for the anti-democratic and anti-aristocratic point that living a good life is a matter of proper training. He thinks this training manipulates the implanted capacity to feel shame. This manipulation occurs through lessons in the school, through the punishments in the legal system, and through the power of persuasion belonging to rhetoric. He says education exists in the city to insure that children become good, that this process begins in the nursery, and that it continues into adult life with the enforcement of the laws of the city, and for those willing to pay to become even better, he says that he himself is "uniquely qualified to assist others in becoming fine and good." Protagoras thus suggests that education is a matter of using threat and reward to develop the implanted sense of shame so that the traditional morality becomes second nature to the children of the city. This transforms the children. It causes them to come to agree in thought and action with their parents, teachers, and lawgivers when they say "this is just, that is unjust, this is fine, that ugly, this pious, that impious, he should do this, he should not do that," and Protagoras can contribute to such teaching because rhetorical persuasion is one way to manipulate the sense of shame (324d–328c).

The Protagorean counterpoint

Protagoras' myth and subsequent argument is interesting in its own right but more so for the counterpoint it provides to Socrates' devotion to knowledge about ethical matters. In the myth, before Zeus has Hermes implant the sense of shame in human beings, no one had an overriding motive to respect the property of others. A person without shame is deterred from taking what he wants only if he thinks the cost outweighs the benefit. The resulting backstabbing destroys the stability of the community, which, in turn, drives human beings back into nature. Without the sense of shame, human beings are not suited for group living. Zeus saw that extinction was inevitable unless he altered human beings so that they would have a strong desire to respect the position of others in society. He implanted the sense of shame to make the necessary change, and he gave it to human beings in more or less equal amounts. Now, with the sense of shame, stable group living is possible because a person no longer tries to take whatever he wants whenever he thinks he can get it. The sense of shame eliminates the otherwise inevitable war of man against man.

Protagoras teaches his students how to manipulate this sense of shame. He says that he himself manipulates this sense to help wayward souls conform to the traditional morality[5] and that he is better than others in assisting a person in "becoming fine and good." Such altruism, however, is not what drove the young men from the aristocracy to pay the Sophists huge sums of money. They were interested in the art of rhetoric so that they could make the crowd, in the courts and in political bodies, share their opinions about what should be done. By using the power of rhetoric to make the many say to themselves that "this is just, that is unjust, this is beautiful, that ugly, this pious, that impious, do this, don't do that," the orator can win support for the policies that, economically and in other ways, favor himself and his friends. If, along the way, the many happen to conform to the traditional beliefs about the just, the beautiful, and the pious, this is purely accidental.

The young men no doubt also thought that expertise in rhetoric was instrumental for their happiness. They assumed that happiness is a matter of changing the world so that it is more to their liking, and the myth helps explain why expertise in rhetoric would be thought an effective way to make such changes. Out of their sense of shame, the many say "this is just, that is unjust, this is fine, that is ugly." These utterances stem from the attitudes of shame that develop and become stable over time because they encourage the city's survival. Over time these attitudes become coordinated because this coordination reduces antagonism and encourages stable group living. The orator, as Protagoras describes him, has a decided advantage in this situation because he can direct the coordination. Because he can use the power of rhetorical persuasion to change what people say is and is not shameful, the orator has the extraordinary power to redirect the resources of group living to satisfy his desires. This is how Protagoras teaches sound judgment in one's affairs, both in the household and in the city. He teaches his student a routine for the satisfaction of desire.

3.3   Rhetoric is Blind to the Good

Like the *Protagoras*, the *Gorgias* is named after an important player in the new education that had become popular in Athens. The discussion in the *Gorgias*, however, is much more tightly focused on the question whether expertise in rhetorical persuasion is the key to the good life.[i] Moreover, in the *Gorgias*, in striking contrast to the *Protagoras* and other early dialogues, Socrates breaks out of his role as a questioner. Now he argues that those who praise rhetoric are confused because, although it might be useful for satisfying desires, it provides no guidance about which goals and plans should be adopted and hence about what is desirable. Socrates argues that rhetoric is dangerous because it is blind to the good. It is a quick way to ruin one's life.

Socrates against Gorgias

Socrates arrives on the scene just after Gorgias has finished the initial part of his display of rhetorical skill. Callicles and Chaerephon are outside, and Socrates tells Callicles that he would like to learn from Gorgias what his art brings about. They go inside to pursue the matter, but Polus jumps in to answer for Gorgias. He boasts that Gorgias is an expert in "the finest of arts" (448c). Socrates rejects this reply because, although it is flattering, it is not an answer to the question he has asked. Gorgias himself is present, and so Socrates puts the question to him.

Gorgias says that his art is "rhetoric," but he has trouble explaining what rhetoric is. He says, first of all, that it is a "producer of persuasion." Socrates asks him what sort of persuasion rhetoric produces, and he also asks him on what subject matter rhetoric produces this persuasion. Gorgias replies that rhetoric produces persuasion in juries and mobs on questions of what is "just and unjust." Socrates distinguishes *two sorts of persuasion*, and Gorgias says rhetoric produces the sort that results in belief as opposed to knowledge:

Do you think that learning and belief are the same or different?

They are different, Socrates.

Right. Here is how you can tell. If someone asked if there is a true and a false belief, you would agree, no doubt.

Of course.

But is there a true and a false knowledge?

Not at all.

---

[i] Like the older Protagoras, Gorgias was a verbal magician. Many of the young men anxious to advance in society were willing to pay him well to teach them this magic. Gorgias, however, unlike Protagoras, seems to have been more rhetorician than sophist. So, for example, in the *Meno*, at 95c, Meno tells Socrates that Gorgias does not undertake to teach virtue or excellence and that he ridicules those who do.

So clearly belief and knowledge are different.

True.

Yet, those who have learned and those who have come to believe have been persuaded?

Yes.

Are there two sorts of persuasion, one producing belief without knowledge, the other knowledge?

Yes.

Now which does oratory produce in law courts and other gatherings concerning the just and unjust?

The one from which we get belief.

So oratory is a producer of persuasion that results in belief, not the persuasion that results in instruction, concerning the just and unjust.

Yes.

And so an orator is not a teacher of law courts and other gatherings about the just and unjust. He only creates belief. For he could not, I take it, teach such a group of so many about matters so important in such a short time.

He certainly could not. (454d–455a)

On Gorgias' conception, the expert in rhetorical persuasion is not an expert about matters of justice. He does nothing more than use his skill to produce belief by making claims about justice and injustice *appear* true. This is how rhetoric is a "producer of persuasion."

Given this conception of expertise in rhetorical persuasion, it looks as if the orator should take direction from the expert on justice. Gorgias himself illustrates the point. He says that rhetoric is like boxing, wrestling, or fighting in armor. Expertise in these arts can be put to vicious ends. Misuse is not supposed to reveal a fault in the art or the teacher. According to Gorgias, in rhetoric, as in boxing and in other such arts, it is not a fault in the subject or the teacher if the student uses what he has learned for ends that run contrary to the traditional morality (456c–457a).

Socrates thinks that Gorgias has contradicted himself, but he leaves the contradiction implicit so that he cannot be accused of being a debater interested in nothing more than scoring points against his opponent. He goes on to say, however, that he would be pleased to continue the discussion if Gorgias, like he himself, wishes to have the "subject become clear," as there is "nothing as bad for a man as having false belief about the things" currently under discussion (457e–458b). This reticence makes it difficult to know what Socrates has in mind, but the contradiction might arise on the assumption that rhetorical skill is the expertise involved in living a good life. Socrates might think, given this much, that expertise in rhetoric must eliminate goals and plans contrary to ethical virtue and hence that the orator cannot exercise his expertise to accomplish bad things.

Gorgias himself does not claim explicitly that the art of rhetoric is the expertise involved in living a good life, but his remarks can easily leave one with this impression. Earlier in the conversation, Gorgias said that rhetoric is concerned with the "greatest of human concerns" and that the expertise in rhetorical persuasion he imparts is "the greatest good":

> What are the speeches used in oratory about?
>
> The greatest of human concerns, Socrates, and the best. (451d)
>
> What is this you say is the greatest good, a thing you claim to produce?
>
> That which is the greatest good, Socrates. It is at once the source of freedom for men and the source of rule over others in their city. (452d)

The great importance Gorgias places on expertise in rhetoric is reminiscent of the importance Socrates himself places on the love of wisdom, the service he believes he provides to the Athenians.[6] This, presumably, is why Socrates, in the lull in the argument, tells Gorgias that he himself does not suppose that any bad for a man is as great as false belief about the things they are discussing. The question is which life is better, a life in the love of wisdom, as Socrates thinks, or a life of ruling over others in the city through the power that accompanies rhetorical persuasion.

Once Gorgias agrees to further questioning, Socrates tries to show him that despite what he has said, he is committed to the belief that rhetoric is in fact *not* like boxing, wrestling, or fighting in armor. To this end, Socrates asks Gorgias whether expertise on matters of "good and bad, admirable, shameful, and just and unjust" is necessary for being an orator. Gorgias admits that it is (459c–460b), and Socrates then argues that this means the "orator will never wish to do what's unjust":

> A man who has learned building is a builder?
>
> Yes.
>
> And a man who has learned music a musician?
>
> Yes.
>
> And a man who has learned medicine a doctor? And is this true with other arts? A man who has learned is the man his knowledge makes him?
>
> Yes.

And so is a man who has learned what is just a just man?

Yes.

And a just man, I take it, does just things?

Yes.

And so is an orator just, and does a just man wish to do what is just?

Apparently.

The just man will never wish to do what is unjust?

Yes.

But we said the orator is just.

Yes.

So an orator will never wish to do what is unjust.

Apparently not. (460b–c)

The orator, therefore, is not like the boxer after all. A boxer might believe that some end is good, when it is not, and he might use his expertise in the art of boxing to secure this bad end for himself. The orator, by contrast, given what Gorgias has said, is not in this situation. He "will never wish to do what is unjust" because he has "learned what is just" and hence is a "just man."

Gorgias now drops out of the conversation rather than face his apparently contradictory beliefs, but perhaps, if he had been more interested in the issues, he could have retraced his steps to provide a more adequate defense of the importance he attributes to rhetoric. He might explain that he does *not* believe that expertise on matters of good, bad, just, and unjust is necessary for expertise in rhetoric. Further, he might distinguish two uses of the term "good." When an end is contrary to the traditional morality, it may be said to be bad; however, in a context in which the interest is in satisfaction of desire, this same end may be said to be good. Indeed, in so far as Gorgias' position is the one Protagoras set out in his myth, Gorgias thinks that happiness is a matter of getting what one wants and that what one wants may run contrary to the traditional morality. Gorgias, however, does not articulate or defend this Sophistical conception of ethics and the good life.

Socrates against Polus

At this point, Polus jumps in to replace Gorgias in the conversation.[j] He asks Socrates what he thinks rhetoric is. One might expect Socrates not to

---

[j] Polus is a student of Gorgias and a teacher of rhetoric in his own right.

answer, but, unlike in the early dialogues, where his role is primarily that of a questioner, he is now quite ready to say and to argue for what he believes. Socrates informs Polus that rhetoric is not an "art." He says that it is a kind of "flattery," that it is a matter of "experience and routine," and that it is an "image" of part of politics:

> I do not believe rhetoric is an art, to tell the truth.
>
> What do you think it is?
>
> What makes art, as you say in the treatise[7] I read not long ago.
>
> What do you mean?
>
> I mean experience.
>
> You believe rhetoric is experience?
>
> I do.
>
> Experience for what?
>
> For producing gratification and pleasure. . . . There is a practice, not an art, that appeals to a soul which guesses, is aggressive, and by nature clever at dealing with people. This practice is flattery, in short. It has several parts, and pastry cooking, for example, is one. It seems to be an art, but, on my account, it is experience and routine,[8] not an art. Rhetoric, too, is like this. . . . It is an image or counterfeit of a part of politics. (462b-463d)

Socrates says that rhetoric is a matter of "experience and routine" and that it is a way of making one think he is doing well when in fact he is not. Socrates goes on to explain that rhetoric is an image of the science of justice in the way pastry cooking is an image of the science of medicine. The science of medicine consists in the knowledge that various drugs in various situations make the body healthy. Among the ignorant, there is difficulty identifying the person who exercises this science. The ignorant are taken in by the image. They have the impression that the pastry baker, not the doctor, is the expert in health matters. The baker, by testing his products in the mouths of the many, learns how to make foods that taste sweet. The ignorant are victims of this sweetness. They become conditioned to eat this food and soon prove unable to break this conditioning even if they realize that the food is bad for them because it ruins their health (464d–465a). The unscrupulous are quick to employ this "flattery" to satisfy their own desires by causing the ignorant to become habituated to act in ways that make their lives worse. This is bad for the ignorant, but it is equally bad for the flatterers because they too satisfy desires they should not satisfy.

The same, according to Socrates, is true of rhetoric. By testing certain ways of speaking against the reaction of his audience, the orator learns how to make speeches that are enjoyable to hear. The ignorant are victims of this ear candy. Hence, rhetoric is really a kind of "flattery." Just as those who have come under the spell of the pastry chef ruin their bodies, those who come under the spell of the orator ruin their souls. In the wrong hands, rhetoric is a tool and means to satisfy one's own desires by habituating the ignorant to act in certain ways. This is bad for the ignorant, but it is also bad for the orators because they too satisfy desires they should not satisfy.

Polus' vanity has been stung by the claim that rhetoric is a kind of flattery. He rejects the analysis out of hand, although he gives no indication he has understood it. Instead, he appeals to the common belief that orators are powerful people, not servile flatterers. Socrates, in reply, argues that orators actually have no real power at all. He admits the orator would be powerful if he acted to make his life good as opposed to following the plan that happens to be salient at the moment. The problem, however, according to Socrates, is that rhetoric cannot provide this ability.

To help Polus understand this fact about rhetoric, Socrates explains that what *seems* good is not necessarily what *is* good. Rhetoric alone, he says, is weak. At best, it provides the power to get what seems good. This pales in comparison to the power to get what is good:

> Is it good if someone does what he thinks is best even when he lacks intellect and intelligence? Is that having great power?
>
> No.
>
> Refute me, then, and show me that orators have intelligence and that oratory is an art, and not flattery. Otherwise, the orators who do what seems good, and despots also, will not benefit from this. Power is good, you say, but you also agree with me that doing what seems good without intelligence is bad?
>
> Yes, I agree.
>
> What I was saying is true, then, when I said that it is possible for a man who does in his city what seems good not to have great power, nor to be doing what he wishes.[9] (466e–468e)

Since rhetoric does not concern itself with what is good, expertise in rhetoric does not provide the power to live a good life. The orator uses his skill to make the world fit his desires, but this is to go through life blindly. Sometimes the orator happens to make his life good, but, more often than not, although he does what to him seems good, he fails to make his life good.

Rather than reply to this argument directly, Polus turns the discussion to happiness and the law. He cites the historical example of Archelaus (a man whose life included vicious behavior to secure his place as King of Macedon) to show that happiness is one thing and that obeying the law is quite another. To attain his seat on the throne, Archelaus had his uncle and his half-brother murdered. This episode suggested to many that crime can lead to happiness:

Do you know of Archelaus, the son of Perdiccas, the ruler of Macedonia?

Well, I do hear things about him.

So is he happy or not?

I do not know, Polus. I never met him.

What! You need to meet him and do not know right off he is happy?

Most emphatically.

No doubt you will not even admit that the Great King[k] is happy!

Yes, and that would be true, for I do not know how he is in regard to education and justice.

Really? Is that what determines happiness?

Yes, by my reckoning. The fine and good human being, man or woman, is happy, whereas the one who is unjust and wicked is miserable.

So, according to you, Archelaus is miserable?

If he is unjust.

Why of course he is unjust! If he wanted to do what is just, he would have remained a slave. And on your reasoning he would be happy! As it is, Socrates, how extremely miserable, according to you, he has become, now that he has committed the most vicious wrongs. (470d–471b)

Polus, in citing this example, has slipped into the rhetorical style, contrary to his prior agreement (461c–462a), as talk of tyrants panders to a crowd

---

[k] This "title refers to the King of Persia, who embodied the popular idea of supreme happiness" (Donald Zeyl, *Plato. Gorgias*, 1987, 34). In the *Euthydemus*, in response to Euthydemus' assertion that he and his brother are in the business of teaching virtue, Socrates says that Euthydemus is "more blessed in his wisdom than the Great King in his sovereignty" (274a). The Athenians knew, though, that not everything had turned out well for the Great King, Darius the Great. He tried to punish the Greeks for their support of the Ionian revolt, but he was defeated at Marathon in 490. His son, Xerxes the Great, led the second invasion, which was put down when the Athenian general Themistocles succeeded in luring the Persian navy into the Straits of Salamis, where they became disorganized and quickly defeated by the allied fleet.

mentality, and Socrates quickly reminds him that the subject matter under discussion should not be treated lightly:

> The matters we dispute are hardly trivial but are ones it is most fine to know and most shameful not to know, as they involve knowing or not knowing who is happy and who is not. (472c–d)

The many may well have been taken in by the spectacle of Archelaus. They may believe that he has made his life good and himself happy, just as Polus himself has supposed, but Socrates insists that this belief must survive in argument. The question of happiness and the human good is a subject for dialectic. It cannot be answered by counting the hands of the many in a vote.

Now that Socrates has set aside Polus' example, he proceeds with his customary method of examination and testing through question and answer. Polus suggests that Archelaus and other such tyrants have made themselves happy by committing crimes and by escaping punishment, but Polus is unable to defend this view against Socrates' pointed questioning. Polus advertises rhetoric as the quick route to the life of a tyrant who can run over others and escape punishment for his crimes, but Socrates gets him to admit that no one really wants such a life. Socrates' questioning forces Polus to admit that to escape just punishment, as Archelaus and other tyrants have apparently done, is actually a way of escaping something good in order to get something bad (478e–479b).

In conclusion, Socrates says that expertise in rhetoric might be useful for acting contrary to virtue, since this so often is the end it achieves, but since breaking just laws and escaping just punishment is no part of living a good life, this fact about rhetoric does not recommend it (480b–481b). And now Polus, like Gorgias before him, is at a loss for words. He does not respond to Socrates' analysis and condemnation of rhetoric. Instead, he drops out of the conversation.

Socrates against Callicles

Now that Polus has been reduced to silence, Callicles jumps into the conversation with both feet. In an extended and uncivil tirade of words, he insists on a point that has been lurking in the background for some time.[1] Callicles

---

[1] Unlike Gorgias and Polus, Callicles is not a teacher of rhetoric. "Callicles of Acharnae is no wandering sophist or rhetorician, but a young Athenian aristocrat ambitious for political power. We know nothing of him beyond what Plato tells us, but there is no adequate reason to think he is fictional; his *deme* is mentioned, and as Dodds remarks, a man at once so ambitious and so frank may well have died in a troubled time too young to be remembered by anyone but Plato, who described him as willing to say what many men believe but are ashamed to say" (R. E. Allen, Euthyphro, Apology, Crito, Meno, Gorgias, Menexenus. *The Dialogues of Plato*, 1984, 190).

proclaims that Socrates has defeated Polus in discussion, just as he previously defeated Gorgias, by illicitly trading on the distinction between what is good by "nature," on the one hand, and what is good by "custom," on the other:

> You appeal to the sympathies of the many with what is fine, not by nature but by custom, instead of pursuing the truth, as you claim. And these, nature and custom, are opposed for the most part, so a man who is ashamed and afraid to say what he thinks contradicts himself. This is the trick you have devised for your refutations. If someone speaks in terms of custom, you question him in terms of nature; if he speaks in terms of nature, you question him in terms of custom. (482e–483a)

> Those who make our laws and customs are weak and the more numerous. And so they do this, and assign praise and blame, with their own advantage in mind. They fear the more powerful, the ones who can take a greater share, and in defense, they say that taking more is shameful and unjust. They do well to get equality, as they themselves are inferior. And so it becomes shameful and unjust to get a greater share, by custom. But I believe nature reveals that it is just for the better and the more capable man to have a greater share than the worse and the less capable man. (483b–d)

Callicles does not draw his distinction between "nature" and "custom" especially clearly, but the leading idea is that what is just by custom is not always good by nature. Nor is what is unjust by custom always bad by nature. Only the customs and laws of the city set the standard for the contrary, and they are promoted by the weak to protect themselves from the strong. Callicles thinks that a life in accordance with the traditional morality is good by custom and that a life of getting what one wants is good by nature, even if what one wants is contrary to the traditional morality.

Socrates takes Callicles' ill-mannered speech in stride. In fact, Socrates too is interested in justice by nature, not simply in what the many as a whole say justice is, so he presses Callicles to explain what justice really is. After several false starts in this direction, Callicles eventually says that justice by nature is for those who have the power to use the force of government to arrange matters in the society so that they themselves get "whatever they have in mind." And so Socrates asks Callicles whether the rulers should rule themselves, i.e., whether they should exercise control over the ends they have in mind for themselves. Callicles answers that they need not. He insists that a ruler should think that satisfying his own appetites is good, whatever these appetites happen to be for, because the good life by nature is a life of pleasure (491a–492b).

Socrates at this point, in his usual way, asks questions to make Callicles contradict himself, but the argument that results in this contradiction is

somewhat convoluted. The crucial point, which Callicles eventually con-
cedes after much discussion, is that if pleasure is understood as the
satisfaction of appetites, then a human being who satisfies his appetites
indiscriminately fills his life with both good and bad. With this concession,
Socrates completes his refutation:

> Polus and I thought that everything is done for the sake of the good. Do you
> concur that the good is the end of all action, and that we should do everything
> for its sake, but not it for the sake of anything else? Are you voting on our side?
>
> I am.
>
> So it is for the sake of the good we should do everything, including pleasant
> things, and not the good for the sake of the pleasant.
>
> Right.
>
> Now, is it for every man to pick out which pleasures are good ones and which
> are bad ones, or does this require an expert?
>
> It requires an expert. (499e–500a)

Callicles has contradicted his prior assertion that rulers need not rule over
their own desires because he now finds himself forced to admit that "the end
of all action is the good" and that only the "expert" can determine whether a
given action is actually part of a good life.

Socrates now returns to the question that informs the dialogue. He
reminds Callicles that the important question on the table is which life is
"better," whether it is the life in the "love of wisdom" Socrates himself
recommends, or the life Callicles recommends (500a–c). Callicles, in a
petulant response, says that he does not know what Socrates has in mind.
And so Socrates patiently explains the essential differences between the two
lives more clearly and completely:

> I was saying that pastry cooking is not an art, but experience, whereas
> medicine is an art. Medicine has investigated the nature of the object it serves
> and the cause of the things it does, and can provide an account of each. The
> other, concerned with pleasure, to which its service is devoted, proceeds
> inexpertly, without having considered the nature of pleasure or its cause. It
> does so without reason, with almost no discrimination. Through routine and
> experience it preserves the memory of what customarily happens, and that is
> how it also supplies its pleasures. And so, Callicles, consider whether you
> think that there are similar practices in the case of the soul. Do some arts
> possess forethought about what is best for the soul, while others have
> disregarded this and have investigated only the way the soul gets pleasure,
> without considering which of the pleasures is better or worse, and indeed

without having any concerns about anything but mere gratification? I think there are, and I say that this is flattery, in the case of the body, the soul, and in any case in which a man is concerned with a pleasure without any thought of what is better and worse. Do you join us in this opinion or not?

I do, so you can finish. (500e–501c)

The practice of acting for the sake of the good is an expertise, a matter of knowledge, and hence is distinct from practices that aim only at pleasure and are "without reason" and work "through routine and experience." These practices lack the ability to evaluate the current situation or the situation that would result from a given course of action. In the absence of this ability, given the contrast between "reason" and "experience," the choice of goals is not an exercise of "reason" and hence not a matter of knowledge. According to Socrates, the life of the sort Callicles recommends is one of acting in terms of plans constructed and executed for whatever goal happens to be in mind, without vetting the goal and the plan by exercising "forethought about what is best for the soul."

This distinction between the two lives is important for what it indicates about how Plato understands psychological functioning in human beings. The lives incorporate a form of Parmenides' contrast between "reason," on the one hand, and "habit born from much experience," on the other. With respect to what exists, Parmenides claimed that "experience" provides no knowledge and that the failure to appreciate this caused the inquirers into nature to take a "backward-turning" path in their inquiries. Socrates, with his focus on definitions of the virtues, works within the general framework Parmenides introduced. Contrary to the more usual assumption that practical wisdom about ethical matters is a matter of experience, Socrates suggests that the knowledge that constitutes this expertise includes knowledge of definitions, which is a matter of "reason," not "experience." Now in the *Gorgias*, the same contrast is at work in the argument against Polus when Socrates says that rhetoric is a matter of "experience" and not an "art." Moreover, it is at work in the contrast between the life in the love of wisdom and the life Callicles recommends.

How Plato understood this is not completely clear, but the leading idea seems to be that expertise in rhetoric can cause a certain kind of irrationality and improper functioning because the cognition involved in "reason" is somehow absent or blocked in a human being who leads the life Callicles recommends. As a result, his decisions about what to do are not a function of knowledge of the good. Rather, his goals are set in terms of desires that themselves somehow arise naturally in the course of living. To achieve these goals, rhetoric may be an effective means. The question, however, is whether achieving these goals can be expected to result in a good life. Socrates argues that there is no such expectation because there is no expectation that the goals are good.

With this much in hand, Socrates argues for the following conclusion: that his life in the love of wisdom is better than the one Callicles recommends. He insists, first of all, that the practice that improves the soul, and hence the human being and his life, is one that makes the soul properly organized by instilling in it the discipline involved in choosing what is appropriate. Callicles goes along with this line of thought initially, but as Socrates hammers the point, Callicles becomes too angry and frustrated to continue the conversation. He has had enough and tells Socrates to finish the discussion himself. Socrates does so, and begins by retracing his steps thus far:

> Listen, then, as I resume the argument from the beginning (506c). Both we and everything else that is good, are good by the presence of some virtue. But a virtue becomes present, not just any old way, but by order and rightness and art. When a certain order, the proper one for each thing, is present, a thing is good. And a properly ordered soul is a self-controlled and a good one, and the man who is self-controlled does what is appropriate with respect to both gods and human beings. For if he did otherwise, he would not be self-controlled. But if he did what is appropriate with respect to men, he would be doing what is just. And if he did what is appropriate with respect to the gods, he would be doing what is pious. Further, he would be brave. For a self-controlled man pursues and avoids what he should, whether these are things, or people, or pleasures and pains. So, it is quite necessary, Callicles, that the temperate and self-controlled man, because he is just and brave and pious, is a completely good man. And the good man does well in what he does. The man who does well is blessed and happy, while the corrupt man, the one who does badly, is miserable. Yet this man, the miserable one, is the undisciplined man you were praising. (506d–507c)

In this summary, Socrates makes several very striking claims. He says that a thing is good just if it is properly organized. In the case of human beings, which he assumes are psychological beings, he says that the proper organization is a matter of discipline and self-control. A human being whose soul is so organized does what is "appropriate," with respect to human beings, to fearful things, and to the gods, and hence is "just and brave and pious and a completely good man." Not only is he "completely good," he is also "blessed and happy." Furthermore, according to Socrates, a human being whose soul has any other organization is "miserable" and unhappy.

Socrates now identifies his own conversations as belonging to the kind of practice that works in terms of "reason," not "experience," and that has the good of the soul in mind. He says that the "conversations in which he engages always aim at what is best." He does not say explicitly that the love of wisdom is the art of living a good life, but this is quite plainly the intended conclusion (508e–509a, 521d–e, 522c–e). On the question of which life is "better," the question Socrates has said that "even a man of little intelligence" would treat with the utmost seriousness, Plato leaves the reader to conclude that the better life is the one Socrates thought the love of wisdom provided, not the life of "political involvement that Callicles and his sort were engaged in."

This conclusion is expected, but the discussion itself leaves many questions unanswered. Even if for the sake of argument one is willing to grant the general claim that good things are all and only the properly organized things, there is still the question of how the love of wisdom provides human beings with the proper psychological organization, whatever exactly this organization is. The idea seems to be that somehow or another the elimination of inconsistency produces this organization by resulting in the psychological organization in which a human being recognizes and chooses the appropriate in the circumstances he encounters. This psychological organization is supposed to constitute rationality in its most expert form, and so it is supposed to follow that a human being is happiest when he is living a life of ethical virtue. Yet, in the absence of a much clearer specification of the human psychology and what the proper organization is, it remains difficult to know why Socrates thought that his claims for the love of wisdom are true. In particular, even if the elimination of inconsistency were to produce the psychological organization Socrates had in mind, it remains unclear why knowledge of the good in this psychological organization is a matter of the cognition involved in "reason" as opposed to "experience." Moreover, in the absence of considerably more discussion and argument about the good human beings seek in rational action, it remains extremely unclear why the good life must coincide with the life of ethical virtue. So although Socrates may have defeated Gorgias, Polus, and Callicles in argument, he does not answer the questions about his own position and hence does not demonstrate its truth.[10]

Notes

1. In Socrates' trial, the jury seems to have been 500 strong. "According to *Apol*[*ogy*] 36a the vote was for condemnation by a majority of sixty, presumably approximately 280 to 220. Once the verdict was reached each side spoke again to propose the penalty, and the jury had to decide between the two. The prosecution demanded the death penalty, while (according to Plato) Socrates,

after having in effect refused to propose a penalty (in *Apol.* 36d–e he proposes that he be awarded free meals for life in the town hall as a public benefactor), was eventually induced to propose the not inconsiderable fine of half a talent, over eight years' wages for a skilled craftsman (38b). The vote was for death, and according to Diogenes Laertius eighty more voted for death than had voted for a guilty verdict, indicating a split of 360 to 140 . . ." (C. C. W. Taylor, *Socrates. A Very Short Introduction*, 1998b, 13–14).

2. Pericles died in 429, shortly before Plato was born, but the dialogues can seem so real that it is easy to misunderstand what was happening in Athens when Plato was writing the *Protagoras* and *Gorgias*. His immediate audience lives after the power and wealth of Athens, which had attracted the sophists, had been dissipated in the Peloponnesian War. "As we read, we can hardly realize that he is calling up a time when he himself was a boy. The picture is so actual that we feel it must be contemporary. That is why so many writers on Plato speak as if the first half of the fourth century ran concurrently with the second half of the fifth. They think of Plato as the adversary of the 'Sophists,' though when he wrote, there were no longer any sophists in the sense intended. They were merely memories in his day; for they had no successors. Even Thrasymachus belongs to the generation which flourished when Plato was a child" (John Burnet, *Plato's* Phaedo, 1911, xxxiv–xxxv). "[It is important] to situate Plato in his own time and place, and thus to overcome what one might describe as the optical illusion of the dialogues. By this I mean Plato's extraordinary success in recreating the dramatic atmosphere of the previous age, the intellectual milieu of the late fifth century in which Socrates confronts the sophists and their pupils. It is difficult but necessary to bear in mind the gap between this art world, created by Plato, and the actual world in which Plato worked out his own philosophy. That was no longer the world of Protagoras and Gorgias, Hippias and Thrasymachus. With the exception of Gorgias (who was unusually long-lived), these men were probably all dead when Plato wrote. Protagoras, in particular, must have died when Plato was a child, and the dialogue named after him is situated before Plato's birth. The intellectual world to which Plato's own work belongs is defined not by the characters in his dialogues but by the thought and the writing of his contemporaries and rivals, such as the rhetorician Isocrates and the various followers of Socrates" (Charles Kahn, *Plato and the Socratic Dialogue*, 1996, 2).

3. The parody of Socrates in Aristophanes' *Clouds* shows that the Athenians were not concerned to distinguish Socrates and his methods from those of the sophists. There is a reflection of this in the *Protagoras*. When Socrates knocks on the door, the servant mistakes him for another sophist (314d). This lumping together was a mistake, as Plato points out in the *Protagoras* and *Gorgias*, but it is also important to realize that despite their very real disagreements, Socrates and Plato shared common ground with the sophists: they all were against the traditional education.

4. Aristotle says that "shame" (αἰδώς) is "defined as a kind of fear of disrepute" and that it "is suitable for youth, not for every time of life, as we think it right for the young to be prone to shame, as they live in terms of feelings, and hence often go wrong, but are restrained by shame" (*Nicomachean Ethics* IV.9.1128b).

5. G. B. Kerferd summarizes the Protagorean position and its essential point that ethical norms constitute a coordination procedure: "[The progression from nature to civilization] is expressed in a particular way in the famous Myth put into the mouth of Protagoras in Plato's *Protagoras* (320c8–322d5), which in all probability is based to some extent on doctrines of the historical Protagoras as published in such works as his treatise '*On the Original State of Man*.' When the first men came up to the light of day, they were sufficiently equipped with innate qualities to enable them to house, feed and clothe themselves. But they lived separately from each other and because of their physical inferiority they were dangerously vulnerable to attacks by wild animals. For self-protection they tried coming together to form groups. But when they did they proceeded to act unjustly towards one another – the groups broke up and they continued to be destroyed. So Zeus sent the two moral virtues *adios* and *dike* – mutual respect and right or justice – to be distributed so that all should have a share in them. . . . And in the explanation and further interpretation which follows the myth it is made plain that the justice which Protagoras is speaking consists of the *nomina* [or customs] of the community. In other words Protagoras has produced a fundamental defense of *nomos* in relation to *physis* [or nature], in that *nomos* is a necessary condition for the maintenance of human societies" (*The Sophistic Movement*, 1981, 125–126).

6. This general observation is common in the secondary literature. "That you need knowledge of good and bad to live well is also a major argument of the *Gorgias*. In contrast to dialogues such as *Euthydemus*, *Charmides*, and *Laches*, Socrates here argues for this conclusion with opponents who explicitly deny it. The famous orator and his Athenian admirers, Polus and Callicles, think that rhetoric (skill at persuasion) is the only knowledge one needs to acquire in order to live well. Rhetoric, according to Gorgias and his devotees, is the finest type of knowledge (Gorg. 448c, e; cf. 466b) and deals with 'the greatest human concerns' (451d). This is to accord rhetoric the same honorific status that Socrates attributes to the knowledge he urges his compatriots to seek" (Susan Sauvé Meyer, *Ancient Ethics*, 2008b, 17–18).

7. The treatise itself has not survived, but presumably the content was devoted to the way in which "experience" underlies expertise. Cf. Aristotle, *Metaphysics* I.1.981a.

8. Michael Frede summarizes the relevant history: "It seems that, at the end of the fifth and in the course of the fourth century, some authors had taken the view that certain important bodies of technical knowledge or expertise were mere matters of experience and that perhaps all knowledge was of this kind. Plato in the *Gorgias* makes Socrates criticize Polus' claim that rhetoric is the highest of all human arts, the master discipline, by arguing that rhetoric, at least as Gorgias

and Polus conceive of it, is merely a matter of experience and knack or practice (τριβή) and not an art (τέχνη). But there is good reason to believe that Polus himself did in fact hold the view that rhetorical knowledge is a matter of experience (Ar. *Met* 981a4), and it is certainly no accident that two terms Plato here uses to discredit Gorgianic rhetoric, namely ἐμπειρία 'experience' and τριβή 'knack' or 'practice,' are both terms later Empiricists used in a positive sense" ("Introduction" in *Galen. Three Treatises on the Nature of Science*, 1985, xxiii–xxiv).

9. This passage can be confusing and perhaps is confused about the role of desire in the human psychology. H. A. Prichard makes the point: "In trying to show that orators and tyrants have the least power in states, [Socrates] lays down generally that what a man wishes for in doing some action is not the action but the result for the sake of which he does it, the man who takes a drug, e.g., wishing not for this but for health, and the man who takes a voyage wishing not for the sailing and the incurring of dangers but for the resulting wealth. Here, however, Plato is plainly going too far in asserting that a man does not want to do the action: what he meant and should have said is rather that though he desires to do the action this desire depends on the desire of a certain result, this latter desire being more properly said to be what is moving him, as being what gives rise to the desire to do the action" ("Moral Obligation," 1949, 113).

10. C. C. W. Taylor makes the general point: "The thesis that the moral life is the best life for the agent thus has the central role of linking Socrates' intuitions of the pre-eminence of morality with the theory of uniform self-interested motivation which is the foundation of the identification of goodness with knowledge. It is the keystone of the entire arch. Given that centrality, it is surprising how little argumentative support it receives. . . . Plato supplies some arguments in *Gorgias*, but they are weak. . . . [I]n order to know which arrangement of psychological components such as intellect and bodily desire is optimum we need first to know what our aims in life ought to be. One conception of those aims may indeed identify the optimum organization as that defined by the conventional virtues, but another, for example, that of Don Juan or Gauguin, may identify a quite different organization, such as one which affords the maximum play to certain kinds of self-expression, as optimum" (*Socrates: A Very Short Introduction*, 1998b, 64–66).

Further Reading for Part II

1. *The Philosophy of Socrates*, Thomas C. Brickhouse and Nicholas D. Smith, 2000
   This is "a general introduction to the philosophy of Socrates" (1). It is informed by some of the current scholarly controversies about Socrates in the secondary literature. The discussion is more philosophical than historical.
2. *A History of Greek Philosophy*. Vol. III: *The Fifth-Century Enlightenment*, W. K. C. Guthrie, 1962
   This volume divides into two parts, *The Sophists* and *Socrates*. Both are general introductions. The discussions are more historical than philosophical.
3. *Plato's Ethics* and *The Development of Ethics. I: From Socrates to the Reformation*, Terence Irwin, 1995
   The first eight chapters of *Plato's Ethics* is a discussion of Socrates and the evidence for his views in the early Platonic dialogues. The "aim of is to expound and examine Plato's moral philosophy" (3). Irwin is a leading historian, and *Plato's Ethics* is a definitive treatment of the subject. *The Development of Ethics* is a critical study of ethics from Socrates to the Reformation. The treatment of Socrates is not new, but the discussion is concise. It is also placed within a longer historical sequence that treats the Cyrenaics and the Cynics before moving on to Plato.
4. *The Sophistic Movement*, G. B. Kerferd, 1981
   This is perhaps the best general introduction to the historical Sophists and their place in Athens in the fifth century.
5. *Socratic Perplexity and the Nature of Philosophy*, Gareth B. Matthews, 1999
   This is a wonderful and thought-provoking discussion of a central aspect of Socrates, as he is presented by Plato in his dialogues, and of the influence of this figure in the subsequent philosophical tradition.
6. *The Religion of Socrates*, Mark L. McPherran, 1996
   This is an investigation into the religious aspect of Socrates. The discussion is both philosophical and historical. The interpretations are sensible.
7. *Socrates: A Very Short Introduction*, C. C. W. Taylor, 1998b
   This is the best general introduction to Socrates. It is historically informed and philosophically sensitive. There is a discussion of the historical Socrates, Plato's Socrates, and the transmission of influence to the subsequent tradition.

Part III

Plato

The Academy

4

Three Platonic Theories

In the middle dialogues, Plato considers possible solutions to the puzzles he encountered in trying to understand Socrates and his love of wisdom. These solutions are traditionally called "theories," but it should not be thought that they are worked out in any detail. Nor should it be thought that Plato believed these theories were adequate. He is not a character in the dialogues.

In the *Meno*, in the *Theory of Recollection*, Socrates considers the possibility that the soul exists separately from the body and that human beings have innate knowledge of certain matters. This knowledge is part of the soul and cannot be eliminated, only obscured by the false beliefs acquired during incarnation. To remove this obscurity, it is necessary to engage in the method of question and answer to eliminate inconsistency in belief. In this way, there is an explanation for the knowledge Socrates presupposes in earlier dialogues. This knowledge belongs to reason, a part of the soul that predates the body.

In the *Phaedo*, in the course of considering arguments for immortality, Socrates sets out his intellectual autobiography. This story is of a piece with the change of perspective in the *Meno*. The lover of wisdom seeks to transform his soul so that it comes to resemble the natural and disincarnate state it enjoyed before incarnation. In this natural and disincarnate state, the soul is free from practical concerns and the need to exercise reason to meet these concerns. Its existence is blessed and completely characterized by knowledge of forms, entities that are changeless and perfect themselves, what Socrates uses his "What is it?" question to ask about. The forms are the subject of the *Theory of Forms*.

In the *Republic*, psychological functioning is a matter of the organization of the parts of the soul: the part with reason and two parts without reason, the appetite and the spirit. All three parts have desire, but only in the part with reason does desire stem from belief. In the other parts, the appetite and spirit, desire is not a matter of reason. Rationality requires that the three parts of the soul are harmonized so that the part with reason rules and so that action is in terms of knowledge of the good, knowledge which is innate in the part with reason but which can be obscured and blocked by improper psychological functioning. This is the *Tripartite Theory of the Soul*.

Ancient Greek Philosophy: From The Presocratics to the Hellenistic Philosophers, First Edition.
Thomas A. Blackson.   © 2011 Thomas A. Blackson. Published 2011 by Blackwell Publishing Ltd.

The middle dialogues mark a new phase in Plato's effort to vindicate Socrates and his love of wisdom. In the course of thinking about Socrates, as the discussion of the good in the *Gorgias* has shown, Plato decides that an adequate defense of Socrates is possible only if the assumption that human beings are psychological beings is placed within a more general conception of reality. The character Socrates continues in his role as chief interlocutor. He sets out and explains the more general conception of reality, but the conception itself is Plato's attempt to make sense of the historical Socrates and his devotion to the love of wisdom.[1]

4.1 The Theory of Recollection

The *Meno* is a lot like an early dialogue, but Meno,[a] Socrates' inter-locutor, has more trouble than usual with the "What is it?" question.[b] After several attempts to answer it, Meno suggests that the problem is with the question. He says neither he nor anyone else can search for the

---

[a] Meno is visiting from Thessaly, north of Athens on the mainland. He may have come to Athens as an ambassador to seek help for his city. Plato portrays him as having youthful good looks, as rich enough to travel with an entourage of slaves, and as having studied with Gorgias (70a–c, 71b–d). "[A]s one might expect from a follower of Gorgias, [Meno's] aim seems to be to impress and catch Socrates out ..." (R. W. Sharples, *Plato*: Meno, 1985, 18).

[b] The trouble starts at the outset of the dialogue. Meno asks whether virtue is acquired by teaching, by practice, by nature, or in some other way. Socrates says that he is far from clear on how virtue is acquired because he is not clear on what it is. Meno thinks that Socrates is not serious. He says that surely Socrates must have heard from Gorgias what virtue is. Socrates says, in reply, that he cannot remember what, if anything, Gorgias has said. Moreover, since Gorgias is not present, Socrates says that it falls to Meno to say what virtue is. Meno is happy to take on the role of instructor. He lists a set of behaviors for different people, that in a man virtue is "to engage in the affairs of the city" and that in a woman virtue is to "manage the house, to look after its contents, and to be subject to her husband" (71e–72a). Socrates finds this answer unsatisfactory. He wants to know what virtue is in general. Meno, although uncooperative, eventually suggests that virtue is "to desire fine things and have the ability to get them" (77b). This is the sort of answer Socrates wants, but Meno is unable to defend the answer against Socrates' subsequent questioning. Finally, out of frustration, Meno says that Socrates is like an "electric ray" because he "causes whoever at any time comes close and comes into contact with him to become numb." According to Meno, although he used to be clear about virtue, and "on many occasions said much about virtue to many people," Socrates has perplexed him (80a–b).

answer because an inquirer either knows the answer already or will not recognize it if he happens upon it (80d–e). Socrates is not persuaded. He turns to certain "speakers" for a response. He does not endorse the position he sets out, but it is easy to get the impression he thinks there is something to it:

> The speakers were among the priests and priestesses who were concerned to account for their practices. Pindar[c] too says it, and many others. They say that the soul of man is immortal. At times, it comes to an end, which they call dying. At times, it is reborn; but it is never destroyed. And as it is immortal, has been born often, and has seen all things here and in the underworld, it learned all things. So it is no wonder it can recollect what it knew before, about virtue and other things. (81a–c)

The "speakers" say that the soul is immortal. This suggests that the search for definitions can be successful. If the soul exists before the body, it is natural to suppose that a human being can "recollect" what he knew before being born in a body. At least, this is what Socrates seems to think.

This is both surprising and interesting. Meno argues that a person either knows or does not know the answer to a given "What is it?" question and that in both cases the result is the same: he cannot search for the answer. Formally, the argument is as follows:

1. Either I know or I do not know the answer.
2. If I know the answer, then I cannot search for the answer.
3. If I do not know the answer, then I cannot search for the answer.

   _____

4. I cannot search for the answer.

In response, Socrates appeals to the poets and others for the suggestion that a human being can "recollect" the answer. This seems to be a denial of the

---

[c] Pindar is a lyric poet who lived in the sixth and fifth century BC. He was among the first of the poets to reflect on poetry and the poet, and presumably this is why Socrates cites him by name.

second premise. Socrates evidently thinks, somewhat paradoxically, that a human being can search for what he knows.[d]

To show that premise (2) is false, Socrates questions one of Meno's slaves. He asks questions to help the slave identify and, at least temporarily, hold in mind the correct solution to a certain problem in geometry. Once the questioning is done, Socrates draws a surprising conclusion. He says that the slave, in "recollecting," is "recovering knowledge" from within himself:

> At the moment these opinions have been stirred up in him, like a dream, but if someone asks him these same things many times and in many ways, you can be sure that in the end he will have as accurate knowledge about these things as anyone.
>
> It seems so.
>
> Then he will know it without having been taught, only questioned, and having recovered the knowledge within himself?
>
> Yes.
>
> And is recovering knowledge within oneself recollection?
>
> Certainly.
>
> Must he have acquired this knowledge or else have possessed it always?

---

[d] This can be confusing. Once he has responded to the argument, Socrates says that he and Meno now think that "one should search for what one does not know" (86c). Yet, the suggestion had been that a human being has the knowledge but searches for it by eliminating the obscurity caused by the presence of false belief. The idea seems to be that the presence of false belief can render knowledge unavailable. The knowledge is not lost. It is obscured. In explanation, R. S. Bluck appeals to a distinction between "actual" and "latent" knowledge. He says that "Socrates in fact assumes that the soul will have been in a state of knowledge for all time" and that the "slave, and of course all other men have been in a state of knowledge (latent or actual) *throughout all time*" (*Plato's* Meno, 1961, 316). Bluck, however, does not explain his distinction between actual and latent knowledge other than to say that latent knowledge "may be aroused into our consciousness" (9) by the sort of questioning Socrates pursued. Michael Frede makes a similar point, but he notes that the "latency," as opposed to the "actual" knowledge, is what Plato thought was in need of explanation: "As to Plato, it would seem that he thinks that a state of knowledge is the natural state of reason, that what needs to be explained is not how it manages to acquire this knowledge, but rather how and why it lost this natural state, how and why the knowledge it somehow has is latent, inoperative" ("Introduction" in *Rationality in Greek Thought*, 1996a, 14).

Of course.

If he always possessed it, he would have always known. If he acquired it, he cannot have done so in this life. Or has someone taught him geometry? For he will perform in the same way about all parts of geometry, and other subjects too. Has someone taught him everything? You ought to know, especially as he was born and raised in your house.

No one has taught him. (85c–e)

Now that Socrates has shown that "recollection" is possible, he leaves Meno to conclude that he should try to answer the "What is it?" question, not construct debater's arguments to show it is unanswerable. Socrates wants Meno to realize that the use of argument to eliminate inconsistency can help an inquirer answer the "What is it?" question because, as the argument shows, pointed questioning and argument to eliminate inconsistency can help the inquirer "recollect" the knowledge he possess innately in his soul but which has become obscured through incarnation.[2]

The assumptions that inform this interlude with Meno's slave supply the content of the *Theory of Recollection*. There is no evidence that Socrates, the historical figure, thought that the human person is an immortal soul imprisoned in a mortal body, but the dialogues suggest that he did think that the human soul is real, that the love of wisdom is the question and answer method, and that this method produces practical wisdom about ethical matters by eliminating false beliefs about what the virtues are. Hence, Plato explores the possibility that the knowledge of the definitions Socrates seemed to presuppose is innate. The problem is always false belief, never the lack of knowledge, and this assumption stands at the core of the Theory of Recollection.[3]

The assumption itself is perhaps the most extreme understanding of the enlightenment principle that a person need not rely on tradition but can think for himself to uncover the truth about things.[e] Plato

---

[e] The Theory of Recollection is also tied to the older tradition. Terence Irwin describes the tradition in a way that makes the similarity clear. "The poets appeal ultimately to divine authority, to the Muses who are the true source of the poet's song, and who transmit to him a true memory (when they choose to)" (*Classical Thought*, 1989, 29). "The Muses have seen what has happened, and tell the poet (Homer, *Il.* Ii.48307, *Od.* 22.347, II.363–8, 13.487–9). But the Muses can sometimes tell the poet plausible lies as well as the truth (Hesiod, *Theogony* 24–8). To distinguish true from false the poet has to rely on memory, the mother of the Muses (*Theog.* 50–5)" (N. 17 on 226).

suggests that such thinking for oneself uncovers the truth because the knowledge is innate. The problem is not that people lack knowledge of what the virtues are. Rather, the problem is that they have false beliefs produced by tradition and ultimately by the experience of being embodied. During its time in the body, the soul becomes so confused with false beliefs that it has trouble acting on its innate knowledge. The trauma of incarnation somehow leaves the soul too weak to withstand the power of misleading impressions. In this traumatized state, the soul assents to these misleading impressions. The false beliefs it acquires in this way obscure its innate knowledge, and hence it fails to act on the basis of this knowledge. To eliminate these false beliefs, and to protect itself against the power of misleading impressions, the soul must take charge of its life in the body by living in a certain way. It must become a lover of wisdom. In this way, the soul restores itself, as much as possible, to the pristine and unconfused state it enjoyed prior to incarnation.

This new conception of the love of wisdom incorporates a line of thought from the Presocratic period. The inquirers into nature thought judgment might be perfected to provide and retain knowledge of what exists. This suggestion appears in Parmenides in the contrast between beliefs made familiar by "much experience" and those that are the judgments of "reason." Democritus built on this suggestion by contrasting two kinds of judgment, the "bastard" and "legitimate." Bastard judgment is a judgment in terms of sense experience. Such judgment is perfectly adequate for getting along in life ordinarily, but it does not issue in knowledge of what exists. For this knowledge, Democritus thought it was necessary to use the legitimate form of judgment. This judgment of "reason" is "separate" from sense experience.[4]

Plato places the love of wisdom within this philosophical context. Socrates' interlocutors invariably fail to hold in mind the universal in some ethical matter. Euthyphro, for example, thinks that his prosecuting his father would please the gods. In his conversation with Socrates, he falls back on this belief for various definitions of piety. This is a mistake. It is a mistake, first of all, because the definitions are open to refutation, as Socrates shows. Secondly, and much more fundamentally, it is a mistake because knowledge of what the virtues are is not acquired in "experience." As Plato now understands the Socratic method of question and answer, it is an attempt to purge the false beliefs a human being acquires during incarnation so that the truth he has known all along is no longer obscured. This knowledge is innate. In this way, knowledge of what the virtues are is a matter of the cognition involved in "reason" rather than "experience," which is absent from the soul in its natural and disincarnate state. This is the import of the Theory of Recollection.[f]

Virtue is not teachable

Once he has removed Meno's resistance to the "What is it?" question, Socrates returns to the question Meno raised initially: whether virtue can be taught. Socrates emphasizes that the answer depends on the nature of the expertise exercised in living a life of virtue. Meno says he is ready to continue the search, but he shows himself unable to engage in serious inquiry.

This, however, does not bring the conversation to a close. Socrates tries something new. He asks Meno to proceed on the conditional assumption that virtue is teachable *if* it is a matter of knowledge. Once Meno agrees, Socrates has him admit that virtue is beneficial because its possession successfully guides one through life. They then conclude that a human being who lives a life of virtue must have wisdom because only those with wisdom meet with success in living their lives. Only they have the expertise to make the right choices in situations that typically confuse others. The wise, for example, proceed confidently or hold back in the face of danger when this is what courage demands, whereas those who are not wise sometimes proceed confidently when they should hold back or hold back when they should go forward (88a–d).

Now that Meno has admitted the point, Socrates sets out to undercut it. He suggests that their conclusion is undermined by the fact that there are neither teachers nor students of virtue. Meno is surprised, since this assertion runs contrary to what is ordinarily supposed. He asks Socrates whether he really thinks that there are no teachers or students of virtue.

---

[f] As a defense of Socrates, the Theory of Recollection leaves certain questions unanswered. It might explain knowledge of what the virtues are, but it does not seem equipped to explain knowledge of what is appropriate in the various situations a human being faces. This knowledge seems to be a matter of "experience" and hence cannot be innate. Furthermore, there is the question of the good a human being aims to bring about in rational action. The brief discussion in the *Meno* leaves it unclear whether Plato intends the Theory of Recollection to explain this knowledge.

Socrates, in reply, says that he can find none, but before he can finish his
thought, Anytus[g] joins the conversation.

Since Anytus is politely assumed to be the son of a "wise and wealthy
father" who "raised and educated his son well" (90a–b), Socrates says that it
is only reasonable to ask him to speak his mind on this vexing subject. Meno
thus temporarily drops out of the conversation, and Socrates and Anytus
attempt to determine whether there are teachers and students of virtue.

Anytus is a man of the people. He is one of the new leaders of the
democracy (that would soon put Socrates to death on trumped up charges),
and he condemns the sophists and announces he knows nothing about
them. He lacks even Meno's ability for intellectual discussion. Socrates
goads Anytus with the suggestion that "those whom men call Sophists"
(91b) are teachers of virtue. Anytus becomes enraged and insists that the
Athenian leaders are the real teachers of virtue. Socrates, in reply, points to
the counterexamples. He goes through a list of Athenian leaders who, by all
accounts, failed to teach their sons virtue. Anytus does not reply. Instead, in
a portent of Socrates' trial and execution, he threatens Socrates and drops
out of the conversation.

Socrates is unfazed and turns to Meno to continue the discussion. Since
the suggestion that there are teachers and students of virtue has not been
defended, and since it seems paradoxical to suppose that virtue is a matter of
knowledge if there are no teachers and students, Socrates suggests that
wisdom is *not* the only thing that can successfully guide one through life:

> A man who knew the way to Larissa[h] or anywhere else you like, and went there
> and guided others, would guide them correctly?
>
> Certainly.
>
> What if someone had the right opinion as to which is the road but had never
> gone there and had no knowledge of it? Would this man also guide correctly?
>
> Certainly.

---

[g] Anytus was a politician and one of the leaders of the democratic revolt of 403 that succeeded
in overthrowing the puppet government known as "The Thirty Tyrants," a government
composed of conservative Athenians sympathetic to Sparta. The Spartan commander
Lysander installed this oligarchy at the end of the Peloponnesian War. Two of Plato's
relatives, Critias (his mother's uncle) and Charmides (his mother's brother), played very
prominent roles in this corrupt regime. Anytus seems to have thought of Socrates as guilty by
association. In the *Apology*, Anytus attacks Socrates "on behalf of the workmen and
politicians" (23e–24a).

[h] Larissa is in Thessaly, Meno's home.

So long as he has right opinion about the matter the other has knowledge, even though he does not have wisdom but only thinks what is true, he will be no worse a guide than the man who has wisdom about the matter in question.

No worse.

So true opinion is no worse a guide to right action than wisdom. This is what we omitted in our investigation of virtue, when we said that wisdom alone guides men in right action. True opinion can also (97a–c). For true opinions are fine as long as they stay, but they do not care to remain long, but run out of a man's soul, so that they are not worth much until one ties them down by working out an account. This, my friend, is recollection, as we agreed. (97e–98a)

A person who has the truth, but not wisdom, is unprotected from error. In some situations, he might make the same choice as the wise and hence act correctly. He might, for example, proceed confidently, rather than hold back, when such action is what virtue requires in the situation. In other situations, however, since he is not wise, the truth may not stay put. He might assent to, and act on the basis of, the impression that holding back is the correct action. Nevertheless, as long as he is not overcome, and so acts on the basis of the truth, the outcome is the same. Thus, contrary to their prior conclusion, wisdom is not the only state that can successfully guide a person.

Since there appear to be no teachers and students of virtue, and since both the wise and the unwise could in principle make the same choices, Socrates suggests that virtue must not be teachable after all. Indeed, instead of being teachable, he suggests that what has passed as virtue must be a gift from the gods, something that comes to be present by a divine inspiration (99b–d). If the great Athenian politicians lived lives of virtue, their choices were a matter of good fortune, not wisdom, despite what the many thought. These politicians may have had the truth, but it was a matter of good fortune that they did not encounter situations in which the appearances over-powered these beliefs. By ruling the city, these leaders may have appeared to the many to be teaching virtue, but Socrates insists that this appearance was an illusion and in fact these politicians taught nothing and hence did nothing, really, to make the citizens good. In comparison with a "politician who could make someone else a politician," he says that these politicians are mere "shadows"[i] (100a).

---

[i] *Odyssey* X.494–495. Plato's Athenian audience would know the reference.

The discussion now comes to an end. The way it ends, however, marks a departure from earlier practice. In the early dialogues, Socrates is ever ready to continue the conversation. Now, in the *Meno*, although the question Meno asked remains without an agreed answer, Socrates says that the time has come for him "to go" and for others to instruct Anytus (100b–c). In this way, Plato signals that the time has past for Socrates to work out and defend the principles that underlie his devotion to the love of wisdom. History shows that Anytus did not become more gentle and that, in Plato's eyes at least, the Athenians were substantially harmed when Anytus, in his anger, brought charges that would result in the execution of Socrates by the city of Athens. Now, with Socrates gone, it falls to his followers to explain and defend the love of wisdom.

4.2   The Theory of Forms

The *Phaedo* is part of this project. It provides more details about the conception of the soul and knowledge mentioned in the *Meno* in the Theory of Recollection. This project begins with the selection of characters, which shows that Plato intends to bring to mind certain Pythagorean doctrines. Phaedo of Elis was one of Socrates' disciples.[j] Echecrates, who is Phaedo's interlocutor, belonged to the Pythagorean community in Phlius. Echecrates seeks more detailed information about Socrates' last day. Phaedo, presumably, is visiting in Phlius on his way home to Elis. Echecrates says that very few from Phlius go to stay at Athens these days (57a), and he asks Phaedo whether he was present on the day of Socrates' death. Phaedo says that he was present

---

[j] There were four minor schools formed by Socrates' followers. Antisthenes founded the Cynic school (he taught in the Cynosarges, a gymnasium near Athens). Aristippus of Cyrene founded the Cyrenaic school. Euclides of Megara founded the Megarian school (he narrates Plato's *Theaetetus*). Phaedo of Elis founded the Elean school. (According to an ancient story, perhaps invented, Phaedo was of noble birth but was subsequently enslaved and brought to Athens as a prostitute. There, he captured Socrates' attention. Socrates persuaded one of his wealthy friends to buy Phaedo and set him free so that he could pursue the love of wisdom.) Phaedo, in the dialogue, tells Echecrates that Antisthenes and Euclides were present during Socrates' last hours. Aristippus, he says, was absent.

and that it would be a pleasure for him to recall Socrates' final conversation.[k]

The participants in Socrates' conversation (the conversation Plato has the preliminary characters Phaedo and Echecrates introduce) also bring to mind various Pythagorean doctrines. Simmias and Cebes are Socrates' interlocutors, and, like Echecrates, they have associated with the Pythagoreans. Socrates says that they must have heard certain things about the propriety of suicide during the period in which they were with Philolaus (61d), and Philolaus seems to have been one of the last Pythagoreans. He was born in Croton in the 470s and seems to have come to mainland Greece and to Thebes when the Pythagorean school in Croton was destroyed. Like Phlius, Thebes was a city of refuge for the Pythagoreans who fled the massacre.

Plato thus represents a connection between Socrates and the Pythagoreans through Simmias and Cebes,[1] but the historical record provides little information about this connection or about the views of the Pythagoreans themselves. Pythagoras himself seems to have written nothing, but he was reputed to be a man of wide interests, in music, mathematics, and astronomy, among other things. Furthermore, and perhaps most strikingly, he seems to have believed in the transmigration of the soul. This was an unusual view in the day. Xenophanes mocks it: "Once they say that he was passing by when a puppy was being whipped, and he took pity and said: 'Stop, do not beat it; for it is the soul of a friend that I recognized when I

---

[k] Plato's activities in the ten years after Socrates' execution are obscure, but it is likely that he wrote many if not all of the early dialogues in this period. In the early 380s, he traveled to Italy and Sicily to meet some of the leaders of the indigenous Pythagorean school, including Archytas of Terentum, who was a student of Philolaus. He returned to Athens within a year or two and soon after founded the Academy in 387. There is an allusion in the *Gorgias* to a view about the soul held by "someone from Sicily" (493a). The view itself is introduced by a quotation from Euripides, so something of these Pythagorean views about the soul was known in Athens. In the *Meno*, in the reference to "wise priests and priestesses" (81a) in connection with the Theory of Recollection, Plato may also have the Pythagoreans in mind. Charles Kahn makes the point: "For the Pythagoreans recollection meant, first of all, remembering one's previous incarnations (as Pythagoras himself was reported to have done) and secondly, remembering the secret passwords and road markers communicated to the initiate for a safe passage in the realm of the dead. Plato has transformed this magical, ritualistic notion of recollection into an epistemology of innate ideas and a priori knowledge" (*Pythagoras and the Pythagoreans*, 2001, 51).

[1] The connection is also attested in other dialogues. In the *Crito*, at 45a–c, Simmias and Cebes are said to have brought money to aid Socrates in escaping from jail.

heard it giving tongue'" (DK 21 B 7; from Diogenes Laertius,[m] *Lives and Opinions of the Philosophers*, VIII.36). By the fifth century, Pythagoras' followers seem to have divided themselves into two groups. There were the "listeners" and the "learners." The content of what the listeners heard was protected by a vow of silence, but it seems to have included various ritual practices. The learners, on the other hand, seemed more connected to the mathematical and scientific part of Pythagoreanism.[n]

The lover of wisdom should not fear death

Plato may conceive of the transmigration doctrine, as it was understood first in Orphic religion, and then in Pythagoreanism, as a precursor to Socrates' pursuit of the love of wisdom in the care of the soul. In the *Phaedo*, which is set on the day of the execution, Socrates suggests that death need not be feared because a human being is really an immortal soul imprisoned temporarily in a mortal body. Those who understand this, he says, realize that the soul can return to its rightful place but only

---

[m] Diogenes Laertius lived in the third century. Nothing is known of his life but what can be deduced from his book. "Diogenes has acquired an importance out of all proportion to his merits because the loss of many primary sources and of the earlier secondary compilations has accidentally left him the chief continuous source for the history of Greek philosophy. . . . Diogenes is a veritable tissue of quotations from all sorts of authors and on most conceivable, and some inconceivable, aspects of philosophers' lives. . . . Much of this quoted material is trivial, merely amusing, or probably false; but some it is very valuable. Hence the importance of Diogenes" (Herbert S. Long, "Introduction," 1972, xix).

[n] Charles Kahn describes this division among the Pythagoreans: "In a passage that can be traced back to Aristotle, Iamblichus reports the existence of two rival schools of Pythagoreans, the *akousmatikoi* and the *mathematikoi*, both of whom claimed to be the true followers of Pythagoras. As their name indicates, the *akousmatikoi* must be those who faithfully preserve the tradition of ritual and taboo. They claim that the mathematical school derives not from Pythagoras but from a renegade Pythagorean named Hippasus. Hippasus is a little-known mathematician and natural philosopher who seems to have lived in the early fifth century. He would thus antedate Philolaus, who appears then as the second name among the more 'mathematical' Pythagoreans. Now the *mathematikoi* do not deny that the 'accusmatic' school are also followers of Pythagoras; they claim only that they are *more* Pythagorean, more truly representative of Pythagoras' teaching" (*Pythagoras and the Pythagoreans*, 2001, 15). Iamblichus is a Neoplatonist philosopher who lived from about 245 to 325. He played a role in folding the Neopythagorian tradition into Neoplatonism.

if it has lived a certain way during incarnation: namely, as a lover of wisdom.°

This conception of the soul begins to emerge during the conversation in the prison cell. Cebes, in giving Socrates the news of the day, reports that Evenus (an elegiac poet[P] and teacher of human goodness) has been asking why Socrates has spent some of his little remaining time putting Aesop's tales to verse. Socrates says that he has had a recurrent dream and has understood it to compel him to engage in this project. He then goes on to to tell Cebes to reassure Evenus that this work was not an attempt to compete with the service Evenus himself provides. Moreover, in an expression of farewell, Socrates bids Evenus to look forward to following after him in death, which in Socrates' case was scheduled for later in the day. Simmias

---

° It was part of the religious movement associated with the name of Orpheus that the afterlife need not be gloomy and that the soul could be improved. In the Pythagorean religious movement, this idea about the soul seems to have been paired with the further idea that the means for improvement are intellectual. Plato, in turn, seems to see Socrates within this general religious framework. John Burnet makes the point: "In this religion the new beliefs were mainly based on the phenomenon of 'ecstasy' (ἔκστασις, 'stepping out'). It was supposed that it was only when 'out of the body' that the soul revealed its true nature. It was not merely a feeble double of the self, as in Homer, but a fallen god, which might be restored to its high estate by a system of 'purifications' (καθαρμοί) and sacraments (ὄργια). . . . [T]he main purpose of the Orphic observances and rites was to release the soul from the 'wheel of birth,' that is, from reincarnation in animal or vegetable forms. The soul so released became once more a god and enjoyed everlasting bliss" (*Early Greek Philosophy*, 1920, 81–82). Burnet provides more detail as follows: "The new thing in the society founded by Pythagoras seems to have been that, while it admitted all these old practices, it at the same time suggested a deeper idea of what 'purification' really is. Aristoxenos said that the Pythagoreans employed music to purge the soul as they used medicine to purge the body. Such methods of purifying the soul were familiar in the *Orgia* of the Korybantes, and will serve to explain the Pythagorean interest in Harmonics. But there is more than this. If we can trust Herakleides, it was Pythagoras who first distinguished the 'three lives,' the Theoretic, the Practical, and the Apolaustic, which Aristotle made use of in the *Ethics*. The doctrine is to this effect. We are strangers in this world, and the body is the tomb of the soul, and yet we must not seek to escape by self-murder; for we are the chattels of God who is our herdsman, and without his command we have no right to make our escape. In this life there are three kinds of men, just as there are three sorts of people who come to the Olympic Games. The lowest class is made up of those who come to buy and sell, and next above them are those who come to compete. Best of all, however, are those who come to look on (θεωρεῖν). The greatest purification of all is, therefore, science, and it is the man who devotes himself to that, the true philosopher, who has most effectually released himself from the 'wheel of birth.' It would be rash to say that Pythagoras expressed himself exactly in this manner; but all these ideas are genuinely Pythagorean, and it is only in some such way that we can bridge the gulf which separates Pythagoras the man of science from Pythagoras the religious teacher" (1920, 97–98).

[P] Unlike the epic poets, who told stories about gods and heroes, the elegiac and iambic poets told stories about more timeless human concerns, such as love and death.

expresses surprise that Socrates would urge such a thing, and Socrates says that he thought Evenus was a lover of wisdom and that "a man who has spent his life in the love of wisdom takes confidence when about to die, and is hopeful that, when he has died, he will gain very great benefits in the other world" (63e–64a).

These remarks provide an important and striking contrast to the remarks the historical Socrates apparently made at his trial. In the *Apology* at 28d–29b, after reminding the jury of his bravery at the battles of Potidaea, Amphipolis, and Delium, he explains that it would be shameful for him now to abandon his love of wisdom out of a fear for his life. In explanation of his calmness in the face of the present situation, he says that the fear of death hinges on the belief that death is bad, a belief that he himself lacks because he does not know what death will bring.

In the *Phaedo*, unlike in the *Apology*, Socrates is no longer so agnostic about death. He now thinks that the lover of wisdom should actually look forward to death. To make his case for this surprising claim, he begins by considering the premise that death is the separation of the soul from the body. Simmias thinks this is obvious. He straightaway registers his agreement with Socrates in thinking that in death the soul is released and comes to "exist itself according to itself" (64c). And part of the reason Simmias assents so quickly is that it was common to think the soul is necessary for life and that it is lost in death. The language Socrates uses, however, suggests that he has in mind the much bolder claim that the soul continues to exist apart from the body. Simmias, nevertheless, does not press the issue, perhaps because of his association with the Pythagoreans.

The next premise in the argument is bolder still. It concerns judgment and the role the senses play in connection with knowledge. Socrates asserts that the body hinders the lover of wisdom because the body both contributes nothing to wisdom and makes it difficult to obtain (65a–d). Socrates goes on to insist that the soul grasps forms through the "intellect alone" and that these forms become manifest by "reasoning" rather than through the use of any of the bodily senses:

Do we say there is such a thing as the just itself, or not?

We do, by Zeus.

And the beautiful and the good?

Of course.

And have you ever seen any of these things with your eyes?

Certainly not.

Or have you ever grasped them with any of your bodily senses? And I am speaking of all things such as size, health, and strength, and, in short, the reality of all other things, that which each of them is. Is what is most true in them contemplated through the body, or is this how it is, whoever of us prepares himself most carefully to grasp the thing he examines according to itself will come nearest to the knowledge of it?

Obviously.

Then the man who does this most perfectly approaches each though the intellect alone, not introducing sight into his thought, or dragging in any of the other senses in his reasoning, but who, using the intellect alone, hunts down each reality. (65d–66a)

He does not explain what he has in mind by "intellect alone" and by "reasoning." Nor does he explain what forms are. Again, however, Simmias does not press the issue.

Socrates now draws his conclusion, but his reasoning is not initially very persuasive. Set out formally, the argument is the following:

1. Death is the separation of soul from body.
2. The lover of wisdom seeks wisdom.
3. The body is no help and is a hindrance in becoming wise.

---

4. The lover of wisdom should not fear death.

This argument looks to be invalid. It seems possible, at least initially, that the soul might perish at death rather than exist apart. So fear might well be warranted after all, and this troubling fact is not lost on Cebes. He tells Socrates he is not yet convinced the soul survives death (69e–70b). He grants the premises of Socrates' argument, but he says that he is not ready to agree with the conclusion because it seems to him that the premises do not determine that, upon death, the soul continues to exist apart from the body and retains its "strength and wisdom."[q]

---

[q] It is a little surprising that Simmias and Cebes challenge Socrates to persuade them of views about the soul that one might expect them to have believed in virtue of their association with Philolaus. What this seems to show is that the scientific emphasis in Pythagoreanism had begun to eclipse the religious aspects of the movement. John Burnet makes the point: "It is a fine historical touch in the *Phaedo* that the young Pythagoreans, Simmias and Cebes, are not very familiar with the mystic doctrine, and require to have it explained to them by Socrates" (*Plato's* Phaedo, 1911, lv).

This initial argument and Cebes' response establish the structure of the rest of the dialogue. Socrates and his interlocutors consider several arguments purporting to show that the soul is immortal. In the end they agree that the soul is immortal, and Socrates says that he is ready to drink the poison, as his death sentence requires. He is composed, but his friends are in tears. He urges them to calm themselves and to behave as befits the wise. Further, he tells Crito not to forget that "we owe a cock to Asclepius."[r] Crito replies dutifully that "it shall be done." He asks Socrates whether he has anything else to say, but Socrates does not respond. He has died, and Phaedo brings his account and the dialogue to a close: "such was the end of our friend, a man who, we should say, was of all those we have known, the best, and also the wisest and most just."

Forms are paradigms fixed in nature

The argument that the lover of wisdom should not fear death is important not only for its continuity with themes in previous dialogues but also for the new ground it breaks. Socrates, first of all, assumes that human beings are psychological beings. This is not new in the dialogues, but the point is now understood in a different way. As in the *Meno*, and now so also in the *Phaedo*, the soul is understood as a persisting object whose existence is not contingent on the body.

Socrates also assumes that the love of wisdom produces a certain psychological functioning, that this includes knowledge of the forms of the virtues, and that "reason" (and not "experience") is the key to achieving this psychological functioning. This too is not new, but once again the point is understood in a different way. Now the psychological functioning is identified in relation to the natural and disincarnate state of his soul. In this state, Socrates suggests that the soul is free of practical concerns and the need to exercise reason to meet these concerns. It is characterized by knowledge of the forms, and the psychological functioning that constitutes human

---

[r] John Burnet suggests that "Socrates hopes to awake cured like those who are healed by ἐγκοίμησις (*incubatio*) in the Asklepieion at Epidauras" (*Plato's* Phaedo, 1911, 147). The sanctuary of Asclepius at Epidaurus was the most famous healing center in the ancient world. (An asclepieion is a healing temple, sacred to the god Asclepius. (Asclepius' father was Apollo. His mother, while pregnant, had an affair. Apollo had the mother killed, but, at the last minute, as the body was about to be burned on the funeral pyre, he rescued the baby by caesarean section. Apollo gave Asclepius to the centaur Chiron to raise, and Chiron taught Ascelpius the art of medicine.).) A person would sleep in the temple, report his or her dreams to the priest, and the priest would prescribe a cure for the disease. Socrates, presumably, hopes to awake "cured" from the difficulties forced on the lover of wisdom by incarnation.

goodness is the one that, as much as possible, resembles the natural and disincarnate state of the soul.

Finally, and perhaps most puzzlingly, Socrates now seems to assume that the forms are the *existence* of certain eternal objects. He talks about the forms in the early dialogues. In the *Euthyphro*, to help his interlocutor understand that the correct answer to the "What is it?" question should be universal (and not apply just in familiar situations), he says that he is interested in the "form" of piety. Now, in the *Phaedo*, Socrates presents an ontology that includes piety and the other things the character uses his "What is it?" question to ask about in the early dialogues.

Plato does not explicitly present a theory of forms, either in the *Phaedo* or elsewhere in the dialogues, but there is a tantalizing remark in the *Parmenides* that seems to express the underlying idea that drives the theory. In this dialogue, which falls in the late period, the tables are decidedly turned on Socrates. He has trouble defending his own views against questioning. He has introduced the forms in response to an earlier argument. And so Parmenides asks Socrates questions about the forms. Socrates has trouble answering them, and now, in a final attempt to explain what the forms are, he says that "what appears most likely" is that "forms are like patterns fixed in nature" (132c–d). Socrates unfortunately does not have this idea worked out in any detail. In fact, he is unable to defend this idea against Parmenides' subsequent questioning. Thus, just as the early dialogues end in perplexity, so also the first part of the *Parmenides* ends in perplexity.

To understand what Plato seems to have in mind, it is helpful to think first about the way forms figure in Socrates' practice in the early dialogues. In these dialogues, to help his interlocutors understand his request for a definition he explains that he is asking about the "form" common to all and only X-things. In light of this explanation, an interlocutor might respond by saying that X-things are X by being X. In fact, Socrates initially even encourages this sort of response in an effort to prevent his interlocutors from identifying X-ness with the way it manifests itself in a range of circumstances. He supposes that being X is how X-things are. He also supposes that being this way admits of a definition, and he uses the "What is it?" question to request this definition.

In the *Phaedo*, the character goes further. He thinks that X-ness itself exists and that being X is somehow the mode of existence X-ness possesses. This is the *Theory of Forms*.[5] In terms of the discussion in the *Euthyphro*, the idea is that piety itself exists and that it exists by being pious. Being pious is its mode of existence. It has this existence "itself according to itself." This existence is the form of piety. In asking what piety is, Socrates is asking about this form.

This ontology is clearly not easy to understand in much detail, but the fundamental point, as the *Parmenides* shows, is that forms do not admit change: they are "fixed in nature." So, since forms are the "patterns or paradigms" specified in definition, and since what is specified is the answer to the "What is it?" question, the primary motivation for the Theory of Forms is that the content of X-ness is immune to change, despite the fact that what is X in one situation may be different from what is X in another situation. Hence, because the answer to the "What is it?" question cannot change, Plato concludes that X-ness itself has an existence incompatible with change.[s]

The mode of existence "itself according to itself" is obscure, but the discussion in the *Cratylus*[t] of whether names are correct by "convention and agreement" (384d) suggests that Plato took seriously the idea that the objects of the "What is it?" question not only exist but exist "themselves according to themselves." Socrates says that things would change with changes in a human being if, as Protagoras says, man is the measure of all things. This, he thinks, has consequences for the love of wisdom. If man is the measure, there is no reality to which the lover of

---

[s] Since it is initially perplexing to think that X-ness exists, one may wonder why Plato did not consider alternative explanations for why the content of the definition cannot change. The answer is not very clear, but it seems likely that Parmenides figures essentially in the explanation. In his poem, as a premise in his argument against the possibility of going out of existence, he seems to say it is absurd to say that something *is no longer*. A thing must exist if it *is* anything at all, according to Parmenides, even if it *is* because it *is no longer*. Since Plato thought that X-ness *is* something, because X-ness *is* definable, perhaps it was natural for him to conclude that X-ness itself exists. Given this much, he would wonder about the sort of existence that could give X-ness its immunity from change.

[t] Socrates discusses names with Hermogenes and Cratylus. Hermogenes is the brother of Callias, and so is part of a wealthy aristocratic family. Hermogenes also seems to have been among Socrates' friends. In the *Phaedo*, he is mentioned as present on the day of Socrates' death. Cratylus was an extreme Heraclitean. According to Aristotle, Cratylus "criticized Heraclitus for saying that it is impossible to step twice into the same river, since he thought it could not be done even once" (*Metaphysics* IV.5.1010a). Heraclitus' views are not very clear, but he stresses experience and so is a counterpoint to the rationalism in Parmendies ("The things of which there is seeing and hearing and perception, these I do prefer" (DK 22 B 55)). Heraclitus also stresses the importance of process in the description of reality ("This world-order did none of the gods or men make, but it always was and is and shall be: an ever-living fire, kindling in measures and going out in measures" (DK 22 B 30)). The exact import of this fragment is obscure, but Edward Hussey understands Heraclitus in this fragment to mean that "process is the basic form of existence of the *observable* world; although something, not directly observable, persists throughout" ("Heraclitus," 99). For this interpretation, Hussey relies in part on the following passage from Aristotle's *On the Heavens*: "These thinkers maintained that while other things are in the process of becoming, and none exists in a determinate way, there is one thing alone that persists, of which all these other things are formed. So we may interpret Heraclitus of Ephesus ..." (III.1.298b).

wisdom can seek to conform. Instead of having a "fixed being of their own," things would be "in relation to us" and "made to fluctuate by how they appear to us" (385e–386e).

Aristotle provides some confirmation for this general approach to understanding the Theory of Forms.[6] His remarks are obscure too, unfortunately, but he seems to say that Plato thought that the "sensible things" – presumably the things salient in ordinary experience – could not be what provide the answer to the "What is it?" question because these things are "flowing":

> In his youth Plato became acquainted with Cratylus and the Heraclitean doctrines that all sensibles are flowing and that there is no knowledge about them, and these views continued to influence him in his later years.[u] Socrates was busying himself about ethical matters, neglecting the world of nature as a whole, and by seeking the universal in these ethical matters, he fixed thought for the first time on definitions. Plato followed him but thought that the problem of definition involved another kind of thing, not sensible things, as no sensible thing is the common definition since sensible things are always changing. Things of the other kind, he called ideas. (*Metaphysics* I.6.987a–b)

Aristotle makes similar remarks later in the *Metaphysics*. He says that Plato thought the forms are apart from the sensible things because the sensible things are somehow not stable enough:

> Socrates did not make the universals or definitions exist separately, but they separated them, and things of this sort they called ideas. (XIII.4.1078b)

> They treat the ideas as universal and as separable and individual. They did not find any substances among the sensible particulars. They thought that the sensibles were flowing and none of them remained, but that the universal must exist beside them and is apart from them. Socrates provided a starting point for this theory, by means of his definitions, but he did not separate them from the particulars, and he was right in this, in not separating them. (XIII.9.1086a–b)

---

[u] Aristotle suggests that the Theory of Forms is a refinement of the Heraclitean idea that observable things are what they are in reference to something not observable. Heraclitus seems to have this sort of conception of observable things in mind in the following fragment. "Of the account which is as I describe it men always prove to be uncomprehending, both before they have heard it and when once they have heard it. For although all things happen in accordance with this account men are like people of no experience, even when they experience such words and deeds as I explain, when I distinguish each thing according to its constitution and declare how it is; but the rest of men fail to notice what they do after they wake up just as they forget what they do when asleep" (DK 22 B 1).

The argument in these passages is compressed and so not easy to understand. Moreover, since his intent is to reject the Theory of Forms, it is always possible that he has not represented Plato's thought sympathetically. Nevertheless, Aristotle's understanding of Plato's theory in these passages seems to emphasize the point that Plato himself has Socrates emphasize in the *Parmenides*: that if the content of a universal is "fixed in nature," then the universal exists and has its being itself according to itself. This being it has itself according to itself is the form, and this form is what Socrates is asking about in his search for a definition.

Some evidence in the Phaedo

The *Phaedo* itself only contains suggestive passages about forms and their existence. In the context of arguments for the immortality of the soul, Socrates twice makes remarks about the forms. He says that they are what he is trying to get straight about when he asks his "What is it?" question and that they themselves always "remain the same" and hence do not change (75c–d, 78d). Subsequently, after Echecrates breaks into Phaedo's narrative to express his admiration for Socrates, Phaedo restarts the story by recalling certain points about the forms. He says that the forms exist and that the other things are named after the forms because they "share in them" (102a).

There is more discussion of the forms in the reply to an objection Cebes raises against one of Socrates' arguments for the immortality of the soul. Socrates says that although in his youth he was at one point interested in "the sort of wisdom known as the inquiry into nature" (96a), he became dissatisfied with this discipline and now concerns himself with the forms:

> This is what I mean, nothing new, but what I have always been saying, earlier in our discussion and other times. I am going to try to show you the sort of cause with which I concern myself, and I will return to the things I have mentioned so often, and proceed from them, assuming the existence of a beautiful, itself according to itself, of a good, a large, and all the rest (100b). I think that if there is anything beautiful besides the beautiful itself, it is beautiful for no other reason than that it shares in the beautiful, and I say so for everything. No longer do I understand or recognize those other sophisticated causes, but if someone tells me that a thing is beautiful because it has a bright color or a shape or any such thing, I dismiss these answers, as they confuse me, but I hold simply and perhaps foolishly to this, that nothing else makes it beautiful other than

the presence of, or sharing in, call it what you please, as I will not insist on the exact nature of the relationship,[v] but only that all beautiful things are beautiful by the beautiful. (100c–d)

Socrates explains that he now pursues wisdom in terms of a method that presupposes the existence of the form the beautiful itself and other such things. He says that he now believes in "the existence of a beautiful, itself according to itself, a good, a large, and all the rest."

As Socrates relates his intellectual autobiography, he says that he abandoned the inquiry into nature because he discovered it was confused in a certain fundamental way. The inquirers into nature tried to get straight about the existence of things, and hence to purge themselves of the false beliefs embedded in the traditional understanding, but they went about it wrongly. He says that, in his youth, when he was high on the inquiry into nature, he tried to follow their inquiry into such questions as whether "we think with air" or "fire" (96a–b). The confusion Socrates finds in answers of this sort is not entirely clear, but the suggestion seems to be that the inquirers into nature exhibit the confusion Socrates himself tries to straighten out in the early dialogues. He explains in these dialogues that he is looking for the universal in some ethical matter, not the way this universal happens to manifest itself in certain circumstances.[7] He tells Euthyphro, for example, not to reply to the "What is piety?" question by citing some one or two of the many pious things, but to tell him about the form itself by which all pious things are pious. By the same token, the suggestion seems to be that it is a mistake for the inquirers into nature to fall back on "air" or "fire" in connection with the question of what thought is. Thought may somehow involve "air," or "fire," but it is a mistake to identify thought with any of these things. According to Socrates, no one of these things, or any combination of them, is what thought itself is.

The love of wisdom, the soul, and its place in reality

Although the intellectual autobiography itself may well be fictional, Plato achieves two goals by setting out Socrates' intellectual story this way. First of all, he credits the historical Socrates for pointing the way to the Theory of Forms. Socrates, according to the story in the *Phaedo*, begins

---

[v] Cf. Aristotle, *Metaphysics* I.6.987b: "Only the name was new. The Pythagoreans say that things exist by imitation of numbers. Plato says they exist by participation, changing the name. But what the participation or imitation is, this they left an open question."

his search for wisdom as an inquirer into nature. Plato seems to understand this inquiry to have the right aim but to be marred by confusion. The aim is to understand what is, and the confusion is one Socrates uncovers. Once he uncovers it, he is said to have abandoned the inquiry into nature for his new interest in forms. In the *Phaedo*, in the autobiography passage, he tells his interlocutors that "if someone tells me that a thing is beautiful because it has a bright color, or a shape, or any such thing, I dismiss these answers, as they confuse me." Socrates himself, the historical figure, presumably did not think that the forms are the unchanging existence of the objects he asks about. Plato sets out the Theory of Forms to introduce this ontology, but he uses the intellectual autobiography passage to credit Socrates for taking the crucial first step in this direction.

Secondly, in a departure from the position the historical Socrates appears to have held, Plato now seems to conceive of the love of wisdom against the background of a Pythagorean conception of the soul and its place in reality. The love of wisdom is now understood to transform the human psychology by introducing a certain intellectual activity into the life of a human being. This activity makes the life good for the human being who lives it. The reason, however, is not just that the lover of wisdom understands what is in his interest and what choices he should make to serve those interests. Now the interest is identified with the existence his soul enjoys in its natural and disincarnate state, a state in which the soul is somehow fixed in knowledge of the forms. In this way, in the *Phaedo*, Plato greatly amplifies and considerably deepens the fundamental change in perspective that appeared in the *Meno* with the Theory of Recollection.

4.3   The Tripartite Theory of the Soul

In the *Republic*, Plato explains the connection of practical wisdom about ethical matters to this new understanding of the love of wisdom. The discussion in this dialogue is devoted primarily to justice, and the theory Socrates develops has its basis in a certain conception of the human soul and its good. Socrates abandons the conception of the human soul he had advocated in the *Protagoras*. Now, in the *Republic*, Socrates argues for a version of the psychological theory he associated with the many and had himself rejected. He argues that the soul has parts and that it is properly organized when these parts work together in harmony. This is the *Tripartite Theory of the Soul*.

The argument for this theory of the soul occurs within the context of a much longer discussion of justice, both in the city and in the individual human being.[w] Socrates and his interlocutors agree, in Book II of the *Republic*, that once they isolate justice in the city, they will search for what justice is in the individual. They reach agreement about justice in the city in Book IV. To apply their results, they appeal to a principle about the use of words according to which things "called by the same name" are alike "with respect to that to which the name applies" (IV.435a–c). Given this principle about the use of words, and given their prior agreement that justice in the city consists in the three parts of the city each doing its own job, Socrates concludes that justice within an individual human being consists in each of the three parts of the soul doing its own job.

This introduction to the Tripartite Theory of the Soul can be confusing. The underlying idea is that a certain organization among the three parts of the soul is appropriate and hence constitutes justice in the individual human being. The problem, though, is that it would not have been plausible to think the soul has parts, and so Plato works to this conclusion by starting from the more familiar and plausible idea that justice in the city is the appropriate organization of human beings in cities. Socrates argues that this organization consists in an arrangement among the three parts of the city that makes the city good. Justice, in this way, is a virtue in a city because the appropriate arrangement of the parts of a city is one that makes its citizens good, to the extent that this is possible. Now, in light of the assumption that human goodness consists in proper psychological functioning, the principle about the use of words opens a path to the Tripartite Theory. It becomes natural to think that proper functioning in the human soul is the proper organization of its parts.[x]

To show that the soul really has parts, Socrates appeals to a principle about "opposites": that since "the same thing is not willing to do or to suffer opposite states at the same time and in the same part of itself in

---

[w] This longer discussion is the subject of the next chapter.

[x] Strictly speaking, even if true (and words with multiple senses seem to provide counter-examples), the principle about words cannot function in the argument in the way required. Justice manifests itself in the city as an organization of the parts of the city, but this organization is not what justice itself is in definition. In definition, justice is what is appropriate with respect to human beings. It is an empirical matter whether the appropriate organization of human beings into cities is the one in terms of the three parts of a city Socrates describes.

relation to the same other thing, if we find this happening we shall know that we are not dealing with one thing but with many" (IV.436b–c). On the basis of this principle, and given the familiar idea that thirsty people sometimes do not want to drink, Socrates concludes that the soul contains two parts: a part with reason and a part without reason but with appetites.

These two parts of the human soul differ importantly in the way they support desire. The desires in the part of the soul with reason stem from judgments about what is best. This part of the soul "reasons," and the idea seems to be that desires in this part are a function of the judgments about goals and the various plans to achieve those goals. Socrates contrasts the part of the soul with reason with another part of the soul, what he calls "the non-reasoning and appetitive part":

> Would we say that sometimes thirsty men do not wish to drink?
>
> Certainly.
>
> What should we say about them, that there is something in their soul, bidding them to drink, and something different, forbidding them, that overrides the thing that bids?
>
> I think so.
>
> And that which forbids arises, when it arises, as a result of reasoning, while the impulse that drags them to drink is a result of feelings and diseases?
>
> Apparently.
>
> So they are two, and different from one another. The part of the soul which calculates and reasons is the reasoning part, and the part with lusts, hungers, thirsts, and has other appetites, is the non-reasoning and appetitive part, friend of indulgences and pleasures.
>
> That seems right.
>
> Then let these two parts be distinguished in the soul. (IV.439c–e)

Unlike desire in the part with reason, desire in the appetitive part does not stem from reasoning. The appetitive part does not reason. The idea seems to be that desire in this part of the soul is produced in reaction to events in the body. These desires result from dispositions, such as those to relieve hunger or thirst. They do not stem from judgments about expected value.

In recognizing the existence of desire in the appetitive part of the soul, Plato rejects the understanding of desire in the human soul that Socrates advocated in the *Protagoras*.[8] Indeed, just prior to distinguishing the reasoning and appetitive parts of the soul, Socrates seems to allude to the early understanding of desire as initially plausible but in fact false (IV.438a). In the *Protagoras*, the view is that all desire in the human soul stems from reasoning and judgment about what is best. Socrates now rejects this view. He recognizes desires that stem from judgment, but in the *Republic*, the character also recognizes desires that stem from bodily dispositions. These desires arise automatically, without the need to engage in any reasoning about expected value.

Once he has established the existence of the appetitive and reasoning parts of the soul, Socrates argues for a third part: the "spirited part" of the soul. To illustrate the existence and functioning of the spirited part, he begins by repeating a story about someone who has a certain desire but is very worked up, and angry with himself, for having this particular desire:

> On his way from the Piraeus along the outer side of the north wall,[y] Leontius saw some corpses near the executioner. He wanted to look but also felt a repugnance and aversion. For a time he struggled, and covered his face, but, finally, overpowered by the appetite, with wide open eyes he rushed toward the corpses, saying, "There, you wretches, take your fill of this fine spectacle!"
>
> I too have heard this story.
>
> It shows that anger sometimes fights against the appetites.
>
> It does.
>
> And we often notice this in other cases, that when appetite forces someone contrary to reason, he reproaches himself and becomes angry with the thing in him that forces him. (IV.439e–440b)

Socrates thinks that this anger is in a part of the soul distinct from the reasoning part because such desire and aversion is apparent in beings who do not act in virtue of reasoning:

> Is this different from the reasoning part, or is it some form of it, so that there are two parts in the soul, the reasoning part and the appetitive part, rather than three? Or, just as there were three classes in the city, is the spirited part a third thing in the soul that by nature is the helper of the part with reason, provided it is uncorrupted by a bad upbringing?

---

[y] Piraeus is the port of Athens. It was connected to Athens by long walls. This helped provide a connection to the sea even in times of siege.

It must be a third.

Yes, provided that we can show it is different from the reasoning part, as we saw earlier it was different from the appetitive part.

That is not difficult. Small children are full of spirit from birth, but as far as reasoning is concerned, some never seem to get a share of it, while the majority do so much later.

Well put. (IV.440e–441b)

Socrates thus concludes that there is a third part of the soul, the spirited part. The anger in the spirited part does not arise from reasoning. This part of the soul, like the appetitive part, does not reason. Instead, the idea seems to be that the desire in the spirted part arises as a matter of conditioning produced in "upbringing."[z] Human beings can develop a disposition to pursue certain ends in certain sorts of circumstances, not because they have engaged in any reasoning about expected value, but rather because socialization has conditioned them to pursue these ends.

Now that the parts of the soul have been distinguished, Socrates draws his conclusion about the nature of justice within the individual. He says that within the just individual each part of the soul does its own job. This means that the part with reason rules. It is naturally fit to rule because it knows

---

[z] John Cooper illustrates this general interpretation of spirited desire in terms of an example from Homer that Socrates himself cites in the remarks that directly follow 441b3: "When Odysseus in disguise comes upon Penelope's maids cavorting with her suitors his immediate impulse is to punish them on the spot: the sight of such disorder in his own household is naturally a blow to his self-esteem (self-respecting noblemen don't permit that kind of thing), and his anger is a response to this affront. It urges him to act immediately to restore order and therewith prove himself deserving of the esteem which he feels is placed in jeopardy by the continuance of this state of affairs. His anger thus represents a traditional view of things to which his continued self-esteem is tied: he will feel bad about himself unless he acts at once to vindicate his honor. Yet his reason does not support this traditional view: from reason's point of view delay does not mean indifference or weakness or cowardly acquiescence, and there is (Odysseus thinks) no *reason* for him to think less well of himself for delaying (in fact, quite the contrary, since he plans eventually *both* to punish the maids *and* to kill off the suitors). But though this is how he thinks, it is not how he feels. The reaction of this *thumos* [or spirited part of the soul] shows that his self-esteem, the way he feels about himself, is tied up with a certain traditional view of the king's dignity, not with the view implied by his own rational planning. Hence reason and spirit in his case are in conflict over what to do. A bad upbringing, Socrates suggests (cf. 441a13), has corrupted Odysseus' spirit, causing him to feel differently about things than he thinks" ("Plato's theory of human motivation," 1999, 134).

the good and hence can "exercise foresight" so that the human being acts for the good:

> Each one of us in whom each part is doing its own work is just.
>
> Of course.
>
> Then, is it appropriate for the reasoning part to rule, since it is wise and exercises foresight on behalf of the whole soul, and for the spirited part to obey and be its ally?
>
> It certainly is. (IV.441d–e)

> And these two parts, having been brought up in this way, and having been educated in their roles, will preside over the appetitive part, which is the largest part and is by nature most insatiable for money and that sort of thing. They watch over it to see that it is not filled with the pleasures of the body and that it does not become so big and strong that it no longer does its own work but attempts to enslave and rule over those it is not fit to rule, and so subvert the life of all of them. (IV.442a–b)

When the ruling part rules, and the other parts do their own jobs, the organization among the parts of the soul is the appropriate one and hence constitutes justice in the individual human being. It is the appropriate organization because it makes a human being good. This organization among the parts of the soul makes a human being good because it is the organization that underlies a certain exercise of reason which involves knowledge of the forms. Plato thought that a life consisting of this exercise of reason is the life in which a human being finds happiness most of all.

Thus, for Plato, justice and happiness are aligned. The more common thought, that they are opposed, drives the discussion in the *Protagoras* and *Gorgias*, but the interlocutors in these dialogues cannot hold their ground against Socrates' questioning. However, it is not enough simply to refute the Sophists. It is necessary to prove that justice is better, and Socrates, the historical figure, as Plato understands him, showed the way forward. He had the crucial insight that makes the proof possible. The common thought that justice and happiness are opposed has its roots in the habits "formed from much experience," not in the knowledge that belongs to "reason." Experience suggests that justice is the same as what is said to be appropriate in some particular range of circumstances, but Socrates, as Plato understands him, showed repeatedly that this understanding of the virtues confuses the particular with the general.[9] Once it is clear in "reason" that justice is what is appropriate with respect to human beings, and further that what is appropriate may vary from one situation to the next, there is no bar to identifying what is appropriate with respect to human beings so that justice is the key to happiness. Plato can argue, as he argues in the *Republic*, that justice pays.

Notes

1. Terence Irwin makes the general point: "Plato begins from Socratic problems, and implicitly claims to find the best arguments for Socratic convictions. . . . Even if he does not openly disagree with Socrates, Plato implies that Socratic convictions are justified only if we accept further doctrines that would have very much surprised, perhaps even repelled, Socrates himself. . . . Plato believes he defends the central Socratic convictions; probably this is why 'Socrates' remains the main character in most of the middle and late dialogues. But to some readers, both ancient and modern, his defense of Socrates has seemed more like a betrayal, a disastrous perversion of the Socratic outlook" (*Classical Thought*, 1989, 85–86).

2. Many commentators have focused attention on this issue. Gregory Vlastos is an influential example: "What Socrates in fact does in any given elenchus is convict p not of falsehood but of being a member of an inconsistent premiss-set; and to do this is not to show that p is false, but only that either p is false or that some or all of the premisses are false. The question then becomes how Socrates can claim . . . to have proved that the refutand is false, when all he has established is the inconsistency of p with premisses whose truth he has not undertaken to establish in that argument: they have entered the argument simply as propositions on which he and the interlocutor are agreed. This is *the* problem of the Socratic elenchus . . ." ("The Socratic Elenchus," 1996, 29). "[T]he 'problem of the elenchus' never bothers Socrates. . . . If he were an epistemologist, he might well have asked, 'What reason is there to believe that those who disagree with me must have those entrenched beliefs which I can use to make them 'see' the falsehood of their misguided theses?' But since he is no epistemologist, he doesn't raise that question. And if he doesn't, why should he be worried? That is Plato's distress, not his. It is Plato, *his* mind 'full of epistemological worries,' who feels the force of that question. *He* reasons that the Socratic method is predicated on frightfully strong methodological assumptions, notably *A*: if the Socratic theses are universally certifiable by the elenctic method, they should be provable to *anyone*, hence *everyone* must have true beliefs which entail the negation of each of his false moral beliefs" ("Afterthoughts on the Socratic Elenchus," 1983, 58).

3. Michael Frede puts the Theory of Recollection into historical context: "Socrates' method of elenctic dialectic turns on consistency as the crucial

feature to be preserved. Not only is inconsistency treated as a criterion for lack of knowledge or wisdom, it also seems to be assumed that the progressive elimination of inconsistency will lead to knowledge or wisdom. This presupposes that deep down we do have a basic knowledge at least of what matters, that we are just very confused, because we have also acquired lots of false beliefs incompatible with this basic knowledge. I take it that in Plato this assumption at times takes the form of the doctrine of recollection, whereas in Stoicism it is supposed to be captured by the theory of common notions and the common sense based on them. Unable to get rid of these notions and the knowledge of the world they embody, the only way to become consistent is to eliminate the false beliefs which stand in the way of wisdom" ("On the Stoic conception of the good," 1993, 83). "Plato, for instance in the *Phaedo* or in the *Timaeus*, suggests a view which would explain the state Socrates seems to presuppose, namely a state in which in some sense we confusedly already know the right answers to the important questions. On this view, when reason or the soul, which pre-exists, enters the body upon birth, it does so already disposing of the knowledge of the Forms, though it gets confused by its union with the body, a confusion it only recovers from to some degree mainly through sustained philosophical effort, recollecting the truths it had known before entering the body. But it is only when it is released from the body, freed from the disturbances involved in its union with the body, and free to pursue its own concerns, rather than having to concern itself with the needs of the body, or other concerns it only has made its own, that it again has unhindered access to the truth" ("Introduction" in *Rationality in Greek Thought*, 1996a, 10). Cf. Tad Brennan, *The Stoic Life*, 2005, 30: "What gives us any reason to hope that the people Socrates speaks with will have a few true beliefs sprinkled among their false ones, and that they will reliably relinquish the false ones instead of the true when Socrates points out their inconsistency? Plato's introduction of Forms provided one way of ensuring that every person would have the rudiments of a true account somewhere present in their mind, ready to emerge from the obscuring overlay of false belief once that was swept aside by dialectic. But remarkably few people in the two centuries after Plato's death seem to have found this solution at all plausible. . . ."

4. Democritus does not seem to understand his distinction between "reason" and "experience" from within a theoretical context in which human beings are psychological beings. Charles Kahn makes the important points: "His description of mental phenomena has not reached the level of a psychological *theory*; he relies entirely on the shifting metaphors of quasi-poetic speech. . . . [T]here is no trace of any *attempt* to escape the limitations of this idiomatic phraseology, no effort to frame a coherent model for psychological description and explanation. This task remained for Plato to undertake. We can see the first step toward such a model in the passage of the *Gorgias* which speaks of "that part of the soul where the desires are located" (493A); but a full-scale model comes

only with the tripartite psychology of the *Republic*. It is the merest beginnings of such an effort that can be recognized in [Democritus] . . ." ("Democritus and the origins of moral psychology," 1985, 14–15).

5. Some scholars say that Plato did not have a theory of forms, and others say that he did and that it is the center-piece of his philosophical thought. The following statements are representative. "It is often said that Plato has a 'Theory' of forms and even that it dominates his entire work. In fact forms appear rarely and are always discussed untechnically; they answer to a variety of needs which are never systematically brought together . . ." (Julia Annas, "Classical Greek philosophy," 1988, 289). "The Theory of Forms is commonly regarded as the center, if not the sum, of Plato's philosophy; and it is on the whole so represented by Aristotle" (W. F. R. Hardie, *A Study in Plato*, 1936, 9).

6. Some scholars have argued that Aristotle's testimony about the development of Plato's Theory of Forms adds nothing to the Platonic texts and may well be mistaken. Charles Kahn insists on this point in *Plato and the Socratic Dialogue*: "There is no reason to suppose that Aristotle had any good evidence for the early development of Plato's thought. . . . The only solid piece of historical information here is that the theory of Forms belongs to Plato, not to Socrates. But that would presumably be a fact well known to everyone in the Academy. . . . The rest of Aristotle's report is more likely to represent his own speculation, based upon his reading of the dialogues and supplemented in some cases by information from Xenophon" (1996, 81–82). Accordingly, Kahn draws the following conclusion: "That means we have both the freedom and responsibility to evaluate these texts from the critical standpoint of modern historical philology, without bowing to the authority of Xenophon or Aristotle" (87). Of course, it does not follow from any of these remarks that Aristotle in fact is wrong. All that follows is the quite plausible point that Aristotle's testimony can only confirm interpretations for which there is independent evidence in the Platonic texts.

7. Terence Irwin offers a version of this sort of interpretation: "If we are asked to say what bravery is, we quite rightly begin with our beliefs about particular brave actions and people, and we think about how we recognize them in particular situations. We observe that in particular situations brave people stand firm, temperate people are quiet, just people pay back what they have borrowed, and so on. These observations of particular situations are quite accurate, as far as they go, but Socrates points out that these observable properties (standing firm, quietness, etc) are not the ones we are looking for, since in other particular situations we can observe the same properties, even though people fail to display the same virtues. How ought we to react to this discovery? We might suppose that we have not yet found the right observable property. Socrates' interlocutors, at any rate, suppose that an account of *F* should mention one and the same observable feature present in every situation where something *F* can be observed; when they find none, Socrates points out that they have given an inadequate

account of *F*, but he does not tell them where they have gone wrong. Does he assume that if we look hard enough, we ought to be able to find the single observable property that the interlocutors have not found? The Socratic dialogues and the *Meno* do not actually say that Socrates assumes that observable properties are needed for definition. But at least Socrates does not discourage the interlocutors from looking in this direction, and we have suggested, by appealing to the *Euthyphro* on disputes and measurement and to the *Meno* on the dialectical condition, that he actually requires definitions to refer only to observable properties" (*Plato's Ethics*, 1995, 163).

8. This view is common in the literature. Hendrik Lorenz makes the point: "One suggestion that has been made by a number of scholars, and that seems clearly correct, is that Plato is making a point against Socrates' view of human desire, as it is presented in earlier Platonic dialogues (such as the *Meno*, the *Protagoras*, and the *Gorgias*). It is part of that view that all human desire aims at 'the good' in a certain way – namely, in such a way that when a person has a desire it always springs from, or consists in, a belief as to what it is good, or best, for them to do in the circumstances in question. If desire fails to be directed at something that is in fact good, this always involves an error of judgment (about what it is good to do) on the part of the person whose desire it is" (*The Brute Within*, 2006, 28). Michael Frede makes similar remarks about Plato and Socrates: "There is reason to believe that Socrates thought that there is no such thing as acting against one's own better judgment. What does happen is that reason in certain circumstances gets confused and, instead of holding on to its better judgment, follows some other judgment. If reason knew the truth, it could never get confused in this way. Thus, according to Socrates, such cases reveal nothing but a failure of reason which in its weakness does not hold on to the true belief, but accepts a false one and acts on it. Plato, Aristotle, and their followers, on the other hand, believed that such cases could not be explained as purely intellectual failures, that one had to assume that besides reason there is an irrational part of the soul with its own needs and demands which may conflict with the demands of reason and which may move us to act against the dictates of reason, if reason has not managed to bring the irrational part of the soul firmly under its control" ("The Stoic doctrine of the affections of the soul," 1986, 96).

9. I think myself Socrates also realized that the virtues are defined in terms of the appropriate, not in some reductive way, but this interpretation of the historical Socrates is controversial. Terence Irwin, for example, argues that Socrates had hoped to find reductive definitions of the virtues: "Reflexion on Socrates' explanatory condition, therefore, might reasonably lead us to doubt whether his epistemological condition is reasonable. The most plausible candidates for reductive definitions meeting the epistemological condition do not seem to satisfy the explanatory condition. Plato might reasonably conclude that we cannot expect a definition to satisfy both conditions and

that we need to choose between them. Plato decides that the explanatory condition is more fundamental, and that we ought to give up the epistemological demand for a reductive definition that eliminates evaluative terms" (*The Development of Ethics.* I: *From Socrates to the Reformation*, 2007, 72). See also *Plato's Ethics*, 1995, 163. The relevant passage is quoted in note 7 above.

5

Justice and its Reward

Socrates attributed supreme importance to the love of wisdom, but it was not clear what it was and why it was so important. As Plato portrays him in the early dialogues, he thought that the expectation of happiness is a matter of proper psychological functioning, that this functioning embodies an expertise, that this expertise includes practical wisdom about ethical matters, and that knowledge of the definitions of the ethical virtues is the knowledge that constitutes this wisdom.

This understanding of Socrates was puzzling for a number of reasons. It was paradoxical to think that the good life is a life of ethical virtue. It was more usual to think that happiness and the demands of ethical virtue not only can, but often do, conflict. In addition, it was very unclear how knowledge of the definitions could be sufficient for action. It was more usual to think that knowledge is sometimes overpowered by desire. Finally, even if knowledge is sufficient, it was difficult to see how knowledge of definitions could exhaust the knowledge involved in choosing wisely among the alternatives. It would seem that knowledge of the good is necessary.

In the *Republic*, some answers begin to emerge. Knowledge is not sufficient. In a proper functioning psychology, the part with reason controls the desires in the two parts without reason. The part with reason knows what the good is. This knowledge is innate. This part also knows that justice is what is appropriate with respect to human beings and that justice in the individual is for the parts of the soul to exist in harmony. When the parts are in harmony, a human being acts for the sake of making his life good and himself happy. He lives a life of reason in which his soul resembles, as much as possible, its natural and disincarnate state in contemplation of the forms.

In the *Republic*, Plato presents a theory of justice. This theory is rooted in previous ideas, but these ideas are developed in novel ways. Socrates, in the early dialogues, supposes that the best life is a matter of proper psychological functioning and that this functioning is a matter of practical wisdom about ethical matters. In the *Republic*, although the best life is a matter of proper psychological functioning, this functioning is understood in terms of the organization of the three parts of the soul. To produce this organization,

Ancient Greek Philosophy: From The Presocratics to the Hellenistic Philosophers, First Edition.
Thomas A. Blackson.   © 2011 Thomas A. Blackson. Published 2011 by Blackwell Publishing Ltd.

human beings must be organized in cities in a certain way. This organization is justice in the city, and it is appropriate for human beings because it promotes the proper organization of the three parts of the soul in an individual human being. This organization of the three parts of the soul constitutes justice in the individual. In the just individual, the part of the soul with reason rules in terms of its knowledge of the good. As a result, the individual arranges his life so that he can expect to spend time in a certain exercise of reason involving the forms, the exercise in which he most resembles the natural and disincarnate state of his soul. Action in accordance with the rules of a just city is part of a plan to maximize time spent in this exercise of reason. This exercise is the activity in which human beings find happiness most of all.

5.1   The Opening Conversation

The first book of the *Republic* sets the stage for the rest of the dialogue. Cephalus introduces the subject for discussion. He remarks, in an offhand way, that wealth is good because it obviates the need to act unjustly.[a] A wealthy person has no need to risk punishment, either in this world or the next. To Socrates, however, this understanding of justice is all wrong. Cephalus, in his remarks, suggests that conforming to the dictates of justice is a burden a human being is often better off without, but Socrates believes that the just life is better than the unjust life. Hence, to determine the truth of the matter, he pushes the conversation to the question of *what justice is*.

The answer Socrates wants to refute takes some time to surface. Cephalus had been involved in a sacrifice before Socrates arrived on the scene. Now that their conversation has taken a serious turn, he quietly returns to the sacrifice. His son, Polemarchus, takes up Socrates' question. Polemarchus

---

[a] Cephalus was a native of Syracuse who settled in Athens to make money. Such resident aliens paid a tax to live and work in Athens, but they enjoyed none of the civic rights and duties of a citizen. By turning his attention to money, and hence away from the excellence of his soul, Cephalus is an example of the sort of human being Plato thought subject to the charge Socrates presses against the Athenians: he attaches little importance to the most important things and greater importance to things that are by comparison worthless. Julia Annas provides the relevant historical detail: "We should remember here that the *Republic* was written much later than the time it depicts. Plato was writing for an audience that knew that the security based on wealth which Cephalus had spent his life building up, and which is so much stressed here, was wholly illusory: only a few years later, when Athens fell, the family was totally ruined, Polemarchus executed, and Lysias driven into exile. (Lysias later became a professional speech-writer, and in his speech *Against Eratosthenes* we can read a vivid account of his family's ruin)" (*An Introduction to Plato's* Republic, 1981, 18).

relies on the poet, Simonides, for the answer, but he cannot defend this understanding of justice against Socrates' subsequent questioning. Polemarchus quickly drops out of the conversation, and Thrasymachus[b] takes his place. Thrasymachus is Socrates' real opponent. He confidently asserts that "justice is nothing other than the advantage of the stronger." Socrates says he is not quite sure what Thrasymachus means, and Thrasymachus explains that the rulers are the strong, that they use the government to satisfy their desires, and that "justice is the same in every city, it is what goes together with the advantage of the established rulers" (I.338c–339a).

Thrasymachus cannot defend this answer. Socrates makes him admit that ruling is for the good of the ruled. The argument is a variation on the prior argument against Polus and Callicles. Socrates forced them to admit that rhetoric, because it is blind, cannot be expected to provide a good life. Now Socrates forces Thrasymachus to admit that rulers sometimes give orders to their disadvantage. This admission (in conjunction with the assumption that obeying the rulers is always just) contradicts Thrasymachus' prior assertion. Once he sees the contradiction, he makes a desperate effort to hold his ground. He insists that rulers do give orders to their advantage because otherwise they do not deserve to be called "rulers." Socrates patiently provides counterexamples until Thrasymachus acknowledges the correct meaning of the word. Once they reach agreement, Socrates forces Thrasymachus to admit that he believes ruling is for the good of the ruled. Socrates then repeats their conclusion. "So, then," he says in conclusion, "no one in a position of rule, insofar as he is a ruler, seeks or orders what to himself is advantageous, but rather orders what is advantageous to his subjects" because "it is to what is advantageous and proper to them that he looks, and everything he says and does he says and does for them" (I.342e).

The conversation now turns away from what justice is and to the question of *whether the just life is better than the unjust life*. Thrasymachus takes the position the reader expects. He says that "the unjust life is better than the just one" (I.347e). He thinks crime can lead to a happier life because it can help a person get "the most he can for himself" (I.349c).[1] Thrasymachus, however, is unable to defend this view against Socrates' questioning. Socrates forces him to admit that he believes the soul has a "function," that this function is "to take care of things, to rule, to deliberate," and that "justice is the soul's virtue" (I.353d–e). Injustice indicates improper psychological functioning

---

[b] Little is known of Thrasymachus, but Plato portrays him unfavorably. Cf. C. C. W. Taylor, *Socrates. A Very Short Introduction*, 1998b, 73: "Thrasymachus, indeed, is a thoroughly nasty piece of work: arrogant, rude, and aggressive (he even tells Socrates to get his nurse to wipe his nose and stop his drivelling (343a)) ...."

and hence irrationality. As such, injustice is not something anyone should expect to improve his life and well-being. "And so, Thrasymachus," Socrates proclaims to make the outcome of the argument clear, "injustice is never more profitable than justice" (I.354a[c]).

Thrasymachus might have fared better in response to Socrates' questioning if he had resisted the identification of justice with proper psychological functioning and rationality. This, in turn, might have put him in a position to argue that injustice is more profitable than justice. If the term "good" is used to say that a given life is enjoyable and happy for the person living the life, then the unjust life may well be better than the just one because, according to Thrasymachus, a life is enjoyable and happy to the extent the person gets "the most he can for himself." Someone strong and smart enough to get away with injustice need not restrict his goals and plans so that his actions remain within the confines of justice. Thrasymachus, however, says none of this. He throws a fit because Socrates has refuted him, and hence the discussion ends unsatisfactorily.

5.2 Justice

The *Republic* itself continues. Glaucon and Adeimantus[d] are not content to let the conversation end unsatisfactorily simply because Thrasymachus has thrown a fit. They challenge Socrates to demonstrate that Thrasymachus is mistaken about injustice and that despite what so many people think about injustice and happiness, the just life really is better than the unjust life.

Since Thrasymachus refuses to speak, Glaucon offers the challenge on his behalf. He suggests that justice is a device. Gluacon says that justice is a matter of the "laws and covenants" that allow human beings to escape the conflict endemic to the state of nature (II.358e–359b). In nature, all that deters a person from taking what he wants is his estimate of success. This leads to enough suffering that the many are convinced it would be better to make everyone respect the positions of others. If, however, someone could get away with breaking the law without being punished, then, as Thrasymachus maintained, he would live the best life of all. Prudence would not force him to respect the positions of others. Nothing would prevent him

[c] Socrates' remarks about the connection between justice and happiness can be confusing. Just prior to this conclusion, he argues for the *sufficiency* thesis. He argues that the just man is happy and that the unjust man is unhappy (353d–354a). He then moves to the *comparative* thesis that injustice is never more profitable than justice. These theses are not equivalent, but Socrates makes no effort to distinguish them.
[d] They are Plato's older brothers.

from getting "the most he can for himself, which is what by nature any natural being pursues as good" (II.359c).[e]

Socrates accepts Glaucon's challenge to "track down the nature of justice and injustice, and where the truth lay as regards the benefits of both" (II.368c). Justice in general is what is appropriate in connection with human beings, and Socrates suggests that he and his interlocutors should search for the appropriate in two domains: in the organization of human beings in cities, and in the organization of the parts of the human soul within the individual human being.

The three parts of the city

Socrates begins the search for justice in the city by first clarifying what a "city" is. He says no one is "self-sufficient" and that human beings arrange themselves into cities because each thinks that cooperation "is better for himself." Each human being thus apparently assumes that some lives are better than others and that a city makes the better ones possible (II.369b–c).

The city must have a way to introduce and enforce rules to produce and distribute material goods and to encourage various forms of behavior. To produce the material goods, Socrates says that the city must have a working class. To introduce and enforce the rules of production and distribution, Socrates says that the city must have a governing or guardian class.

The guardian class has another job as well. The production and distribution of material goods is not the only behavior in the city. Socrates says that the guardian class is responsible for introducing and enforcing the rules that determine all forms of acceptable behavior, not just for introducing and enforcing the rules for the production and distribution of goods.

To produce the guardians, a certain system of education is necessary. Socrates describes this in detail, but the main points are these. The education begins with training in literature, whose content is highly restricted. Stories with falsehoods about the gods are not allowed. Similarly, stories that discourage virtue are not allowed. This training in literature is followed by physical training. This training, like the training in literature, is highly regimented. The goal in both cases is to induce the psychological organization in which the part of the soul with reason executes its function of

[e] Glaucon illustrates his point with the legend of the Ring of Gyges. Gyges was a shepherd in the service of the king of Lydia. Gyges, after an earthquake, found and entered a cave that entombed a corpse who wore a golden ring. Gyges soon realized that the ring, when turned a certain way, made him invisible. He used this new power to seduce the queen, murder the king, and take the throne for himself. Glaucon says that everybody would like to be in Gyges' place.

ruling properly. At a certain point, testing occurs to determine which of the trainees can best hold on to the truth about justice in situations where a person might be "confused by pleasure or fear" (III.413c). Those who fare best in these tests will be rulers. Those who fare less well will be auxiliaries. The auxiliaries serve to enforce the rules the rulers introduce.

With the city and its three parts established – the ruling class, the auxiliary class, and the working class – Socrates looks for where "justice resides in it." He says the "city, if rightly founded, is completely good," and then he quickly concludes that his city is "wise, brave, moderate, and just" (IV.427d–e). He provides no explanation, but the idea is that a "rightly founded" city is one in which knowledge of the good governs the lives of citizens. This interpretation makes sense of Socrates' central idea that his city is good because it is rightly founded and properly organized. There is more evidence for the interpretation later in the dialogue. Socrates goes on to say that "unless lovers of wisdom rule in cities as those who speak in council to set public policy, and political power and the love of wisdom coincide, cities will continually be plagued with problems" (V.473c–d). And so Socrates' city is rightly founded because all the citizens in his city train to be wise but only the wisest rule. Since the rulers rule, the auxiliaries are brave in enforcing the rules, and the workers are moderate, knowledge in the rulers determines that the citizens live as well as possible.

Socrates thus concludes that the organization he has described is justice in the city. The appropriate arrangement of human beings in cities defines justice in the city, and since the appropriate arrangement of human beings in cities is the one that results in the citizens living good lives to the extent that is possible, Socrates concludes that "doing one's own job by the working, auxiliary, and ruling groups, is justice and makes the city be just" (IV.434c).

The rulers in a just city are lovers of wisdom

Now that he has identified justice in the city, Socrates identifies the rulers in the just city. He says that the rulers must be lovers of wisdom. Plato's Athenian audience would have been surprised by this assertion. To them, it was not clear what it is to love wisdom. Moreover, to the extent that it was clear, it seemed to them that lovers of wisdom do not make good rulers. Hence, to defend his surprising and paradoxical claim, Socrates explains what a lover of wisdom is.

He initially characterizes a lover of wisdom as someone who "gladly turns to learning things," but Glaucon immediately objects to this description as a qualification to rule. He tells Socrates that this characterization of the lovers of wisdom would not distinguish them from other "strange people," people who would not be appropriate rulers of the city. These people are immersed in popular culture, they "run around to all Dionysiac festivals,"[f] but Glaucon complains that they are incapable of understanding the way things really are. Socrates agrees with Glaucon's assessment and explains that the lover of wisdom is interested in truth, but since "all of the forms each is itself one but appears to be many because they each manifest themselves in actions, bodies, and one another," these "strange" people appear to love wisdom (V.475c–476e).

The import of Socrates' explanation is not easy to understand, but the leading idea seems to be that the "strange" people Gluacon mentions mistake appearances for reality. These people are like dreamers who think they are in touch with reality when in fact they are fast asleep. The lover of sights recognizes particular beautiful things, but he is not willing to admit that beauty itself is invariant in all the many different beautiful arrangements of things, such as sounds, colors, and shapes. Hence, the lover of sights has "opinion" (V.476b–d). To prove this point, Socrates goes on to imagine how the lover of sights would respond to questions of a certain sort. He maintains that the lover of sights is forced to say that just things appear unjust and, more generally, that things participate in their opposites (V.478e–479b[2]). The argument is difficult to reconstruct, but the fundamental point seems to be that the features people ordinarily take to indicate the presence of X-ness in various circumstances are not the same as what X-ness is. Otherwise, it would follow that things "will in a way appear both beautiful and ugly, and so with the other things included in the question." Hence Socrates concludes that the lover of sights is not really concerned with what X-ness is. His interest is not in the reality but in the features commonly thought to indicate X-ness is various circumstances. Beliefs of this sort constitute what Socrates terms "the many customs of the many" (V.479d–480a).[3] In this way, the "strange" people Glaucon mentions have opinions, not knowledge. They live in terms of "customs," not in terms of the forms, which are the reality of things.

---

[f] These festivals, associated originally with the god Dionysus, had become important venues for various spectacles, including theatrical performances, trains of sacrificial animals, and choral songs and dances. The grandest of these festivals, the City Dionysia, took place in Athens. It occurred in March. There were many visitors in the city at the time, since the seas had become navigable again. This was also the time of the year when allies came to Athens to pay tribute. The festival thus took on a kind Panhellenic significance (although unlike the Olympics it was not a Panhellenic festival), and Athens seized on the opportunity to use the festival to showcase her wealth and cultural supremacy.

Socrates does not say so explicitly, but the contrast he draws between the lover of wisdom and the lover of spectacles appears to be part of a more general analysis of the failure of the traditional education. The "many customs of the many" constitute the traditional beliefs about ethical matters. The Sophists, when they teach the traditional morality, promote these customs:

> Not one of those private teachers, who work for money, and whom the people call sophists and consider to be their superiors, teaches anything but the opinions the multitude expresses when they are together, and they call this wisdom.[g] It is as if a man were learning the moods and appetites of a huge beast, which he had in his keeping, how to approach and handle it, when it is most difficult or most gentle and what sounds soothe or anger it. Having learned this by living with the beast over time, this routine he calls wisdom. He gathers this information together as if it were an art, and starts to teach it. In truth, he knows nothing about which of these opinions is fine or shameful, good or bad, just or unjust, but he applies all these names in accordance with how the beast reacts. He calls what pleases it good and what vexes it bad, and he has no other account to give. (VI.493a–c)

The problem, according to Socrates, is that this "wisdom" is illusory. And so the lover of sights who thinks he recognizes what "is beautiful or ugly, good or bad, just or unjust" charges ahead on the basis of this illusion and inadvertently ruins his life. The situation is made all the worse with the addition of rhetorical persuasion acquired through a sophistical education, as this allows the lover of sights to promote his "wisdom" to the public and hence to ruin more lives.[h]

The lover of wisdom, by contrast, has what it takes to make his life good. It is puzzling why this is true in the early dialogues, but now a clearer picture has begun to emerge. Previously, even if it were granted that the lover of wisdom knows that the virtues are a matter of what is

---

[g] Plato does not have Socrates name Protagoras explicitly, but Socrates may well have had him particularly in mind when he says that "those private teachers" teach nothing different from "the opinions of the multitude." In the *Protagoras*, as part of a proof that virtue can be taught, Protagoras says that he teaches his students to live successful lives. He is an expert in the art of rhetorical persuasion, and this art helps him make his students conform with the many when they say "this is just, that is unjust, this is beautiful, that ugly, this pious."

[h] As R. S. Bluck notes, "[t]he general purpose of the *Republic* V passage is to reject mere 'culture' in favor of ἐπιστήμη [or knowledge] as a qualification for *ruling the state*..." (*Plato's Meno*, 38).

appropriate, it remained unclear why this knowledge alone allows the lover of wisdom to recognize what "is beautiful or ugly, good or bad, just or unjust" in particular situations. He also needs to know what is appropriate. It was tempting to suppose that the lover of wisdom has the "measuring art," but this still left the problem of how the lover of wisdom is supposed to determine, or "measure," what is appropriate in a given situation. Now, in the *Republic*, it appears that Plato thinks that the lover of wisdom has the necessary additional information. The lover of wisdom not only knows what the good is, he knows that the appropriate is what in the circumstances secures the good.[4]

This interpretation explains how Socrates chooses the particular educational system and social arrangements for his city.[i] Socrates, of course, is a lover of wisdom. He is the paradigm example that Plato, from the early dialogues onward, has been trying so hard to understand. As a lover of wisdom, Socrates is not confused about justice or about the virtues generally. He knows what justice is. He knows that justice is what is appropriate in matters involving human beings. Socrates also knows that the appropriate secures the good. Furthermore, he knows what the good is in a human being and in a city. This knowledge is innate, and through his practice of asking questions Socrates has managed to rid himself of the false beliefs that typically obscure this knowledge in others. He is thus in a position to conclude that the educational system and social arrangement he identifies is the appropriate organization of human beings in cities.

Socrates nowhere points to specific empirical evidence to justify his choice of the educational system and social arrangement in a just city. Instead, he seems to rely on very general impressions of how human beings behave in various situations. He is, however, careful to mention the importance of experience in connection with the training program for the rulers. Socrates insists that those who are in training to rule shall "not fall short of others" in "experience":

---

[i] In addition to the general education program for producing guardians, Socrates introduces several arrangements that departed significantly from Athenian tradition. He says, for example, that the guardians will have nothing substantial in the way of private property, that they will not have money, and that their needs will be provided through taxation (III.416d–417b). He says that among the guardians wives and children will be held in common and that intercourse will be controlled as part of a eugenics program (III.423e–424a, V.449c–460b).

Is it enough if someone continuously, strenuously, and without distraction devotes himself to the arguments, as he did in the bodily physical training, for twice as long?

Do you mean for six years or four?

Well, it does not really matter, so make it five years. After that you must send them into the cave again, and compel them to command in matters of war and occupy the other offices suitable for youth, so that they do not fall short of others in experience.[j] And during this time too they must be tested to determine if they will remain steadfast or waver...

How long should this last?

Fifteen years. At fifty, those who have survived the tests and been successful both in practice and in knowledge must be led to the goal and compelled to turn upwards to what provides light for everything, and when they have thus seen the good itself, they must each in turn put the city, its citizens, and themselves in order, using it as their model. (VII.539d–540a)

It is not clear exactly what Socrates means by saying the rulers shall "not fall short of others in experience," but it would not be surprising if Plato had the "measuring art" in mind. The lover of wisdom identifies the appropriate alternative in situations in which others might become confused. He is able to make this identification because in addition to knowing what the good is, and that the appropriate is what secures the good, he has experience in assessing the kinds of alternatives he is likely to face. In this case, given the possession of this sort of "measuring art," the lovers of wisdom would have the expertise necessary to rule in the city.

5.3　The Just Life is Better

Justice in a city is for the happiness of its citizens. Plato follows Socrates in thinking that the expectation of happiness is a matter of proper psychological functioning. Plato however, unlike Socrates, thinks that the proper functioning consists in the psychological organization in which action is for the sake of returning to the state the soul enjoys outside the body.

This new, unearthly perspective shows itself in the *Phaedo* in connection with whether the lover of wisdom should fear death. Socrates indicates that

---

[j] Socrates first insists on the point at VI.484d–485a.

the love of wisdom, properly understood, requires the lover of wisdom to undergo a fundamental change in orientation (66b–e, 69a–d, 79d, 80d–81a, 82b–c). Socrates explains that the lover of wisdom has replaced his old outlook with a new conception of himself and of his purpose in life. Once he is a lover of wisdom, he no longer concerns himself with money and other such things. He now conceives of himself as a soul temporarily lodged in a body. During his time in the body, his aim is to master his "bodily passions" and to follow "reason . . ., contemplating the true" (84a–b). The lover of wisdom sees his present life as connected to his state in death when his soul is separate from the body.[5]

This same general idea is evident in the *Republic*. In passages very similar in tone to the passages in the *Phaedo*, Socrates says that the lover of wisdom wants the part of his soul with reason to be "fastened to that which is of each nature itself" and wants to "imitate" the forms and "become as like them as he can" so that he "becomes divine and ordered as far as a man can" (VI.490a–b, VI.500c–d, VII.518d–e). And the explanation here is the same as in the *Phaedo*. The lover of wisdom thinks of himself as a soul and thinks that a certain transformation is his goal. He wants to restore himself to the natural state of contemplation he lost upon incarnation.

Justice is the key to this transformation. In becoming just, the lover of wisdom sees what he is and what his interests are. This knowledge belongs innately to the part of the soul with reason, but incarnation obscures this innate knowledge. Through the training involved in becoming just, this obscurity falls away as the parts of the soul become harmonized. Once the parts of the soul exist in harmony, the part with reason has control and hence action is for the good.

When the lover of wisdom is engaged in the love of wisdom, he acts for the good because he acts to make himself and his life better. The details of this improvement are unclear, but the idea is that he takes on ever more knowledge of reality. Justice has given him some knowledge not obscured by false belief. Now it is up to him, through the use of "dialectic" in the love of wisdom, to gain more clarity and so to become more like his disincarnate soul. Through the use of "dialectic," he seeks to grasp the structure of reality generally. He seeks to reach "the first principle of all that exists" and to understand "what follows from it" by moving in terms of "forms and through forms to its conclusions which are forms" (VI.510c–511c). In this way, by grasping ever more of the structure of reality, the lover of wisdom increases his happiness.

Yet, even given all this, it remains unclear that Socrates has established the conclusion that has driven so much of the discussion: that the just life is better than the unjust life. Glaucon raises this issue with respect to the lovers of wisdom in Socrates' city. He asks if the obligation to rule prevents them from living the best life and having the most happiness possible. In reply, Socrates says that in other cities, cities in which the lover of wisdom has become a lover of wisdom "against the will of the government and constitution," the lover of wisdom has no obligation to rule (VII.519d–520c). In his city, however, the lovers of wisdom are obligated to rule in turns:

> In the remainder of their lives, each will spend much of his time in the love of wisdom, but, when his turn comes, he must labor in politics and for the sake of the city, not as something fine, but as a necessity. And when each has thus educated others like himself to take his place as a guardian of the city, he will depart to dwell in the Islands of the Blessed. The city will establish memorials and sacrifices to him as a god, if the Pythia[k] agrees, but if not, then as a happy and divine human being. (VII.540b–c)

In this case, however, it can seem that justice is not always better. Given what Socrates says, it looks as if justice and happiness can conflict and that the lovers of wisdom in a just city would have better and happier lives were they to forsake ruling to spend more time in the love of wisdom.

Despite the appearance, this cannot be what Socrates thinks. Since he and his interlocutors have agreed that the organization of human beings in the city he describes is appropriate for human beings and hence is justice in the city, the idea must be that time spent in the love of wisdom is most likely maximized in the city Socrates describes as the just city.[6] He says that the lover of wisdom will rule in public affairs for the sake of the city "not as something fine, but as a necessity." The necessity itself is left unexplained, but the idea must be that the lover of wisdom chooses to rule as part of a plan to change the world so that he can maximize time spent in the love of wisdom, the exercise of reason involving the forms that, according to the argument, makes the dominant contribution to how much a human being likes his circumstances. Hence, were the lover of wisdom not to take his turn in ruling, he would be acting contrary to his good. By not taking his turn, he would be increasing the likelihood of spending less time in the love of wisdom.

---

[k] The Pythia is the prophetess at the sanctuary for Apollo at Delphi. She made the will of Apollo known on Earth to believers who had questions about what to do. The Greeks often consulted the Pythia on important matters.

In this case, although the lovers of wisdom can conceivably have better lives than the ones they have in the just city, it is not rational for them to abandon their posts. The added value given in terms of increased happiness is more than discounted by the low probability of actually attaining these lives. This is true for two reasons. First of all, by abandoning their posts, the lovers of wisdom yield to temptation. They choose the pleasure in love of wisdom over ruling, thereby undermining proper psychological organization, and thus becoming unjust. This initial disorganization among the parts of the soul is a cancer that leads to ever more disorganization in the future and hence to the increased likelihood of action contrary to what the part with reason knows is good.[1] Moreover, the increased likelihood of improper psychological organization (and thus of action contrary to the good) is not the only obstacle to confront the lover of wisdom who considers leaving his post to spend more time in the love of wisdom. The resources in the city Socrates describes are largely directed to the support and maintenance of the rulers in their love of wisdom. Life outside this city is likely to be much more difficult and unhappy for lovers of wisdom than life inside it.[m]

This interpretation is confirmed to some extent by Socrates' claim that anyone who has managed to become a lover of wisdom "against the will of the government" bears no obligation to go into political life and to promote the laws in this city. It seems likely that in a city in which the rules discourage and stand in the way of the love of wisdom, a life in politics cannot be expected to increase the time spent in the love of wisdom. In this case, it is unsurprising that the lover of wisdom bears no obligation to go into political life in this city. Given the circumstances, it

---

[1] "[Plato insists that] unjust actions tend to eventuate in psychic discord, while just actions promote psychic harmony. So, the just person, who has an interest in psychic harmony, will prefer those actions which are just to those which are unjust" (Christopher Shields, *Classical Philosophy*, 2003, 94).

[m] Socrates himself provides the example. In the *Apology*, in contemplating the counter-assessment he should propose to the jury, the character says that he deserves "free meals in the Prytaneum" (37a). (The Prytaneum was the hall in Athens in which Olympian victors were honored with meals at the public's expense.) In justification, he says that whereas the "Olympian victor makes you think yourself happy, I make you be happy," and that although "the victor does not need the food, I do" (36d–e). Not surprisingly, the jury rejected this counter-assessment in favor of the original penalty of death.

would be contrary to reason because there are alternatives with greater expected value.[n]

Nevertheless, the central question remains. One may grant that ruling in turns is rational for the lovers of wisdom in Socrates' city, but it still seems possible that some unjust lives are better than some just ones. Because the just human being is not confused about what he is and what is in his interest, his actions are directed toward the good. The same cannot be said for the unjust human being. He does not always make the best choice among the available alternatives. In this way, relatively speaking, he is less happy than he could be. Yet, for all that, in the absence of a much more detailed specification of what contributes to and detracts from human happiness, something which Plato does not provide in the *Republic*,[7] it remains in doubt whether Socrates establishes the comparative thesis that a just life is more profitable and hence better and happier than an unjust one. It seems possible that a just life might be pretty miserable in certain circumstances. Equally, it seems possible that in certain circumstances, an unjust life might not be all that bad.

Glaucon, however, has been taken in by the argument. When he issued the challenge, he wanted Socrates to show that a just human being who suffers what are popularly understood as great misfortunes is still better off than an unjust human being who suffers none of the misfortunes but who instead is showered with what are popularly understood as the good things in life:

> We must deprive him of any reputation for justice, as this would bring honor and awards, and we could not be sure whether he is acting for the sake of justice itself or for the honors and awards. So we must strip him of everything except justice and make his situation opposite to that of the unjust man who does no injustice, but has the greatest reputation for it. (II.361b–c)

> The just man, in these circumstances, with his reputation for the greatest of injustices, will have to endure the whip, being stretched on a rack, blinded with fire, and finally, after extreme suffering, being impaled. (II.361e–362a)

---

[n] So, in the *Apology*, in explanation of why he interferes in private affairs, but does not venture to go to the Assembly and advise the city itself, Socrates says this: "Be sure, gentlemen, that if I had gone into politics, I would have been put to death long ago, and benefitted neither you nor myself" (31d–e).

And now, in view of what Socrates has said about justice and injustice, Glaucon thinks that the challenge has been met and that there is no need to carry the argument further:

> From this point on the inquiry is absurd, now that justice and injustice have been revealed, since even with all manner of food and drink, lots of money, and every sort of power to rule, life is not worth living when the body is ruined. So, even if someone can do whatever he wishes, save what will free him from vice and injustice and make him have justice and virtue, it cannot be worth living when his soul, that by which he lives, is disordered and ruined. (IV.445a–b)

Glaucon believes that injustice, or an improper organization among the three parts of the soul, is so bad that the just human being who is whipped, tortured on the rack, has his eyes burned in their sockets, and is run through, is still better off than the unjust human being. The implied conception of happiness is obviously quite paradoxical, but Glaucon, at this point, believes that the more ordinary conception is based on a misconception of what a human being is.[8]

Notes

1. Cf. G. B. Kerferd, *The Sophistic Movement*, 1981, 122: "Thasymachus does not actually use the terminology of the *nomos-physis* [or custom-nature] antithesis. But he is rightly to be placed among those who employ it, since in rejecting vulgar justice in favour of vulgar injustice he is elevating vulgar injustice to the status of what is right by nature, and what is right by nature is, in the language of the *nomos-physis* antithesis, natural justice. This is recognized in Book II (359c3–6) where Glaucon does not hesitate to express the problem raised by Thrasymachus in the actual terms of the *nomos-physis* opposition. What we have in the *Republic* is a restatement of the position assumed by Callicles in the *Gorgias* without the complication of alliance with the doctrine of fulfilment of desires."

2. This passage is similar to Socrates' remarks at 100b1–d8 in the *Phaedo*. Terence Irwin stresses the similarity in "Plato's Heracleiteanism" (1977). See also his *Plato's Ethics*, 1995, 154–168.

3. J. Adam provides a plausible explanation of the meaning of the phrase: "The words refer to general rules, standards, canons, believed by the multitude (cf. τὰ τῶν πολλῶν δόγματα VI 493 A), who have on every single subject many such standards (πολλὰ νόμιμα), mutually inconsistent and uncoordinated, because they do not know that τὸ καλόν, τὸ αγαθόν etc. are each of them ἕν" (*The Republic of Plato*, 343).

4. Terry Penner argues for a version of this interpretation: "I have presented a picture of the Form of the Good (as the Form of Advantage or Benefit) which is quite different from the moral or quasi-moral picture that has tended to dominate the interpretation of Plato – especially since Prichard's great 1928 paper 'Duty and interest.' I applaud Prichard for forcing interpreters to confront the possibility that the *Republic* might be working with two opposing pictures of justice: (1) justice as morality, and (2) justice as what makes each individual happier. In forcing us to choose here, I claim that he – and his most distinguished successors (if we include under morality the quasi-moral notion of agent-independent good) – make exactly the wrong choice, opting for morality. What I have been arguing here, by contrast, is that what the Form of the Good is the Form *of* is not the moral good or some quasi-moral good, but quite simply advantage: a notion that involves the kinds of means/end considerations that are normally consigned to the dustbin as speaking merely to instrumental goods – a purely prudential notion of good that lies entirely outside of the realms of morality. I regard putting this purely factual notion of advantage at the center of ethics as a valuable departure on the part of Plato from the strong belief in morality almost universal in Greek thought as in Western thought generally. In my view (which I believe I inferred from my studies of Socratic doctrine), it is not clear that morality and the moral good (as opposed to what is quite simply good *for* humans, regardless of any supposed *moral* good) are intrinsically involved in the human good" ("What is the form of the good the form *of*? A question about the plot of the *Republic*," 2007, 36).

5. Michael Frede makes the general point: "The soul is conceived of as preexisting and as just temporarily joined to the body. It thus has two lives and two sets of concerns. Its own concern is to live a life of contemplation of truth. But, joined to the body, it also has to concern itself with the needs of the body. In doing this it easily forgets itself and its own needs, it easily gets confused so as to make the needs of the body its own. To know how to live well is to know how to live in such a way that the soul is free again to clearly see and mind its own business, namely to contemplate the truth. Thus we have an extremely complex inversion of the relative weight of one's theoretical understanding of reality and one's practical knowledge of how to live. It is one's understanding of reality, and the position of the soul in it, that saves the soul by restoring it – to the extent that this is possible in this life – to its natural state, in which it contemplates the truth. Hence a good life will crucially involve, as part of the way one lives, contemplation of the truth. Practicing the right way to live will also be a means to enable the soul to free itself from the body, to see the truth, and to engage in the contemplation of truth" ("The philosopher," 2000, 9). Cf. "Introduction" in *Rationality in Greek Thought*, 1996a, 13: "[W]hereas Socrates had thought that there was no need to gain theoretical knowledge about the world or reality and that perhaps it was even impossible to do so, since it was not the function of reason to gain such knowledge, both Plato and Aristotle disagreed. They thought that it was crucial not only for a good life, but also for an understanding of how to live well, to have

an adequate general understanding for the world. Moreover, though they granted that it was a function of reason to determine the way we live, they, each in their own way, did not think that this was the sole function of reason. Plato rather seems to have thought that guiding us through our embodied life is a function which reason takes on, but that it, left to itself, is concerned to theoretically understand things quite generally."

6. This is not the only possibility. Some scholars have thought that ruling is not contrary to happiness because rational action is for the sake of the good as such, not for the good of the individual. John Cooper and Richard Kraut are important examples. "[The just human being] knows the good-itself and therefore whatever he values he values strictly in the light of a comparison between that thing and the good. ... [But the just human being need not] always choose to live a contemplative's life, retired among their mathematical books and constantly engaging in philosophical discussions. Perhaps one would choose this if all he cared about was *his* realizing the good so far as possible. But a just person is a devotee of *the* good, not *his own* good; and these are very different things. Knowing the good, what he wants is to advance the reign of rational order in the world as a whole, so far as by his own efforts, alone or together with others, he can do this. He recognizes a single criterion of choice: What, given the circumstances, will be most likely to maximize the total amount of rational order in the world as a whole? And here he has a wide arena for possible activity. He can not only impose rational order on his own soul, thinking rational thoughts and satisfying rationally controlled appetites of his own; he can help to bring rational order to the souls of other individuals, and to their social life" (John Cooper, "The psychology of justice in Plato," 1999, 145–146). "[Socrates] tells us at one point that when philosophers look to the harmonious arrangement of the Forms, they develop a desire to imitate that harmony in some way or other (500C). And then he adds that if it becomes necessary for the philosophers to imitate the Forms by molding human character in their likeness, they will be in an excellent position to do this job well. So it is clear that when the philosophers rule, they do not stop looking to or imitating the Forms. Rather their imitative activity is no longer merely contemplative; instead, they start acting in a way that produces a harmony in the city that is a likeness of the harmony of the Forms. Furthermore, were they to refuse to rule, they would be allowing the disorder in the city to increase. Were any single philosopher to shirk her responsibilities, and let others do more than their fair share, then she would be undermining a fair system of dividing responsibilities. The order that would be appropriate to their situation would be undermined. And so failure to rule, whether in an individual philosopher or in a group of them, would create a certain disharmony in the world: Relationships that are appropriate among people would be violated. And in creating this disharmony, the philosopher would in one respect cease to imitate the Forms. She would gaze at the order that is appropriate among Forms but would thereby upset an order that is appropriate among human beings" (Richard Kraut, "The Defense of Justice in Plato's *Republic*, 1992, 328).

Cf. Donald Morrison, "Happiness, rationality, and egoism in Plato's Socrates," 2003, 21: "It is reasonable to read the *Republic* as implying that philosopher-kings will be motivated to promote the good as such, to increase the goodness around them as much as they are able."

7. Terence Irwin makes the point: "Plato does not tell us in any detail what he takes happiness to be ..." (*The Development of Ethics*, I: *From Socrates to the Reformation*, 2007, 91).

8. Plato does give further argument in *Republic* IX. For a brief statement of the arguments, see C. C. W. Taylor, "Platonic Ethics," 1998a, 68–69. For a more thorough discussion, see Julia Annas, *An Introduction to Plato's* Republic, 1981, 305–320.

Further Reading for Part III

1. *An Introduction to Plato's* Republic, Julia Annas, 1981
   Annas concentrates "on bringing out the lines of moral argument" in the *Republic* (v). The discussion is beautifully written. The interpretations are sensible.
2. *Plato's Ethics* (1995) and *The Development of Ethics. I: From Socrates to the Reformation* (2007), Terence Irwin
   Chapters 9 and 10 of *Plato's Ethics* discuss, among other things, the Theory of Recollection and the Theory of Forms. Chapters 11–18 discuss the *Republic*. The book is a definitive treatment of the subject. It is not, however, always easy going. Irwin himself makes the point: "Though I have tried not to presuppose extensive acquaintance with philosophy, some parts of the book are fairly detailed, and may try the patience of less experienced readers" (11).
3. *Pythagoras and the Pythagoreans. A Brief History*, Charles Kahn, 2001
   This is a wonderful "survey of the whole [Pythagorean] tradition, period by period, reflecting contemporary scholarship" (x). The early part of this tradition is important for understanding Plato, and Kahn provides a clear and thoughtful explanation of this tradition. He also provides a nice explanation of the subsequent Neopythagorean tradition and its connection to Neoplatonism.
4. "Plato," Richard Kraut, 1992 (http://plato.stanford.edu/entries/plato/)
   This is a brief but insightful general introduction to Plato.
5. *Unity and Development in Plato's Metaphysics*, William J. Prior, 1985
   This is a nice introduction to one of the more difficult parts of Plato's philosophy. The focus is on "the Theory of Forms and the doctrine of Being and Becoming" (1).
6. *Plato*, Christopher Rowe, 2003
   This is probably the best general introduction to Plato. "The book attempts to provide a connected account of Plato's main themes and arguments." It is historically and philosophically informed.
7. *A Companion to Plato's* Republic, Nicholas P. White, 1979
   This discussion is analytical. White attempts "to follow step by step . . . the main argument, to show how that argument is articulated, to show the important connections among its elements, and, above, all, to show thereby that there is a coherent and carefully developed train of thought which motivates virtually everything in the work" (1).

Part IV

Aristotle

*The first great Platonist and Plato's first
great critic*

6

Second Philosophy

A teleological conception of natural bodies and their specific behavior

Aristotle reinvigorated the philosophy of physics. This part of philosophy had emerged in reaction to the Milesian revolution, but it was almost immediately pushed into the background when Socrates took up ethical matters and the good life. Plato turns to the philosophy of physics late in the corpus. He worked out the beginnings of a conception of the reality of natural bodies, and Aristotle tried to remove the problems he thought he perceived in Plato's work. One of these problems concerns the forms, objects Plato introduced with great enthusiasm but whose existence he never clearly explained. Aristotle thinks there are forms, but he conceives of these objects and their relation to natural bodies differently than Plato. He argues that the forms are particular objects. According to Aristotle, the forms of natural bodies are in matter and are separable only in account.

Aristotle[a] is the first great Platonist and Plato's first great critic. Plato recast the love of wisdom as an exercise of reason in connection with forms. He thought that the human good is psychological organization in imitation of the disincarnate soul. In this state, the soul is free from practical concerns and the need to exercise reason to meet these needs. It is fixed in an exercise of reason that involves knowledge of the forms and hence is fixed in the

---

[a] Aristotle was not an Athenian. He was born in 384 in Stagira on the Chalcidice peninsula, which extends into the northern reaches of the Aegean Sea. His father, a physician, died young. In 367, Aristotle was sent to Athens to study in the Academy. When Plato died in 347 the Academy passed to his nephew, Speusippus, so Aristotle left to join a philosophical circle in Assos on the Aegean coast. Later he moved to Mytilene on Lesbos, an island in the Aegean, to join Theophrastus, whom he knew from the Academy. In 343, Philip of Macedon invited Aristotle to serve as tutor to his son Alexander. After Philip died in 335, Aristotle returned to Athens and established his school, the Lyceum. When Aristotle left the Lyceum and Athens in 323, the school passed to Theophrastus. Alexander's death in 323 had allowed anti-Macedonian sentiment to surge in Athens. Aristotle left to save his life. He died a year later.

Ancient Greek Philosophy: From The Presocratics to the Hellenistic Philosophers, First Edition.
Thomas A. Blackson. © 2011 Thomas A. Blackson. Published 2011 by Blackwell Publishing Ltd.

contemplation of reality itself, as the forms are the reality of things. Plato, in the middle dialogues, does not have this conception of reality fully worked out. He provides more detail in the late dialogues, but the conception remained underspecified and perplexing in certain ways. It was left to his followers to solve the problems and work out the details, and Aristotle is the first and greatest philosopher in this tradition.

There is broad agreement on this general understanding of Aristotle, but the textual evidence is difficult to present in a clear and concise manner. The problem is that the Aristotelian corpus, as it now exists,[1] is composed of esoteric works[2] and is organized systematically. It is possible to start at the beginning with the logical works, but since these works are formal and preliminary for the most part, it is better to begin with the physical works (which follow the logical works) and to understand the logical works as anticipating the physical works. The physical works themselves are devoted to "second philosophy" or, to use a more literal translation, the "second love of wisdom" (or "the love of wisdom in a secondary way"). This inquiry provides a vantage point from which to understand how Aristotle transforms the conception of forms, and of reality more generally, which he inherited from Plato. Aristotle conceives of second philosophy so that it approximates first philosophy (or the "first love of wisdom", or "the love of wisdom in the primary way"[b]) and he conceives of first philosophy as the legitimate offspring of Plato's attempt to recast the love of wisdom.

6.1   Natural Bodies and their Specific Behaviors

Second philosophy is about natural bodies and their fundamental behaviors. Aristotle pursues this knowledge in the physical works, beginning in the *Physics*, which is the first and most general work in a long series of works

---

[b] In the *Metaphysics*, Aristotle says that "the theory of sensible substance is the work of physics and second philosophy (δευτέρας φιλοσοφίας)" (VII.11.1037a). In the *Physics*, he says that "the student of nature ... should confine himself to things which are separable in form, but which are in matter" and that "what is separable, and how things are with it, is the work of first philosophy" (II.2.194b). Aristotle understands the difference between first and second philosophy in terms of the difference in the "being," or existence, of the objects in their respective domains. In the *Metaphysics*, he says that "there are as many parts of philosophy (φιλοσοφίας) as there are kinds of substance ... For being falls into genera, and the sciences will correspond to these genera" (IV.2.1004a). Aristotle's conception of "being" in connection with first and second philosophy is the subject of a subsequent chapter.

devoted to natural bodies.^c These works unfold against the background assumption that natural bodies are real and that their fundamental behaviors are those they possess in virtue of their inclusion in natural kinds. In the *Physics* itself, Aristotle investigates the principles common to all natural bodies. In subsequent works in the sequence, he investigates the principles common to specific groups of natural bodies, such as living natural bodies.

Aristotle's belief in the reality of natural bodies may seem unexceptional, but it was a departure from the approach the inquirers into nature pursued.[3] As the inquiry into nature was understood in response to Parmenides' arguments, the natural bodies traditionally thought to exist are eliminated from the ontology. In the new conception of reality, there are only the objects that constitute the nature of reality. Nothing else exists. The significance of this conception of reality is particularly striking for living bodies. Such bodies and their behaviors are understood as appearances of the arrangements of the objects that constitute the nature of reality.

Aristotle, by contrast, understands natural bodies and their behavior from within the broad ontological framework of forms Plato introduced in his repudiation of the ontology the inquirers into nature had developed in their response to Parmenides. Aristotle begins with the idea that natural bodies are more than heaps of material. They have a certain unity or oneness. The material that constitutes a natural body is organized so that there exists a body that instantiates the natural kind to which the body belongs. This organization persists through the changes in the material that constitutes the body at various points in its history. Aristotle says that this organization is a *form*.^d Moreover, in the case of living bodies and perhaps in the case of all natural bodies, he says that the fundamental behaviors of these

---

^c In the Aristotelian corpus, the *Physics* is followed by *On the Heavens, On Generation and Corruption*, and *Meteorology*. This sequence is organized systematically. In the opening lines of the *Meteorology*, Aristotle says that he has discussed the first causes of nature (*Physics* I and II), natural movement in general (*Physics* III–VIII), the movements of the heavens (*On the heavens* I and II), the number and nature of the sublunar elements and their transformation into each other (*On the heavens* III and IV), and coming to be and passing away generally (*On Generation and Corruption*). In the *Meteorology* itself, Aristotle turns his attention to the next subject in the sequence: the things in the region nearest to the heavens.

^d Aristotle's doctrine is difficult, but it helps to keep in mind the way Plato had extended the use of the word. In Homer, the word occurs in connection with the human figure to connote visual form. It is the characteristic look that allows a person to be recognized despite the fact that strictly speaking he appears differently at different times, depending on whether he is standing, sitting, and so on. Plato extends this use of the word to cover the universal in ethical matters. The form underlies the various manifestations. Piety, for example, is a certain thing in one situation and a different thing in another, but the form is always the same. Aristotle applies this idea to natural bodies.

bodies are *for the sake of* an end fixed in nature. The form is the organization of the material so that there exists a natural body that functions, or works, in the ways that characterize the natural kind. This functioning is teleological. It is for the sake of an end that belongs to the body by nature.[4]

Demonstration

Aristotle has something of this conception of natural bodies in mind even in the logical works[e] in connection with the syllogisms[5] he calls "demonstrations."[6] Definitions are starting points for demonstrations. A definition expresses the "essence" of the species of the natural bodies under consideration, and a demonstration is a syllogistic argument that shows the natural bodies in question to have their specific behaviors because these bodies instantiate the essence. Natural bodies of a certain kind have a certain organization in their material, and this organization is the cause of their specific behavior.[f]

Aristotle's extant discussions of natural bodies are investigations, not finished science, and so these discussions do not contain demonstrations. The following example, however, which turns on the familiar Aristotelian idea that "man is the rational animal," indicates what he seems to have in mind. Where rational animal is the essence of human beings, and judgment in terms of sensation is the specific behavior in question, the demonstration takes the following form:

(1) Human beings are rational animals   (All A are B)
(2) Rational animals make judgments in terms of sensation. (All B are C)
_____   _____

(3) Human beings make judgments in terms of sensation.   (All A are C)

This syllogism displays some of the structure that informs the bodies within the natural kind, human being. Each human being has a recognizable unity, or oneness, that persists through the changes it undergoes at various points in its history. Aristotle, in the physical works, explains this oneness in terms

---

[e] The logical works precede the physical works and are arranged systematically. The *Categories* is first. It discusses terms, the parts of sentences. The *Categories* is followed by *On Interpretation*, which discusses sentences, the parts of syllogisms. *On Interpretation* is followed by the *Prior* and *Posterior Analytics*. The *Prior Analytics* discusses the syllogism. The *Posterior Analytics* discusses demonstration, which is a kind of syllogism.

[f] *Prior Analytics* I.1.24b, 1.4.25b, *Posterior Analytics* I.2.71b, *Topics* I.5.101b, *Physics* II.3.194b, *On the Soul* I.1.402b, *Metaphysics* VII.6.1031b, XI.7.1064a.

of a form that unifies the material constituting the body. This form is specified in the account of what a human being is. The form is the organization of the material so that the power to make judgments in terms of sensations is part of the organization that makes the material be a rational animal. In this way, the form is the organization of the material so that there exists a human being who, by being human, has the power to make judgments in terms of sensations.

Induction

Aristotle supposes that the definitions necessary for demonstration are known in a process he calls "induction." There must, he argues, be knowledge of the starting points if there is knowledge of the demonstrations themselves. Furthermore, according to Aristotle, this knowledge of the starting points of demonstrations cannot itself be demonstrative knowledge. Otherwise, the knowledge of the demonstrations would be circular or constitute a vicious regress (*Posterior Analytics* I.3.72b). It would be "absurd," he says, to have this knowledge and to suppose it "escapes notice." Aristotle thus denies that knowledge of starting points is an innate part of the human psychology. Instead, he maintains that this knowledge is acquired over time in a process he calls "induction":

> It is impossible to know through demonstration if we do not know the starting points. If we already know them, it is absurd. We would have knowledge more fundamental than demonstration and yet this escapes notice. But if we somehow get them, we cannot have learned them without prior knowledge. So it follows that we must get them in some other way and have some other sort of capacity to acquire knowledge of them. And in fact all animals have the capacity for perception. If perception is present, in some there is the retention of the precept, but in others there is not. For those in which there is no retention, there is no knowledge outside of perceiving. For those in which there is retention, when many such things come about, then a difference comes about, so that some gain reason,[7] and others do not. From perception comes memory, and from memory, when it occurs many times in connection with the same thing, comes experience, as memories which are many in number form a single experience. And from experience, or from the whole universal that has come to rest in the soul, the one apart from the many, the one which is the same in those things, there comes a starting point for art and knowledge, for art when the starting point concerns how things come about, and for knowledge when it concerns what is. Thus it is clear that it is necessary for us to know the first things by induction. (*Posterior Analytics* II.19.99b–100b[8])

Aristotle thinks that human beings are naturally subject to a certain causal process, a process that begins with sense impressions, involves memory and experience, and somehow ends with the presence of "reason" and the knowledge of the definitions necessary for demonstration.[9]

Aristotle provides few details about induction, in the *Posterior Analytics* or elsewhere in the corpus, but it is possible to understand his theory of induction as part of an attempt to correct what he regards as Platonic mistakes. Plato thought that some knowledge is innate, and he joined this thesis about the structure of the soul with a thesis about the relation of the soul to the body. Aristotle rejects both theses. The soul does not preexist the body. Nor are human beings born with knowledge of the definitions necessary for demonstration. Instead, according to Aristotle, they come to possess this knowledge through the process of "induction." Aristotle says that "experience" is necessary for the presence of this knowledge, but this "experience" is not evidence for the knowledge. Aristotle is a rationalist. The knowledge is a matter of the cognition involved in "reason," but this cognition occurs only after there is a certain amount of "experience."[8]

6.2   Natures are Forms

Aristotle sets out some of the argument for his conception of natural bodies in a discussion of the "nature" and "cause" of natural bodies. He begins with the assumption that natural bodies have a certain unity, or oneness, that functions as a "starting point of change and staying unchanged." Aristotle says that this "starting point" is the "nature" of the body (*Physics* II.1.192b). The "nature" is the "cause" of the unity, or oneness, that characterizes natural bodies. It is the unifying factor in the history of a natural body so that this history is a sequence of changes in *one* object. In the absence of the nature, there is only a sequence of different arrangements of material.

To determine what the nature of a natural body is, Aristotle considers the two historically prior approaches to the question. The first is from the Presocratic tradition. Instead of recognizing the existence of the natural

---

[8] As Michael Ferejohn says in his discussion of induction in *The Origins of Aristotelian Science*, "the 'inductive' process ... [occurs] not just [in] the Aristotelian scientist, but [in every] ... well-developed mature human specimen ..., solely by virtue of having a rational soul..." (1991, 47–48). Induction, in this way, as a natural process, is an instance of teleological causation. There is more discussion of this point in the next chapter.

bodies salient in experience, this tradition eliminates these objects in favor of an ontology in which the only objects are the ones that constitute the nature of reality:

> Some identify the nature and substance of a natural body with the material, so the wood is the nature of the bed, the bronze the nature of the statue. A sign of this, says Antiphon,[10] is that if you bury a bed and the thing acquires the power to send up a shoot, what comes up will be wood, not a bed. This shows that the arrangement is accidental and that the substance is what persists. So some say earth is the nature of things, others fire, air, water, some or all of these. This or these they declare to be the whole substance, everything else its affections, states, or dispositions. (*Physics* II.1.193a)

The second approach is Platonic. It identifies the reality underlying change with form. Aristotle says that this second answer is superior to the answer he associates with the inquirers into nature:

> Another account is that nature is the shape and form, which is specified in the definition. What is potentially flesh or bone has not yet its own nature, and does not exist by nature, until it receives the form specified in the definition, which we name in defining what flesh or bone is. So on this understanding, the nature of things that have in them a starting point of change is the form, something not separable except in account. The form is more the nature than the matter because a thing is something when it is actually, not when it is potentially or in possibility. (*Physics* II.1.193a–b)

In the absence of the form (which is specified in the account), there is only a heap of materials, or, as Aristotle himself says, a natural body "in possibility." The form unifies the materials so that there exists a natural body of a certain kind. Such forms, however, according to Aristotle, do not exist in the way Plato supposed. Aristotle believes that the forms of natural bodies are *in matter* and are *separable only in account*. They are not separable completely and without qualification.

The picture from the Academy

To get a clearer understanding of what Aristotle has in mind, it is helpful to contrast his conception with the one Plato sketches in the *Timaeus*.[h]

---

[h] The *Timaeus* is a late dialogue in which there is detailed discussion of the natural world. The participants in the dialogue are Socrates, Timaeus, Critias, and Hermocrates. Socrates, the previous day, described "the state and its citizens" (17c). Now it is time for Timaeus and Critias to speak. Timaeus goes first, and it is agreed that his discussion will begin with "the birth of the world and end with the nature of man" (27a).

Socrates, in this dialogue, has given up his role of chief interlocutor. Timaeus now leads the discussion,[11] as he has "made knowledge of the nature of the whole his chief object" (27a), and in the ensuing lecture on cosmology, Timaeus develops a conception of natural bodies in terms of the forms and what he calls the "receptacle."

Timaeus introduces the forms in his discussion of the ontological framework he presupposes. To theorize about the nature of the whole properly, he says it is necessary to distinguish "that which is always and has no birth" and "that which is becoming always but never is" (27d–28a). Timaeus does not name the forms in this passage, but it is clear, in light of two subsequent passages in which he alludes to the distinction he has just made, that the forms are "that which is always":

> A new starting point in my account is necessary. We distinguished two kinds but now must declare a third. In the earlier account, one was the model or paradigm, intelligible and ever changeless. The second was as an imitation of the model, becoming and visible. (*Timaeus* 48e–49a)

> That which has not been brought into being and is not destroyed, which neither receives into itself anything else from anywhere else, nor itself enters into anything else anywhere, is invisible and cannot be perceived by the senses, it is for intellect to regard. The second is named after the former and so it is similar, perceived by the senses, begotten, constantly borne along, coming to be in a certain place and then perishing out of it, it is apprehended by opinion with the help of sensation. (*Timaeus* 52a)

In these passages, the form of X-ness is the being or existence of X-ness. X-ness has this being according to itself. The existence of X-ness is incompatible with change. It "is always and has no birth." The many X-things do not so exist. Each "is becoming always but never is."[12]

The new starting point Timaeus mentions is the "receptacle." He says, in the continuation of 49a, that "a third we did not distinguish, thinking that two would suffice, but now, it seems, the argument compels us to attempt to bring to light and to describe a kind difficult and obscure, the receptacle of all becoming." The natural bodies, in this way, are not starting points in reality. They are "born," and the receptacle plays a role in this birth. Timaeus' description of this ontology is difficult to understand, but the general idea is that natural bodies are products of two more basic parts of the ontology: the receptacle and the forms. Over time, parts of the receptacle become like the separately existing forms fire, air, earth, and water, and as these parts of the receptacle become like these forms, portions of fire, air, water, and earth are "born" (48b–c, 50b–d, 51a–b, 52b–c). The non-elemental bodies are compounds made out of these elemental bodies.

Aristotle too conceives of natural bodies in terms of forms, but he tries to remove problems he perceives in the ontology Plato sketches in the middle dialogues and later supplements in the *Timaeus*. Aristotle eliminates the receptacle. And further, whereas Timaeus seems to conceive of the opposition between unchanging forms and changing images in the receptacle in terms of the the opposition between unchanging general objects and changing particular objects, Aristotle denies the existence of general objects. They are not part of his considered ontology. Aristotle supposes that the forms of natural bodies are numerically distinct but specifically identical particular objects. Each form is the reality of the organization of different material, but the organization itself is the same because it is the one specified in the definition of the natural kind. Thus, for Aristotle, but not for Plato, the forms of natural bodies are separable from matter only in account.

6.3   Teleology in Nature

Despite this difference in the ontology of forms, Aristotle stands squarely with Plato against the inquirers into nature. Thales and the Milesian inquirers into nature broke from the older school of thought represented by Hesiod and the theologists. Unlike Hesiod and the theologists, Thales and the Milesian inquirers into nature did not invoke the traditional pantheon of gods in their explanations of natural phenomena. Moreover, although Anaxagoras may be an exception, the inquirers into nature did not replace the purposes of the gods with any sort of teleology. Aristotle argues that this ontology is mistaken. Specific behavior, he insists, is not a "coincidence." This behavior does not simply appear in coincidence with the necessary behavior of the objects that constitute the nature of reality. According to Aristotle, this understanding of reality is "impossible":

> Why should not nature work, not for the sake of something, nor because it is better, but as it rains, not to make the corn grow, but of necessity? What is drawn up must cool, and having cooled, must turn to water and descend, and that the corn grows happens together with this. Equally, if someone's corn rots on the threshing-floor, the rain did not fall for the sake of this, so that the corn rots, but this happens concurrently with the rain. And why should not the same be true with the parts in nature, that our front teeth come up of necessity sharp and fit for biting, the back teeth broad and fit for grinding, not for the sake of this, but as a coincidence, and so also with other parts in which the "for something" seems present? When things turned out just as if they had come to be for the sake of an end, they survived, being organized automatically in a fitting way; when

they did not, they perished, just as Empedocles says of his man-faced ox progeny.[i] This argument, or others of the kind, might cause difficulty. Yet it is impossible for things to be this way. (*Physics* II.8.198b)

The problem, as Aristotle understands it, is that according to the conception of reality the inquirers into nature invoke in their explanations, what is ordinarily thought of as an instance of specific behavior is really nothing more than the coincidental behavior of the objects that constitute the nature of reality. The natural bodies ordinarily thought to exist do not themselves do anything. They do not take in food or reproduce. They do not exercise these, or any other, specific behaviors because in reality these natural bodies do not exist.

In *On the Parts of Animals*,[j] Aristotle explains why the inquirers into nature went wrong and why their mistake went uncorrected. In "ancient times," he says, those who talked about generation concerned themselves only with the material parts. Thus, as Aristotle understands the prior philosophical tradition, the importance of the essence and definition in connection with natural bodies went unrecognized because the "love of wisdom" was in its infancy. Socrates introduced some clarity into this discipline by searching for answers to the "What is it?" question with respect to ethical matters, but this did not result in the proper understanding of natural bodies because Socrates himself was not interested in nature (*On the Parts of Animals* I.1.640b, 642a).

It is difficult to know whether Aristotle is correct about the "ancient times." The work on the generation of natural bodies is fragmentary. There is, however, a treatise in the medical tradition that supports Aristotle's understanding of the history. According to *On the Nature of the Child*, representative bodily "parts" from the parents heap up in the female. Once there, the embryo results from two naturally occurring processes involving the elements "air" and "fire":

> If the seed . . . remains in the womb . . ., it acquires breath, since it is in a warm environment. . . . [T]he breath makes a passage for itself in the middle of the seed and escapes. . . . [It then] inspires from the mother a second quantity of breath, which is cool. It continues to do this. . . . The warmth of its

---

[i] DK 31 B 61.

[j] In the works devoted to the study of natural objects, there is a series devoted to the study of living natural bodies. This series begins with *On the Soul* and includes several more specific studies of animals. *On the Parts of Animals* is one of these more specific studies. It is preceded by *On the History of Animals* and followed by *On the Movement of Animals*, *On the Progression of Animals*, and *On the Generation of Animals*.

environment heats it, and it acquires cold breath from the mother's breathing (12.1.[13]). The seed, then ... grows because of its mother's blood, which descends to the womb (14). [F]lesh begins to be formed, with the umbilicus, through which the embryo breathes and grows ... (15). As the flesh grows it is formed into distinct members by breath. Each thing in it goes to its similar.... Each settles in its appropriate place.... The bones grow hard as a result of the coagulating action of heat.... The head begins to project from the shoulders.... The sex of the genitals becomes plain. The entrails too are formed into distinct parts.... Now the formation of each of these parts occurs through respiration – that is to say, they become filled with air and separate, according to their various affinities. Suppose you were to tie a bladder to the end of a pipe, and insert through the pipe earth, sand, and fine filings of lead. Now pour in water, and blow through the pipe. First of all the ingredients will be thoroughly mixed with the water, but after you have blown for a time, the lead will move towards the lead, the sand towards the sand, and the earth towards the earth.... Now the seed, or rather the flesh, is separated into members by precisely the same process. (17)

According to the picture in these passages, the representative parts from the male and female are blown to their respective places by the "air" that moves in and out of the heap as the female breathes. As these parts are blown to their respective places, the "fire" that heats the female body cements the resulting heaps together into the organs, bones, and other parts of the embryo.

This account of sexual generation, although primitive, can appear to a modern reader as a step in the direction of progress. Aristotle, however, supposes otherwise. He does not deny that accounts in terms of the elements are possible. Rather, he is convinced that such accounts are not explanations of specific behavior because these accounts contain no natural body to exercise the behavior being explained. To understand this, two points must be kept in mind.

First of all, if these accounts from the medical tradition are to be taken as representative of the accounts the inquirers into nature gave, then the references to the male, the female, the embryo, and so on, must be understood in terms of the notion of "custom" the inquirers into nature employed in their response to Parmenides. That is to say, in *On the Nature of the Child*, the references to the male, the female, and so on, must be understood as the customary, but literally false, way to talk about what is an arrangement of the objects that constitute the nature of reality.

Secondly, it is important to notice that some events presuppose the existence of certain objects because the events are essentially a matter of someone, or something, doing something. Consider the building of a house. One could describe the movements of the nails, boards, and other materials, without mentioning the builder who directs the movement of these materials, but this set of movements is not the same as the event of building a house. The movement of the materials is compatible with an indeterminate number of processes other than house-building. The materials could have become arranged because someone was picking through a pile and throwing the various items aside as he searched for treasure. In this case, a house came into existence, but not by being built. The same is true if the arrangement were the result of an earthquake or a storm.

In the *Phaedo*, in the intellectual autobiography passage, Socrates makes this sort of point in connection with the explanations of human actions. He tells his interlocutors how very excited he was when he first heard that Anaxagoras[k] appealed to something he called "Mind" in his explanations of things. Socrates, however, immediately goes on to say that his initial excitement quickly gave way to extreme disappointment once he actually read what Anaxagoras had to say. He had hoped Anaxagoras was an exception to the ongoing trend to eliminate ordinary objects. In fact, however, as Socrates says, with his characteristic biting humor, Anaxagoras made no use of his "Mind." To Socrates, Anaxagoras is absurd. He is like someone who tries to understand human actions in terms of the various ways the parts of the body are organized and disposed:

> It seemed to me like saying that Socrates does with his mind whatever he does, but then, in citing the causes of what I do, saying that I am sitting here because my body consists of bones and sinews, because the bones are hard and separated by joints, that the sinews contract and relax, and so on, but neglecting the true causes, that the Athenians decided it was better to condemn me, and so I have decided it is better to sit here and more just to remain and endure the penalty they ordered. (*Phaedo* 98c–e)

Socrates insists, invoking common sense, that his actions are things he himself does. He is the cause of his action. An account of the motion of the bones, sinews, and so on, might describe the motion of the parts of his body, but his action is not the same as the motion of the parts of his body. Socrates insists that his actions are things *he* does because *he thinks it better*.

---

[k] "Ionian science was introduced into Athens by Anaxagoras about the time Euripides was born ... " (John Burnet, *Early Greek Philosophy*, 1920, 10). "Anaxagoras was the first philosopher to settle at Athens, where he spent some twenty years (under the patronage of Pericles) until his prosecution or persecution for impiety" (A. A. Long, "Lives and writings of the early Greek philosophers," 1999a, xvii). His accounts of the heavens brought him into conflict with the traditional religion. In the *Apology*, Socrates says that Anaxagoras' books sold for a "drachma, at most, in the books shops" (26d10–e1). A drachma seems to have been worth a day's work for a laborer.

Aristotle generalizes this position. His interest is in the behavior that characterizes the kind, and he thinks that the motion of bodily parts is compatible with an indeterminate number of processes that are not instances of the natural body itself exercising the behaviors characteristic of the kind to which it belongs. To use a modern example, the changes in the materials involved in an instance of something digesting something could take place in glassware in a laboratory, but these changes would not be an instance of digestion because nothing digests anything.[14] Aristotle is convinced that there is specific behavior only if there exist natural bodies to exercise this behavior. In addition, for at least some and perhaps all natural bodies, he is convinced that there are natural bodies to exercise specific behavior only if the exercise of this specific behavior is *teleological*.[15] Natural bodies have a certain unity or oneness, according to Aristotle. This unity or oneness consists in the organization of the materials so that there exists an object that persists and functions in the ways that define objects of the natural kind. This functioning is in the exercise of specific behavior, and Aristotle thinks that this behavior is *for the sake of* an end fixed in nature.

In an effort to remove the resistance to his conception of natural bodies, Aristotle argues that the lack of deliberation in nature does not undercut the belief that "art" and "nature" function in the same way. The example of a doctor who heals himself is supposed to illustrate the point:

> It is absurd to suppose that purpose and the "for something" is not present because we do not observe deliberation. Art does not deliberate. If the ship-building art were in the wood, it would produce the same results by nature. And so if the "for something" is present in art, it is also present in nature. An example is when a doctor doctors himself: nature is like that. (*Physics* II.8.199b)

In certain circumstances, a doctor automatically takes action that results in the elimination of an illness that has befallen him. The doctor has no need to deliberate because he has seen the problem and its remedy so many times in the past. Yet, despite the lack of deliberation in the particular case, the doctor's action would be regarded as rational and for the sake of eliminating the illness. Hence, Aristotle concludes that the lack of deliberation is no bar to teleology in nature.

Aristotle, in this way, has the beginnings of a solution to a problem that had confounded Plato in the middle dialogues. In the *Phaedo*, Socrates says that he hoped Anaxagoras would show him why "Mind" placed and arranged things in the best way possible. This hope, however, was disappointed, and Socrates himself is unable to construct such explanations, so he settles for the kinds of explanations he discovers as a "second best" in his search for understanding:

> I was pleased with this cause and it seemed to me somehow right that Mind should be the cause of all things. If this were so, I thought, Mind would arrange everything and establish it in the way it was best for it. And so if one wished to know the cause of each thing, why it comes to be or perishes or exists, he had to find what was the best way for it to be. And as I considered these things I was delighted to think that I had found in Anaxagoras a teacher about the cause of things in accordance with my own mind, and that he would tell me, first, whether the earth is flat or round, and then would explain why it is so of necessity, saying which is better, and that it was better to be so.[1] (*Phaedo* 97c–e)

> I would gladly become the student of any man who taught me that kind of cause, but since I was denied that, and could neither discover it myself nor learn it from another, do you wish me to give you an explanation of how, as a second best, I conducted my search for the cause of things? (*Phaedo* 99c–d)

The explanations he discovers are in terms of forms. They are not the kind of explanations he had hoped to find because they do not explain why things happen in terms of the relation of the change to what is best. Aristotle, by contrast, given his conception of natural bodies, can avoid this disappointment if he can work out a way in which specific behavior in natural bodies is exercised for the sake of the best existence possible. The way Aristotle works this out begins to become clear in his discussion of the form of living natural bodies, which is the subject of the next chapter.

Notes

1. The Aristotelian corpus became organized by content at some point after Aristotle's death. The logical works come first. They are followed by the physical works. The ethical and political works are last. This systematic organization may not stem from Aristotle himself. The history of the corpus and its organization is uncertain. Pierre Pellegrin sets out the story: "The history of this transmission is of the most romantic sort, and it is impossible completely to disentangle the true from the legendary in the accounts that have come down to us. Theophrastus, Aristotle's successor as head of the Lyceum, left his library containing Aristotle's works in particular to Neleus of Skepsis, the son of his

---

[1] David Gallop sets Socrates' discussion in the intellectual autobiography passage in its proper historical context: "[*Phaedo* 97b–98b] marks the transition from a mechanistic to a teleological conception of the natural order that was to dominate European science for the next two thousand years" (*Plato*, Phaedo, 1986, 175).

former co-disciple Coriscus. This is no doubt the same Coriscus whom Aristotle often takes as an example of an individual man. As the kings of Pergamum, the Attalids, wanted to build a library able to rival that of Alexandria, and to that end conducted a veritable hunt for books, the heirs of Neleus, fearing their possessions would be stolen from them, hid Aristotle's works in a cellar, from which they were not removed until a century and a half later by a certain Appellicon of Teos, who was in the employ of the king Mithridates. Appellicon had copies made of Aristotle's texts. When Mithridates was defeated by the Romans, the library in question ended up in Rome in the hands of Tyrranion, a remarkable man who was Cicero's librarian and the tutor of his son, who took up the project of editing Aristotle's works. But the enterprise was really brought to completion only by Andronicus of Rhodes, the eleventh successor to Aristotle as head of the Lyceum (from about 70 to 50 BCE). Andronicus corrected and edited the texts of Aristotle and, most important, set them in the order in which they have been transmitted to us" ("The Aristotelian way," 2006, 239–240). For discussion of the texts and the revival of Aristotelianism, see Michael Frede, "Epilogue," 1999b, 772–776.

2. The distinction between "esoteric" and "exoteric" works is a distinction between works written for insiders – people in the place – and works written for outsiders – people outside the place. "According to evidence supplied by various ancient sources, and confirmed by references in the extant writings themselves, Aristotle's works fall into two broad categories: finished literary productions intended for circulation among a general audience outside the Lyceum – the so-called 'exoteric works' (*exoterikoi logoi*); and a variety of more specialized studies apparently intended to support the research and teaching activities of Aristotle's school. To the first category belonged dialogues and treatises dealing primarily with moral, political, and literary subjects. With the exception of a treatise in defense of the study of philosophy – the *Protrepticus* – which has been substantially reconstructed in recent years from other ancient sources, these works have been almost entirely lost. To the second category belonged a series of 'catalogues' or compilations of historical and other information, and a large number of more or less elaborate and finished treatises on all subjects. Apart from a study of Athenian constitutional history discovered less than a century ago, and generally assumed to form part of the massive catalogue of 'constitutions' (*politeiai*) that was produced by Aristotle and his students, most of the catalogue material has also been lost. The Aristotelian corpus as it exists today consists overwhelmingly, then, of the specialized treaties" (Carnes Lord, "The character and composition of Aristotle's *Politics*," 1981, 460–461).

3. Susan Sauvé Meyer makes the essential point. She says that Aristotle's opponents, as he understands them, impugn "the ontological credentials of plants and animals" because they say that plants and animals do not exist or occur in their own right, but only insofar as something else exists or occurs. "In claiming that such a development is accidental, Aristotle's opponents relegate it to a

category of entity beyond the scope of science, for science does not deal with the accidental (*APst.* 87b19–22; *Met.* 1026b4–5). This is not to admit that the development is due to supernatural causes, for they can specify material causes sufficient for its occurrence. Rather, it is to claim that if we consider the development of an animal (or plant) to be something other than the simple conjunction of independent activities of the material elements, there really isn't anything to explain. This is why Aristotle says that accidents are close to nonbeing (*Met.* 1026b14–15); they do not exist or occur in their own right, but only insofar as something else exists or occurs (1025a28–29). . . . [Thus, by] claiming that the development of the parts of plants and animals is accidental and hence inexplicable, Aristotle's opponents impugn not the explanatory power of their own physical theory, but the ontological credentials of plants and animals" ("Aristotle, teleology, and reduction," 2008a, 824–825). Other commentators have made similar points. Michael Frede is an important example: "Aristotle wants to hold on to the metaphysical primacy of objects, natural objects, living objects, human beings. He does not want these to be mere configurations of more basic entities, such that the real things turn out to be these more basic entities. But to look at an object just as the configuration of material constituents transiently happen to enter into is to look at the material constituents as the more basic entities. So since Aristotle, against the view of practically all his predecessors, wants to hold on to the ontological priority of objects, he introduces essences which guarantee this status. This might be tied to, as we should put it, an epistemological point. What we try to understand when we do science are the ordinary objects around us. There might be something radically misguided about any view which interprets scientific theories which we develop in order to understand these ordinary objects and their behaviour in such a way that these objects are no longer of any significance in our scientific view of things" ("On Aristotle's conception of the soul," 1992, 146–147).

4. Aristotle seems to have living things primarily in mind. "Aristotle nowhere maintains that everything which is due to nature is for an end; on the contrary, as we have seen, he holds that things which are due to nature in the sense of matter are not for anything, but are just necessary unconditionally. What he maintains is that *some of the things* which are due to nature are for something. This is the sense of his cautious remark that 'the "for something" is present in things which are and come to be due to nature' (199a7–9; cf. 30, b10, 200a8). The things due to nature which Aristotle holds are for something are in fact the organic parts and the natural or unconstrained changes in respect of size, shape, place, etc., of plants and animals, and not even all of these: eyes, for instance, are for something, but they may not be blue for anything (*De gen. an.* V 778a30–b1, 616–19)" (W. Charlton, *Aristotle's* Physics I, II, 1970, 120–121).

5. The doctrine of the syllogism is due to Aristotle and marks the beginning of formal logic. "[Aristotle's] primary interest was in laying down the conditions of scientific knowledge; this is announced as his purpose at the beginning of the

Prior Analytics, and towards this the formal study of syllogism is the first step" (David Ross, *Aristotle*, 1949, 32).

6. Aristotle's theory of demonstration is complex, and my discussion is necessarily brief and indicates the general idea only. For a detailed discussion, see Michael Ferejohn's *The Origins of Aristotelian Science*, 1991.

7. It is easy to misunderstand what Aristotle means when he says that human beings acquire "reason" through the process of induction. Michael Frede provides some of the necessary explanation. He stresses that what human beings acquire is a certain expertise: "Aristotle quite explicitly says (*APo.* B19.100a2) that reason only comes into being as we acquire the appropriate concepts of things and thereby the knowledge of things and their principles which the mastery of these concepts embodies" ("Introduction" in *Rationality in Greek Thought*, 1996a, 11). "Now, one crucial point for my purposes is this: I have talked a lot about 'reason,' but in the passages I have discussed so far, in particular in *Metaph.* A1, the word 'reason' itself does not actually occur. Now, in B19, the crucial word '*logos*' finally does occur, namely in 100a2. It is used to refer to precisely the disposition of the mind or soul in virtue of which, or perhaps rather in which, we know first principles, and he talks of this disposition as something we come to acquire. I infer from this, though the conclusion seems striking and surprising (given our intuitions about, and our understanding of, reason), that Aristotle assumes that we are not born with reason, but acquire it, and that, in Aristotle's view, to have reason, to be fully rational or reasonably, is to know first principles" ("Aristotle's rationalism," 1996b, 169).

8. References to lines in a work of the Aristotelian corpus are to the edition Immanuel Bekker produced in 1833. This standard edition of the Greek text of Aristotle has been superseded, but scholars still use the Bekker numbers as a common reference. My translations aim for understanding, not literalness. This makes the texts more readable, but the result is often more paraphrase than translation. The current standard collection of translations is *The Complete Works of Aristotle*, but the editor does not give them a very strong endorsement. He prefers a strictly literal translation into what he calls "tough English" (Jonathan Barnes, *The Complete Works of Aristotle*, 1984, ix–xi). For an example of such a rendering of the Greek, see Montgomery Furth, *Aristotle's* Metaphysics. *Books Zeta, Eta, Theta, Iota (VII–X)* (1985). The Clarendon Aristotle Series at Oxford University Press also provides very close translations, as well as philosophical commentary. In constructing my translations, I have consulted all of these as well as the older translations in the *Perseus Digital Library* and the *MIT Internet Classics Archive*.

9. Aristotle here seems to depend on elements of an earlier empirical tradition. This tradition itself is not well preserved and hence is not well understood. Plato mentions it in the intellectual autobiography passage at 96b in the *Phaedo*.

10. Antiphon was a speech-writer, primarily in the area of homicide law, active in Athens in the last quarter of the fifth century BC. He played a role in the

revolution of the Four Hundred in 411 and, as a result, was brought to trial and convicted on charges of treason. He apparently made a great speech in his own defense but was convicted and executed nevertheless (Thucydides, *History of the Peloponnesian War*, 8.68; Plutarch, *Moralia* 834a–b).

11. The character Timaeus seems not to have corresponded to any historical person. "There is no evidence for the historic existence of Timaeus of Locri. If he did exist, we know nothing whatever about him beyond Socrates' description of him as a man well-born and rich, who had held the highest offices at Locri and became eminent in philosophy (20A), and Critias' remark that Timaeus was the best astronomer in the party and had made a special study of the nature of the universe. This is consistent with his being a man in middle life, contemporary with Hermocrates. The very fact that a man of such distinction has left not the faintest trace in political or philosophic history is against his claim to be a real person. The probability is that Plato invented him because he required a philosopher of the Western school, eminent both in science and statesmanship, and there was no one to fill the part at the imaginary time of the dialogue. Archytas was of the type required, a brilliant mathematician and seven times *strategus* at Terentum; but he lived too late. Plato first met him about 388 BC" (F. M. Cornford, *Plato's Cosmology*, 1937, 2–3).

12. It is extremely difficult to see what exactly Plato has in mind in this ontology. In "Being and becoming in Plato," Michael Frede offers the following suggestion: "Why should we not say that Socrates has such a nature as to have the marks of a human being and hence really is a man? It is not clear what the answer is supposed to be. There seems some wavering on Plato's part. But if we come to the *Timaeus* the answer seems to be the following: if we look at Socrates to find what it is that is a man and to see whether it is a man of its own nature, all we find is some material which only temporarily takes on the form of man, and ultimately, if we push the analysis further, some matter which is nothing in its own right and which can only be described metaphorically as part of some randomly shifting chaos. So underlying the marks or looks which the world around us displays there are no natures or essences which would produce these marks. To put the matter grossly: there is no reality underlying the appearances" (1988, 50).

13. For translation and commentary, see I. Lonie's *The Hippocratic Treatises On Generation, On the Nature of the Child, Disease IV: A Commentary* (1981). My translations follow Lonie's translations.

14. Michael Frede gives this example. "There . . . is nothing in Aristotle to prevent us from saying that this process can be understood and explained in terms of the appropriate kind of chemistry. And yet to understand the process this way is not to understand it as the natural process it is. Presumably the same process, as described in material terms, could be reproduced artificially. But if it were, it would not be a case of digestion. And this not because it lacked some details or some mysterious quality the natural process has, but because it, as a whole and its details, would have to be explained differently. What makes the digestion of

food the process it is, and hence is essential to our understanding of it, is that it is the exercise of the capacity or ability of this kind of organism to digest food. And similarly for the other life functions. In each case there is a material description in terms of material parts of the organism and of what happens to them in terms of their properties. But in each case the process is the natural or physical process it is, rather than a materially equivalent but formally different process only, because it is the exercise of an ability the organism has in virtue of its form or soul" ("On Aristotle's conception of the soul," 1992, 150).

15. Many commentators offer an interpretation along these general lines. Christopher Shields is a recent and influential example: "[Aristotle thinks that] there are general metaphysical reasons for supposing that at least some biological facts will ultimately, at least implicitly, rely on teleological principles. That is because he regards it as a non-conventional fact that some living organisms, substances like this particular woman or this particular horse, exhibit both synchronic and diachronic unity. . . . Aristotle supposes that this non-conventional fact requires explanation; and he doubts that it can be given in anything other than teleological terms" (*Classical Philosophy*, 2003, 132).

7

Psychology

Aristotle places the study of psychology within the study of natural bodies. Plato thought that human beings were psychological beings and that rationality is a matter of the organization of the parts of the soul. This presupposes that the human psychology might be disorganized, and hence it was necessary to consider the nature of the human psychology and the various organizations that were possible. Aristotle continues this work in psychology, but he rejects Plato's ontology of the soul and its relation to the body. Because the soul is the form of the living body, Aristotle supposes that it is separable only in account. Moreover, like his conception of natural bodies generally, Aristotle's conception of human beings is teleological. He argues that the soul is the cause of the behaviors a body possesses by virtue of its inclusion in a natural kind and that bodies of a given natural kind have their specific behaviors for the sake of becoming like the unmovable first mover.

On the Soul is the first in a series of works devoted to life. Socrates thought human beings are psychological beings. Plato took this a significant step further. He argued that the soul is a persisting object that exists independently of the body.[a] Aristotle both amplifies this general line of thought and tries to correct certain problems within it. He argues that the soul is the form of the living body. In addition, he argues that the various behaviors characteristic of living bodies (such as nutrition and propagation) are for the sake of its becoming like the divine. In this way, Aristotle has a solution to a problem that vexed Plato. He has teleological explanations of the kind that Socrates, in the autobiography passage in *Phaedo*, says he had tried to learn from Anaxagoras.

---

[a] In the *Phaedo* at 78b4–84b8, when Socrates argues that the soul must be immortal in virtue of its affinity to the forms, there is no indication he supposes the soul is a form. Later, however, in the *Theaetetus* at 184d, in a tantalizing remark in connection with perception, Socrates seems to show a change of mind. He says it would be strange if "there were not some one form, soul or whatever one ought to call it, to which all these converge, something with which, through the senses, as sort of instruments, we perceive all that is perceptible."

Ancient Greek Philosophy: From The Presocratics to the Hellenistic Philosophers, First Edition.
Thomas A. Blackson. © 2011 Thomas A. Blackson. Published 2011 by Blackwell Publishing Ltd.

7.1   The Soul is the Form of the Body

Aristotle works against the background assumption that natural bodies are real. He supposes that a natural body exists by having a nature.[1] In the case of living bodies, the nature unifies the material so that there is a living body. The question is what this nature is, and Aristotle concludes that it is a *soul* and hence that the soul is the "substance as the form of the natural body":

> Bodies are thought to be among the substances, especially natural bodies, as they are the starting points of all other bodies. Of natural bodies, some have life in them, others not. By life we mean self-nutrition and growth and decay. It follows that every natural body which has life in it is a substance as a composite. Since a living body is one having life, the body cannot be the same as the soul. The body is the subject and matter, not something attributed to it. So the soul must be the substance as the form of a natural body having life potentially within it. Substance is actuality, and thus soul is the actuality of the body. But actuality is of two kinds, corresponding to knowledge and to contemplation. The soul is an actuality like knowledge. Sleeping and waking presuppose the soul, and waking corresponds to contemplation, sleeping to knowledge, since it comes before. So the soul is the first actuality (ἐντελέχεια ἡ πρώτη) of a natural body having life potentially in it. (*On the Soul* II.1.412a)
>
> The substance is the cause of existing, and here, in the case of living things, to exist is to live, and the soul in them is the cause and starting point. (*On the Soul* II.4.415b)

As the "substance as the form" of the living body, Aristotle supposes that the soul is the "cause and starting point" of propagation and the other specific behaviors involved in the activity of living. The soul is the organization of the material so that there is an object that exercises the behaviors involved in living. In Aristotle's words, the soul is the "cause and starting point" of life.

The soul is the first actuality of the living natural body

Just after Aristotle describes the soul as the form of the body, he says that it is "the first actuality" of the body. This language is puzzling but, in asserting that the soul is an "actuality," the idea seems to be that the soul is the organization of material so that the material constitutes an object for which "in-end-hold" (ἐν-τέλος-ἔχειν)[b] is true. The material is organized *for the sake of* living. Living is the end for the sake of which the material in the body has its organization and form.

Although living is the end, in saying the soul is the "first" or initial actuality (as opposed to a complete actuality or an actuality simply and without qualification), Aristotle seems to mean living is an end with qualification. He uses an analogy to make the point. A human being cannot always be awake. Some time must be spent in sleep. Hence, given that contemplation is the end without qualification, it does not coincide with the presence of the soul in the material that constitutes the body.[2] Moreover, since not all living bodies are capable of contemplation, which is an exercise of reason, there must be another way in which the soul is a first actuality. Aristotle must mean that the soul is the first actuality, as opposed to an actuality without qualification, because the behaviors that constitute living somehow only approximate the final end, the end without qualification.

Aristotle's discussion of living (in plants and animals) provides confirmation for this interpretation. He believes that to be a living body is, first of all, to be organized so that various things can be ingested for the sake of "propagation and the assimilation of nutriment" (II.2.413b, II.3.414a–b). This is plausible enough, but Aristotle also believes something much more striking. By organizing the material so there is a living body with the ability to take nutriment and reproduce, the soul unifies material into an object that "partakes in the eternal and divine":

> First of all we must treat of nutrition and reproduction, for the nutritive soul is found along with all the others and is the first and most common, that by which all have life. It manifests itself in reproduction and the use of food, as a living thing that has reached its normal development and which is unmutilated, and whose mode of generation is not spontaneous, naturally produces another like itself, an animal an animal, a plant a plant, in order that, as far as its nature allows, it may partake in the eternal and divine. That is the goal toward which they all strive, that for the sake

---

[b] Aristotle seems to have invented the word ἐντελέχεια. According to David Ross, it is "probably derived from the phrase τὸ ἐντελὲς ἔχον, 'having completeness'" (*Aristotle*, De Anima, 1961, 15).

of which they do whatsoever their nature renders possible.^c However, since none can partake of the eternal and divine by uninterrupted existence, as nothing perishable can ever remain one and the same, they try to achieve that end in the only way possible, so it remains not as the same individual but continues in existence in something like itself, not as one in number but one in species. (*On the Soul* II.4.415a–b)

The soul is not the organization of material so that a living body is "one in number" with any eternally existing object. Rather, the soul is the organization of material so that a living body is "one in species" with the living bodies that exist at every moment in time. The use of food in nutrition and reproduction is thus a qualified way to "partake in the eternal and divine" because it is a qualified way to exist eternally. The soul is the *first* actuality of the body.

The soul is separable from the body only in account

This distinction between a first actuality and an actuality without qualification helps makes sense of Aristotle's otherwise puzzling discussion of whether the soul, or any part of it, exists separably from the body. At certain places in the corpus, he can seem to make an exception to the universal claim in the *Physics* that form is "not separable except in account" (II.1.193b4–5). Aristotle can seem to say that the part of the soul that underlies "contemplation" is separable from the body, just as Plato had supposed,[3] because this part is not the organization of any material:

About the intellect and potential for contemplation, the situation is less clear. It seems to be a different kind of soul and alone can exist separately. It is evident, though, from what we have said, that the other parts of the soul cannot exist separately. (*On the Soul* II.2.413b)

---

^c Aristotle's idea seems to have its roots in Plato. Timaeus suggests that natural bodies exist in terms of "the craftsmanship of mind" but that "mind" must contend with "necessity" in crafting these bodies (47e–48a). Aristotle does not believe in a divine craftsman who works with preexisting material to bring about the best result possible. He does, however, think that specific behavior is for the sake of an end and that this end is to exist like the divine mind as much as possible. Aristotle's idea that the soul is a first actuality thus seems to be a more precise version of the somewhat indeterminate idea in Plato that although "mind" does what it can, "necessity" entails that not every existence is perfect.

That it is impossible for them all to exist before is clear. Those starting points whose actuality is bodily cannot exist without a body, just as there is no walking without feet. And so to enter from outside is not possible. For neither is it possible for them to enter by themselves, being inseparable, nor yet in a body, since the semen is a residue of a change in the nutriment. It remains, then, for the intellect alone so to enter and alone to be divine, for no bodily actuality takes part in the actuality of intellect. (*On the Generation of Animals* II.3.736b)

Unlike in the case of perceptual beliefs, Aristotle says the "intellect" itself has no organ (*On the Soul* III.4.429a). The sense organs, for example, are involved in the formation and retention of the belief that some particular in front of a given human being is water. The same, however, according to Aristotle, is not so clearly true of the belief that such-and-such is the essence of water:

Since a magnitude and what it is to be a magnitude are not the same, nor water and what it is to be water, and likewise in many other cases, we judge flesh and what it is to be flesh by different faculties, or by the same faculty in two different states. It is by the faculty of sense perception that we judge the hot and the cold, the factors which combined in a certain ratio constitute flesh, but what is to be flesh is judged by something different, either separate from this faculty or related to it, as a bent line is related to itself when it has been straightened out. (*On the Soul* III.4.429b)

He says such judgments involve "something different," either separate, or, if not separate, related as "a bent line is related to itself when it has been straightened out."

This analogy does not make the relationship very clear, but rather than revert to the Platonic understanding of the soul and its relationship to the body, which would run contrary to the general theory of the existence of natural bodies in the *Physics*, maybe Aristotle is struggling to distinguish *two* kinds of dependence. One way for a psychological ability to depend on the body is for the exercise of this ability to involve some part of the body directly. Judgment in terms of sensation involves the sense organs in this way. This is the point of his remarks in *On the Generation of Animals* where he says that the "starting points whose actuality is bodily cannot exist without a body, just as there is no walking without feet." The idea is that "just as there is no walking without feet," so also there cannot be judgments in terms of sensation without sense organs. Hence, the part of the soul that is the organization of the material for perception cannot exist apart from the sense organs organized out of this material. The "intellect" does not depend on the body in this way, according to Aristotle, but it does depend on the body in some way. In the *Posterior Analytics*, to explain how induction issues in knowledge of the definitions, he says that "reason" comes to be present in the body from "experience" and that "experience" comes from "sensation and memory." So the "intellect" does depend on the body. The ability to grasp the essence does not directly involve any organ, but it does require "experience" and "sensation and memory" for its existence.[4] Judgment in terms of sensation is for the sake of theoretical knowledge because such judgment is part of the inductive process that ends in the presence of what Aristotle calls "reason." Thus, although the "intellect and the potential for contemplation" can appear separable in existence from the body because it is not embodied in any particular bodily organ or organs, it in fact is dependent on the body. Human beings acquire knowledge in the process of induction. This is how the human soul, as a first actuality, holds the material together for the sake of the end that exists by nature.

There is no motion in the soul

Given this understanding of the soul, Aristotle is able to insist on a point that Plato may have misunderstood. Plato sometimes seems to suggest that the soul, not the human being, is the proper subject of the attribution of various changes. Aristotle was convinced that this conception of the soul is confused and that ordinary forms of speech to the contrary should not be taken literally:

> We say that the soul is pained or pleased, confident or afraid, angry, perceives, and thinks. All these seem to be movements, and so one might infer that the soul is moved. But this does not follow. Even if being pained or pleased, or thinking, are movements due to the soul, to say that the soul is angry is as to say the soul weaves or builds houses. It is better not to say that the soul pities or learns or thinks but to say that it is the man who does this with his soul. (*On the Soul* I.4.408b)

Aristotle says, as an example, that the human being is the proper subject for anger. The living body, not the soul itself, can undergo the changes that realize anger.[d] The soul is necessary for anger because only living bodies can be angry. The soul itself, however, cannot be angry.

---

[d] Aristotle seems to have thought that anger, in its material aspect, involves "a boiling of the blood around the heart" (*On the Soul* I.1.403a).

Thus, contrary to the Platonic picture, the soul cannot regain a pure state it lost through incarnation. A human being can change in various ways. In particular, a human being can become more rational, and becoming more rational might be understood to be a matter of proper psychological functioning. Aristotle seems to accept all of this. Plato's mistake, from Aristotle's point of view, is in the idea that such exercises are changes in the soul itself.[5] Aristotle insists that, properly speaking, it is the human being, not the soul, that undergoes certain changes. The soul makes this possible by organizing the parts so that these changes occur naturally.

7.2 Induction

This interpretation of the soul as an actuality, and as something that itself does not change but which is the organization of material so that certain changes occur naturally, helps put Aristotle's theory of induction into somewhat sharper focus. Induction is a process. It is the way the human soul organizes the bodily parts so that human beings acquire the knowledge of definitions necessary for demonstration. According to Aristotle, in the natural course of human development, a certain sequence of events unfolds for the sake of the existence of this knowledge:

> All men by nature desire to know. A indication of this is the delight we take in our senses, especially sight because it makes us know and brings to light many differences between things. And by nature animals are born with the capacity for sense perception, and from sense perception memory is produced in some of them, though not in others. And therefore the former are more intelligent and apt at learning than those which cannot remember. The animals other than man live by appearances and memories, and have but little connected experience, but man lives also by art and reason. And from memory experience is produced in men, for many memories of the same thing produce finally the capacity for a single experience. Experience seems to be very similar to knowledge and art, but really knowledge and art come to men through experience. (*Metaphysics* I.1.980a–981a[e])

---

[e] Cf. *Sense and Sensibilia* 1.436b–437a.

This sequence raises many questions, but one of the most puzzling concerns the contrast between "experience" on the one hand, and "reason" and "knowledge" on the other hand. It is not immediately clear just what Aristotle has in mind in drawing this particular contrast.

One might well think that, by "experience," Aristotle has in mind the justification that underwrites the expertise of a practitioner in some field. This interpretation is initially tempting because to explain what he means when he says that "[e]xperience seems to be very similar to knowledge and art," Aristotle appeals to an example from medical practice:

> Experience made art, as Polus says, and inexperience luck. Art arises when from many notions gained by experience one universal judgment about similar things is produced. To form a judgment that when Callias[f] was ill of this disease this is good, and similarly for Socrates and other cases, is a matter of experience. To judge that this is good for all persons of a certain sort, when they were ill of this disease, is a matter of art. For action, experience seems in no respect inferior to art. We even see men of experience succeeding more than those who have theory without experience.[g] But knowledge and understanding belong to art more than experience, and artists are wiser than men of experience. The former know the cause, but the latter do not. For men of experience know that the thing is so, but do not know why, while the others know the why and the cause. (*Metaphysics* I.1.981a)

In this passage, Aristotle explains the contrast between "experience" on the one hand, and "reason" and "knowledge" on the other hand, in terms of the difference between a practitioner and a theorist. Experience with patients gives a practitioner the expertise to make the correct diagnosis in circumstances in which the layman is more likely to make a mistake. The medical theorist has an expertise too, but it is not the expertise of a practitioner. The theorist knows "the why and the cause." He knows why certain treatments work in certain situations. This sets him apart from the layman and the practitioner. Neither of them is likely to give the correct explanation.

Given this understanding of "experience," there is an obvious puzzle. It seems part of Aristotle's idea that human beings, over time, as a matter

---

[f] Callias was a wealthy Athenian, one of the generals in the Peloponnesian war, and a patron of culture. His house is the scene of Plato's *Protagoras*.

[g] Cf. *Nicomachean Ethics* VI.7.1141b.

of natural development, come to have the sort of theoretical expertise characterized by the possession of demonstrations. Yet, as a matter of common observation, it is clear that human beings in general do not naturally become practitioners, medical practitioners or otherwise. Moreover, even in the cases in which a human being does acquire the expertise of a practitioner, he does so relatively late in life. Hence, contrary to what Aristotle seems to suggest, it appears to follow that human beings rarely if ever acquire the theoretical expertise that is supposed to follow "experience" in the inductive process.

It is not completely clear how this puzzle should be solved, but maybe Aristotle understands "experience" in such a way that the experience that underlies the expertise of the practitioner is a special case. The medical practitioner knows certain empirical generalizations. This knowledge requires careful observation, but the same is not so clearly true for every empirical generalization. For example, all normal adult human beings can reliably discriminate human beings from the other things they typically encounter in their lives. Yet, this ability does not seem to be the product of careful and systematic observation. Hence, in having "experience" precede "knowledge" in induction, maybe the point is that the knowledge generated in experience is insufficient for the knowledge involved in demonstration. The knowledge exercised in discriminating human beings from other things does not essentially involve knowledge of the essence of what it is to be a human being.[6] This knowledge of "the why and the cause" is required for demonstration, and Aristotle's idea may be that this knowledge is a matter of "reason," not the cognition involved in "experience."

If this is what Aristotle has in mind, there are certain points to notice. First of all, in the *Posterior Analytics*, when he says that "reason" follows "experience" in induction, he must conceive of "reason" as something different from what human beings are now ordinarily thought to possess when they are said to be rational. Induction is for the sake of knowledge of "the why and the cause." It would not ordinarily be thought that this knowledge is necessary for rationality, even if human beings are psychological beings and rationality is proper psychological functioning.

Secondly, even given that the understanding of "experience" is a special case of the expertise which characterizes a practitioner, Aristotle cannot think the inductive process always comes to completion, despite the fact that it is a natural process. It is obvious that human beings do not normally end up with "reason and its knowledge" as they normally end up with their adult teeth as a matter of the natural processes involved in maturation. Rather, Aristotle must think that human beings themselves do something to advance beyond the "experience" stage in induction. It is not clear what this is, but it does seem clear that "reason and its knowledge" is not something that just happens to a human being as he becomes an adult. The inductive process is *teleological*. It occurs for the sake of the knowledge of the "why and cause," but this knowledge does not naturally become present in every normal adult human being. It becomes present, if at all, as a human being somehow gets insight into his "experience."[h] Thus, by conceiving of this insight into reality as a matter of the cognition involved in "reason," Aristotle remains squarely within the framework of the rationalist tradition he inherited from Plato and that originates with Parmenides.[7]

7.3 Becoming Like the Unmovable First Mover

In thinking about the end in nature for which induction works, although he develops the details differently, Aristotle retains the general idea Plato had taken initial steps to work out in the *Timaeus*. It is unclear just how literally Timaeus should be understood,[8] but he argues for the remarkable claim that the cosmos has a divine maker, that this maker is good, and that he made things as much like himself as possible because he wanted to bring into existence as much good as possible (28b–c, 29d–30a). In addition, as an example of how the maker made things

---

[h] Aristotle may follow a procedure he expects to result in this insight. "The natural way to proceed ... is to begin with inquiry (*historia*), with the aim of grasping the differences between, and attributes of, all the animals; and then to attempt to discover their causes. This is natural because, given that our goal is demonstrative understanding, we want to end up with a clear distinction between the *explananda* (the *peri hon*) and the *explanans* (the *ex hon*). The *History of Animals* characterizes itself as a contribution to the first of these two inquiries, and looks forward to investigations that aim to discover the causes – the reasons why animals have the attributes they have and differ in the ways that they do. In the language of the *Posterior Analytics*, HA establishes the *fact*, e.g., *that* all animals with lungs have windpipes, or *that* all cetacea have lungs and are viviparous, typically seeking to identify groups by means of discovering co-extensive differentiae with the aid of the method of division. Works such as *Parts of Animals* or *Generation of Animals* seek to establish the reason why – the cause – of the fact. If he is following the method described in the *Analytics*, these causal explanations should aim at the same time to give us an essential definition of what it is to be a windpipe or to be viviparous" (James G. Lennox, "Aristotle's biology and Aristotle's philosophy," 2006, 297–298).

as much as possible like himself, Timaeus says that the maker included the sense of sight in the human design so that human beings, through exercise of this ability, could transform themselves so that their minds were more orderly. The experience of seeing is part of a process that gives rise ultimately to the "love of wisdom" and hence to a transformation of the human soul so that it is more like "god"[i] (46e–47c).

Aristotle has this general view in mind. He does not believe the cosmos has a divine maker,[j] but he accepts the fundamental point: that the exercise of specific behaviors in natural bodies is for the sake of becoming like some divine object whose existence is perfect. In the *Metaphysics*, which (in the traditional arrangement of the corpus) comes after *On the Soul* and the other physical works, Aristotle argues for the existence of what he calls "the unmovable first mover":

> The first mover exists out of necessity, and as necessary; it is good and in this way a starting point. On such a starting point, depend the heavens and the world of nature. And its life is such as the best which we enjoy, and enjoy for but a short time. For it is ever in this state, which we cannot be. And thought in itself deals with that which is best in itself, and intellect thinks itself because it shares the nature of the object of thought, so that intellect and the object of thought are the same. The god is always in that good state in which we sometimes are, and life belongs to God, for the actuality of thought is life, and God is that actuality. (*Metaphysics* XII.7.1072b)

These remarks are perplexing in many ways, but the main points Aristotle seeks to establish are clear enough. The unmovable first mover has the perfect existence. Its state is good without qualification, and other things are good to the extent that their existence is like this perfect existence.[9]

Aristotle's disagreement with Plato is over the model for teleology. For Aristotle, as for Plato, perception is part of a process in which the human mind becomes like "God." Aristotle, however, does not explain this process in terms of the Platonic idea that there is a divine craftsman and

---

[i] The reference here is confusing. In the account Timaeus gives, the cosmos is alive and hence, like all living things, has a soul in it. The "god" appears to be this soul. It animates the body of the cosmos. The divine maker, the craftsman who makes the cosmos because he is good, includes the power of sight in the human design as part of a causal process that transforms human beings so that their cognition becomes like that of the cosmic soul. In this way, since the divine maker makes the cosmos because he wants things to be as good as possible, and hence as much like him as possible, human beings indirectly become like the divine maker by becoming like the cosmic soul.

[j] This is not always so clear. See *On Generation and Corruption* II.10.336b–337a.

that this craftsman has arranged things so that they naturally become as good as possible. In the *Metaphysics*, Aristotle argues that motion must exist eternally. He argues that time is a function or mode of motion, that there can be no first or last moment of time, and that the explanation for the necessity of eternal motion requires the existence of a cause that itself is free from change.[k] This understanding seems to rule out the craftsmanship model of teleology. A craftsman changes when he crafts, so a craftsman, even a divine one, is not free from change. Yet, according to Aristotle, the cause of the eternal motion must cause this motion without itself changing.[l]

For this reason, Aristotle introduces the unmovable first mover. It is unchanging, but its existence entails that there is motion. The natural bodies exist because bodies of these kinds are what the existence of the unmovable first mover entails. The unmovable first mover enjoys a perfect existence, and this fact somehow entails that nature contains changing bodies which naturally become like the unmovable mover. Since the unmovable first mover is fixed in a certain exercise of reason, in nature there are animals with reason. Bodies of this kind acquire demonstrative knowledge on the basis of perception and memory through the inductive process. This is how necessity permits them to become like the unmovable first mover, and this is how they become good by exercising their specific behavior. This behavior is for the sake of an exercise of reason that makes their existence like the perfect existence of the unmovable first mover.

---

[k] *Metaphysics* XII.7.1071b–1071a.

[l] D. N. Sedley provides some explanation: "Plato had left the matter awkwardly poised. On the one hand, his cosmic god, the world soul, is enmeshed in world government, and hence concerned with the particular and the changeable – inevitably, given that the world is providentially structured by it all the way down. On the other hand, in recommending assimilation to that cosmic god, Plato is advising us to emulate him, not as administrator, but as something better, a pure intellect directly contemplating eternal truths. What could be more natural, for someone thinking through the tensions within this doctrine, than to ask why the cosmic god need adulterate his perfection by having to turn his thought to the changeable at all? If the best human life is godlike purely in virtue of being contemplative, it should follow that god is purely contemplative. Aristotle's exclusively intellectual god is very probably the outcome of that reflection. And, if so, we even have a plausible explanation of how Aristotle's cosmology as a whole evolved from Plato's. For Aristotle's contemplative god now moves the entire world, not by directing his thoughts downward, but purely in virtue of the fact that the world, at every level from the stars down to the elements, is striving upwards to become like him so far as it can" ("'Becoming like god' in the *Timaeus* and Aristotle," 1997, 335–336).

Notes

1. This point is common in the secondary literature. The following remarks, respectively from Terence Irwin and Christopher Shields, are representative: "In Aristotle's view, disputes about soul and body are simply a special case of the more general disputes about form and matter" (*Classical Thought*, 1989, 130); "Aristotle regards soul–body relations simply as a special case of form–matter relations, an attitude which, he thinks, allows him to position himself as a moderate between what he regards as the excesses of Presocratic materialism and Platonic dualism" (*Classical Philosophy*, 2003, 134).

2. Michael Frede makes the point: "The forms of sensible substances and separate substances are both substantial forms and they are both actualities, i.e., the reality of the object they are is constituted by their reality. But whereas separate substances turn out to be substantial forms and actualities without qualification, the substantial forms of sensible objects have to be understood as substantial forms and actualities of a certain limited kind. ... The forms of sensible substances involve potentiality in two ways, and hence are not pure actualities, though it is the essence of a form to be an actuality. They need matter to be realized in, and thus are the forms of objects subject to change. But, what is more, when we turn to the paradigms of sensible substances, living beings, it turns out that their forms themselves essentially contain an element of potentiality. When Aristotle in *De Anima* II.1 defines the soul as the 'first actuality' of a certain kind of body, this very language reflects the fact that the soul in a way is constituted by the various abilities to exercise the life-functions characteristic of the kind of living being in question, but that not all these life-functions are exercised all the time. What is more, some of the abilities that characterize the soul, like virtue and knowledge, are only acquired. Thus, the forms of sensible substances are not pure actualities; they in part are constituted by unrealized possibilities and in that sense are not fully real. The form that is the unmoved mover, on the other hand, is pure actuality. It neither needs matter to be realized nor does it involve any abilities that might or might not be realized or exercised. The unmoved mover is just eternally thinking the same thought" ("The unity of general and special metaphysics: Aristotle's conception of metaphysics," 1987e, 89–90).

3. Timaeus describes the human person as a preexisting soul that the lesser gods somehow received and placed within a mortal body of their construction (*Timaeus* 42e–43a).

4. Michael Frede makes this point: "Aristotle's view turns out to be this: the exercise of the intellect, Aristotle wants to say (cf. *DA* 429a18ff, esp. a24–25), unlike the exercise of the other so-called mental faculties, does not involve the use of a bodily organ. For otherwise our cognitive abilities would be hampered by the restrictions the organ puts on them, the way the sense-organs limit what we can perceive. But this does not mean that the exercise of the intellect does not presuppose a body. It is Aristotle's view that we could not think the way we do unless, for example, we were capable of perception and could remember, and

somehow process, what we perceive. Thus our ability to think presupposes a body" ("On Aristotle's conception of the soul," 1992, 155). "Aristotle does not believe in a providentially ordered world, but he does think that organisms have to be understood teleologically, as naturally tending to achieve full development and perfection in their kind, unless handicapped or their development is thwarted. Since we naturally do have reason and since reason functions best, and serves its function best, if we do have the requisite knowledge, he assumes that we must be constructed in such a way as to be able to acquire the knowledge reason needs to function well. And he, too, thinks that he can explain this by assuming that there is a process which leads, on the basis of perception and memory, not only to our having concepts, but to our having concepts which are adequate to the way things essentially are, and which thus provide us with basic knowledge about things, but also with the ability to think and reason about things, properly speaking, instead of, for instance, just having impressions or even generalized impressions of things" ("Introduction" in *Rationality in Greek Thought*, 1996a, 14).

5. Many commentators have made the general point that the soul, as the form of the body, figures in the explanation of change but does not itself change. Hendrik Lorenz is a recent example: "It is in fact a central commitment of Aristotle's psychology, and indeed of his physics, that souls are immune from change. Like other principles of change and rest, they play a crucial role in accounting for certain forms of change without themselves engaging in or undergoing change. Something that itself undergoes change could not be a *principle* of change" (*The Brute Within*, 2006, 204).

6. Michael Frede uses this example in his interpretation of Aristotle's rationalism: "On Aristotle's view it does not seem to suffice for thinking that we have a notion of, say, a human being which allows us, by and large, to distinguish successfully between human beings and other things; the notion rather has to be based on a sufficient grasp of what it is to be a human being, of the crucial feature or features of human beings, and of how these features are related to each other and to a whole network of features. ... To grasp what it is to be a human being, on Aristotle's view, is more than just to grasp what human beings have in common; it is to grasp something which figures prominently in the explanation of human beings and their behavior" ("Aristotle's rationalism," 1996b, 164).

7. This is controversial. Jonathan Barnes says that Aristotle is an empiricist: "Aristotle was a thoroughgoing empiricist in two senses of that term. First, he held that the notions or concepts with which we seek to grasp reality are all ultimately derived from perception, and 'for that reason, if we did not perceive anything, we would not learn or understand anything, and whenever we think of anything we must at the same time think of an idea.' Secondly, he thought that the science or knowledge in which our grasp of reality consists is ultimately grounded on perceptual observations" (*Aristotle*, 1982, 58). Michael Frede, on the other hand, says that Aristotle is a rationalist: "To say that it is somehow a natural process by means of which we arrive at first principles is to exploit

Aristotle's generous conception of what is natural and to focus on just one aspect of it. This becomes particularly clear if we keep in mind that on Aristotle's view it also is the case that by nature we are meant to be virtuous and are thus constructed as to naturally be virtuous. Nevertheless, Aristotle also assumes that it takes a great deal of effort on our part to come to know the first principles in general (and thus to become wise), or even just the first principles in some domain. What is needed for this is a great deal of often highly specialized observation and of often highly technical reflections. But this should not obscure the fact that the insight, if it is an insight, does not derive its epistemic status from these observations and reflections which lead up to it. What makes it an insight is not the support it gets from observations or considerations, but that one finally sees in a way which fits how the features in question are related to each other and to other relevant features" ("Aristotle's rationalism," 1996b, 172). "Aristotle's own view seems to be that to recognize reason as something apart from perception would involve a recognition of the intellect (νοῦς) with its distinctive active power to grasp terms or universals and thus the basic terms and the immediate truths about them from which all other scientific truths can be deduced, a power which, though (at least in the case of human beings) causally linked to, and in a way based on, perception, nevertheless epistemologically is an independent source of knowledge, in fact the source of all knowledge properly speaking" ("An empiricist view of knowledge: Memorism, 1990, 236). Some of Frede's remarks about the Stoics also cast light on his understanding of reason in Aristotle. The following statements are representative. "[R]eason, in the first instance, is not conceived of as an ability to reason, to argue, to make inferences from what we perceive; it rather, in the first instance, is conceived of as being a matter of having a certain basic knowledge about the world, which then can serve as the starting point for inferences. . . . Thus, to be rational is not solely, and not even primarily, a matter of being able to reason, to make inferences; it, to begin with, is a matter of having the appropriate knowledge about the world. Correspondingly, the perfection of reason does not consist primarily in one's becoming better and better in one's ability to reason correctly; to be perfectly rational rather is to be wise . . ., and this involves, first of all, an articulate understanding of, or knowledge about, the world" ("The Stoic conception of reason," 1993–4, 54). "It is quite true that the Stoics assume that it is ultimately perception which gives rise to the natural notions and the knowledge embodied in them. . . . But this knowledge is not arrived at by inference from what we have perceived. Nor does it owe its epistemic status to the fact that it stands in the appropriate relation of justification or confirmation to the data of observation. It, according to the Stoics, rather owes its epistemic status to the fact that nature has constructed human beings in such a way as to arrive at these notions and the assumptions they involve. So, in this sense, the basic knowledge embodied in the natural notions is not empirical, but *a priori*. And correspondingly the knowledge we arrive at by reasoning from what we know by nature is *a priori*. So in this sense the Stoic position clearly is rationalist" ("The Stoic conception of reason,"

1993–4, 55–56). For a helpful discussion and argument against the recent tendency among scholars to see Aristotle as an empiricist, see Michael Ferejohn's "Empiricism and the first principles of Aristotelian science," 1991.

8. There is disagreement over whether Plato actually believed in this divine "maker and father of the whole." "As is well known, there have been, from the very first age of Platonic study, two directly opposed opinions on the main point. Aristotle seems to regard it as a plain, incontrovertible fact that Plato described the universe as having come to be; whereas his contemporary Xenocrates, the third Head of the Academy, held that the account put into the mouth of Timaeus ought to be interpreted as analysis of the world's existing structure in the guise of a story of its construction in the past, Plato's object being to facilitate exposition . . ." (R. Hackforth, "Plato's cosmogony (*Timaeus* 27dff.)," 1959, 19).

9. Aristotle's position in *On the Soul* is much less definitive, perhaps because the unmovable first mover is a subject for first philosophy, not second philosophy, but he does seem to have the unmovable first mover in mind in III.5.430a. The "immortal intellect" in this passage seems to play the same role as the unmovable first mover. Both appear to be the object in terms of which induction is understood as a natural process by which human beings become like the divine. Just as the presence of light is necessary for things with the potential for color to show their color, the immortal intellect is somehow necessary for the potential for "reason" (that belongs by nature to human beings) to show itself through induction. This identification, however, is controversial. It seems first to have been suggested by one of Aristotle's ancient commentators, Alexander of Aphrodisias. For a helpful discussion of the main interpretative options and their most prominent historical proponents, see Victor Caston's "Aristotle's psychology," 2006, 338–339.

8

First Philosophy

It is a principle of second philosophy that natural bodies are forms in matter. These forms underlie the specific behavior of natural bodies, the behavior natural bodies exhibit in virtue of their inclusion in natural kinds. The question arises whether these forms are substances, and to answer this ontological question, Aristotle conducts a general inquiry into existence. The outcome of this inquiry is a matter of considerable scholarly dispute, but one likely possibility is that Aristotle continues to play the role of Platonist and Platonic critic. Aristotle, it seems, is working his way toward a teleological conception of the universe in which forms are the reality of things but in which there are no general objects and perhaps nothing general at all.

In the *Metaphysics*, Aristotle considers what "substance" is.[a] Previously, in the physical works, forms in matter are the substances of natural bodies. In the *Metaphysics* which, in the traditional ordering, follows the physical works, he reconsiders this assumption within the more general inquiry into whether there are things more substantial than forms in matter. His discussion is difficult, and a matter of scholarly controversy, but he seems to decide that substances are "immovable and separable" and that the forms of natural bodies are substances with qualification because they are in matter and hence immovable and separable with qualification.[1] Aristotle, in

---

[a] The English word "substance" is an etymological descendent of the Latin word *substantia*, which means roughly "thing that stands under." This Latin word was the traditional translation of the Greek word οὐσία, which itself is a noun formed from a participle of the verb to be, εἰμί. Michael Frede explains the translation: "Traditionally οὐσία has been rendered by 'substance.' The reason for this is that, on the view Aristotle puts forward in the *Categories*, properties depend for their being on objects in that objects are their ultimate subjects, they are what ultimately underlies everything else. Indeed, objects in the *Categories* are characterized by the very fact that they are the ultimate subjects which underlie everything, whereas there is nothing that underlies them as their subject. It is because of this characterization that the rendering 'substance' seems appropriate" ("Substance in Aristotle's *Metaphysics*," 1987d, 73).

Ancient Greek Philosophy: From The Presocratics to the Hellenistic Philosophers, First Edition.
Thomas A. Blackson.   © 2011 Thomas A. Blackson. Published 2011 by Blackwell Publishing Ltd.

this way, corrects what he sees as the fundamental mistake in the ontology Plato sketches in the middle and late dialogues. Forms exist and are the reality of things, but they are particular.[2]

8.1 The Science of Being

Aristotle describes his inquiry in the *Metaphysics* in two ways. In Book I, the inquiry is theology. He says that "wisdom is about the first causes and starting points of things" (I.1.981b) and hence that wisdom most of all is about "divine objects ... because God is thought to be among the causes and starting points of all things" (I.2.983a). In Book IV, he says that his inquiry is the study of "being as being,"[b] a study which aims to produce "knowledge theorizing about being as being, i.e., that which belongs to being according to itself" (IV.1.1003a). This knowledge about existence is "first philosophy" or, more literally, the "first love of wisdom" (IV.2.1004a).

These identifications are initially puzzling, as Aristotle himself recognizes. He says that "one might be perplexed as to whether the first love of wisdom is universal, or only deals with a certain kind of being" (VI.1.1026a). The problem is that theology and first philosophy seem to have distinct subject matters. The study of "being as being," as Aristotle characterizes it in his discussion in Chapters 1 and 2 of Book IV, would seem to be a theory of the principles of existence itself. Theology, on the other hand, would seem to be a theory of only part of what exists because it would seem to be a theory of all and only those things whose existence is divine.

Aristotle tries to resolve this puzzle by saying that theology and first philosophy are one and the same science if the objects of study in both theology and first philosophy are the same. Theology, in this case, is or at least includes the study of "being as being" because divine objects exist

---

[b] The study of "being as being" is an inquiry into existence in general. It is an inquiry into what it is *to be* or *to exist*. "By distinguishing between a kind of beings and a way of being I mean to make a distinction of the following sort. Horses are a kind of beings, and camels are a different kind of beings, but neither horses nor camels have a distinctive way of being, peculiar to them; they both have the way of being of natural substances, as opposed to, e.g., numbers that have the way of magnitudes, or qualities which have yet a different way of being" (Michael Frede, "The unity of general and special metaphysics: Aristotle's conception of metaphysics," 1987e, 85). The study of "being as being," for Aristotle, is the study not of a qualified way of being, the way that belongs to natural substances, for example. Rather, it is the study of being without qualification or, as he says, "being as being."

in the primary way. The existence of the objects in the domain of physics and mathematics are qualifications of the mode that characterizes divine objects:

> If there is no substance other than those formed by nature, physics will be the first knowledge. But if there is an immovable substance, the knowledge of this is prior and the first love of wisdom, and universal in this way, because it is first. And it will belong to this to consider being as being, both what it is and the things that belong to it as being. (*Metaphysics* VI.1.1026a)

If there are divine objects, according to Aristotle, it follows that the objects in the domains of physics and mathematics must be understood in terms of the primary way of existence that characterizes the objects in the domain of theology. This primary way of "being" belongs to the science of theology to describe as part of its theory of divine objects. Because this description is the description of "being as being," and because first philosophy is the study of "being as being," theology is first philosophy. There is one science because the objects of study are the same.

Given that Aristotle says he intends "to prove" there are divine objects (objects that are "immovable and separable"), it is clear that he thinks first philosophy is theology (XI.7.1064a–1064b). He believes that there are divine objects and hence that the objects in the domains of physics and mathematics do not possess existence or "being" as such. Instead, according to Aristotle, their existence is a restriction of the mode of being of divine objects. The objects in the domain of physics and mathematics are "immovable and separable" in a qualified way.

The restriction on "immovable" is the easiest to understand. The objects in the domain of physics are the forms of natural bodies. According to Aristotle, these forms are causes of certain changes in natural bodies. For example, in the case of the human soul, where this is the organization of material so that a human being exists, the form underlies the changes which characterize a human being as a member of the natural kind, human. No human soul, however, according to Aristotle, exists eternally. Hence, although a human soul is "immovable," it is *immovable with qualification*. The human soul is not fixed throughout all possible changes. It is fixed relative to the changes that occur in the specific behavior of the kind.

Now consider the other conjunct, "separable." There are two ways to be "separable." An object can be immaterial, or it can be material but have no material parts. Again, consider the human soul. As the organization of the material so that a human being exists, the soul is material. It does not exist in the absence of material organized into a human being. In the absence of the material, there is nothing organized so that a human being exists. This, however, is not to say that the account of the soul must mention some material part. Having a human soul is not the same thing as having flesh, bones, and so on, in a certain arrangement. Rather, it is having the specific behavior characteristic of a rational animal. In this way, although a human soul is "separable," it is *separable with qualification*. The human soul cannot exist separately from matter. It is in matter and is separable only in account.

Even given this much, it is not easy to understand either the argument Aristotle presents for the existence of divine objects or the mode of existence he attributes to them. The argument for existence depends on certain assumptions about time and motion. Aristotle supposes that time is an attribute of motion, that there can be no first or last moment of time, and that the necessity of everlasting motion requires an explanation. To provide the explanation, there must be unmovable movers to function as the source of motion of the celestial spheres (the spheres in which the heavenly bodies are located). Since the motion of the heavenly bodies in their spheres is imparted from one sphere to another, this requirement for unmovable movers reduces to a requirement for one unmovable mover to move the first celestial sphere, the sphere of the fixed stars.[3]

Now that Aristotle thinks he has established that there is at least one unmovable mover, he sets out to prove there is only one and hence that it is separable without qualification. The unstated premise in the argument is that the ultimate cause of motion cannot itself be subject to change. From this premise, Aristotle concludes that there is one unmovable mover:

> It is evident that there is but one heaven. If there are many, as men, the starting point of each will be one in form but many in number. But all things many in number have matter. For one and the same account applies to many things, as the account of man, whereas Socrates is one. But the first essence has no matter, for it is actuality. So the unmovable first mover is one both in account and in number. (*Metaphysics* XII.8.1074a)

This unmovable first mover, because it is unique, exists without being embodied. Unlike the substances in the domain of physics, which are separable only in account and cannot exist apart from matter, the unmovable first mover is separable without qualification. In this way, the mode of existence of the substances in the domain of physics is a qualification of the primary mode of existence, the mode of existence that characterizes the unmovable first mover.

8.2   Substances are Forms

Aristotle's understanding of substantial existence in terms of form seems to be a view he reached in the interval from the *Categories* to the *Metaphysics*. In the *Categories*, which is a study of words and their referents, Aristotle discusses substances as the referents of certain words. To avoid confusion about what substance itself is, he explains that that which is called substance most "strictly, primarily, and most of all, is that which is neither said of nor in a subject." His idea seems to be that the substances are the ultimate subjects in terms of which other things exist:

> Substance, that which is called most strictly, primarily, and most of all, is that which is neither said of a subject nor in a subject, e.g., a particular man or horse. The species in which the things called substances primarily belong, and also the genera of these species, are called substances secondarily, e.g., a particular man belongs in a species, man or human, and animal is a genus of the species, and so man and animal are called substances secondarily. Thus all the other things are either said of the primary substances as subjects or in them as subjects. So if the primary substances did not exist it would be impossible for the other things to exist. (*Categories* 5.2a–b)

This general conception of substance continues to be present in the central books of the *Metaphysics*, the books in which Aristotle begins his investigation into whether theology or physics is first philosophy. In these books, which seem to have been written after the *Categories*,[4] Aristotle conceives of substance as that in terms of which everything else exists:

> Being is said in many ways, as we pointed out. It signifies what a thing is or this something, It signifies that a thing is of a certain quality or quantity, or has some such predicate asserted of it. Being is said in these ways, but obviously primary is the what a thing is. This indicates the substance of the thing. All other things are said to be because they are, some, quantities of what is in the primary way, others, qualities of it, others afflictions of it, and others something else. Clearly, then, it is because of substance that each of those others is. And therefore that which is in the primary way, not is something, but is without qualification, is substance. (*Metaphysics* VII.1.1028a)

A substance "is in the primary way." Other things "are said to be because they are, some, quantities of what is in this way, others, qualities." So, for example, according to Aristotle, the quality of being white is in a secondary way: the quality is said to exist because some substances are white.

Although Aristotle's general conception of what substance is does not change from the *Categories* to the central books of the *Metaphysics*, he does change his mind about what objects are substances. The reasons for this change of mind are not easy to reconstruct, but it is clear that Aristotle became dissatisfied with the ontology he had set out in the *Categories*. The ontology in the *Metaphysics* is Aristotle's subsequent and more settled view about what exists.

In the *Categories*, Aristotle divides reality (or what exists) along two dimensions and hence into four groups of things. There are particular and general objects, and there are particular and general properties. Aristotle sets out this division in the following remarks:

> Of things some are said of a subject but are not in any subject, e.g., man is said of a subject, the man, but is not in any subject. Some are in a subject but are not said of any subject. By in a subject, I mean what is in something, not as a part, and cannot exist separately from what it is in – e.g. the knowledge of grammar is in a subject, the soul, but is not said of any subject, and the white is in a subject, the body – for all color is in a body – but is not said of any subject. Some are both said of a subject and in a subject, e.g., knowledge is in a subject, the soul, and said of a subject, knowledge of letters or grammar. Some are neither in a subject nor said of a subject, e.g., the particular man or particular horse – for nothing of this sort is either in a subject or said of a subject. Without exception things that are individual[c] and numerically one are not said of any subject, but there is nothing to prevent some of them from being in a subject. The knowledge of letters is in a subject. (*Categories* 2.1a–b)

Particular objects are "neither in a subject nor said of a subject." These things are the primary substances in the ontology. Nothing else is a primary substance because everything else is either "in a subject" or "said of a

---

[c] The Greek is ἄτομα. It transliterates as *atoma* and is the ancestor of the English word "atomic." The translation "individual" goes back to the Latin translation as *individuum*, which means "indivisible." Aristotle uses the Greek term for "the particular man or particular horse," what would now be called "individuals." This is a striking first in the extant literature and is part of an attempt, on Aristotle's part, to explain the oneness that characterizes what we now, in our debt to him, call "individuals." He uses forms of the word again at 3a35, 38, 39, and 3b 2, 7, and 12.

subject." General objects, according to Aristotle, are "said of a subject but are not in any subject." Particular properties, he says, are "in a subject but are not said of any subject." Lastly, he says that general properties are "said of a subject and in a subject."

Now the first thing to notice about this ontology is not which things Aristotle identifies as substances, but rather that the ontology itself is much more striking than one may initially realize. In addition to *objects*, Aristotle thinks that there are *properties* of objects. So, for example, if the statement "Socrates is pale" is true, it is supposed to follow that there is a particular object, Socrates, and that there is a particular property in Socrates, his paleness. Properties themselves are not objects, according to Aristotle, but they stand in relation to objects.

In addition to the distinction between object and property, Aristotle recognizes a distinction between *particular* and *general*. So, for example, if the statement "Socrates is a man" is true, it is supposed to follow that there is a general object, man. Man is general, but man is not a property. Socrates and man are both objects. Socrates is supposed to be a particular object, and man is supposed to be a general object. Furthermore, given the fourfold division of what exists, not all properties are general. Some properties are particular.[d]

Aristotle's motivation for this fourfold division of reality is not completely clear, but it is natural to think that at least in part he is attempting to improve the ontological framework he inherits from Plato. By contrasting the *X*-ness itself with the many *X*-things, Plato emphasizes an ontological distinction between *general* and *particular*. As part of his attempt to remove what he took to be the tensions and outright mistakes in Plato's conception of reality, Aristotle seems to think that the distinction between *objects* and their *properties* is at least

---

[d] Aristotle's ontology is suspect for many reasons, but perhaps his recognition of particular properties stands out above the others. When nouns for kinds are in the plural, they apply to particular individuals. "Man" refers to a kind, human being, and the plural "men" refers to individuals of this kind. Terms for qualities, by contrast, do not easily take the plural form, and hence do not seem to refer to particulars. Furthermore, when terms for qualities do take the plural, these terms seem to refer either to kinds of the quality or to individuals with the quality. Illnesses are kinds of illness, and beauties are beautiful people or things.

equally if not more important.[e] Moreover, Aristotle seems to think that Plato should not have privileged the general over the particular. In the *Categories*, Aristotle abandons the direction of ontological dependence enshrined in Plato's ontology. Aristotle restricts primary substances to particular objects, such as "the particular man." Although species and kinds are substances in his ontology, Aristotle says that they are secondary, not primary, substances. Finally, the things Socrates asks about in his search for definitions are neither primary nor secondary substances.

In the interval from the *Categories* to the central books of the *Metaphysics*, Aristotle seems to once again distance himself from Plato's ontology. In the *Categories*, some things are general. In the *Metaphysics*, either nothing is general or no object is general. Since Aristotle does not think that the properties are all and only the general things, this view about what is general does not entail that the ontology of the *Metaphysics* is restricted to objects. Aristotle seems to have held on to his prior belief that there are particular properties and perhaps also general properties.

This view about what is general forces Aristotle to rethink his earlier explanation of the individuality of the particular objects he identified as primary substances. A human being, such as Socrates, is one thing, not a heap of things. The problem is to explain this oneness. Aristotle's expla-

---

[e] It is important not to overlook the significance of this result. Wolfgang-Rainer Mann stresses the point: "In two of his early works – in the *Categories* especially, but also in the *Topics* – Aristotle presents a revolutionary metaphysical picture. This picture has had a peculiar fate. Its revolutionary theses are so far from being recognized as such they have often been taken to be statements of common sense, or expressions of an everyday, pretheoretical ontology. The most striking and far-reaching of those theses is the claim that, included among what there is, among the entities (τὰ ὄντα), there are *things*. Aristotle, famously, goes on to maintain that these things are ontologically fundamental. All other entities are (whatever they are) by being appropriately connected to the things, for example, either as their *features* (their qualities, sizes, relations-to-each-other, locations, and so on), or as their genera and species, that is the *kinds* under which things fall. These further claims and their proper interpretation have received considerable discussion. Yet the fundamental one has gone virtually unnoticed. To formulate it most starkly: before the *Categories* and *Topics*, there were no things. Less starkly: things did not show up as things, until Aristotle wrote those two works" (*The Discovery of Things*, 2000, 3–4). Other scholars have made this same general point. "If Aristotle, then, is the first writer to call individuals 'individuals,' the question arises what is it he had in mind when he calls them 'indivisible'; for that is just what 'individuum,' rather 'atomon,' means" (Michael Frede, "Individuals in Aristotle," 1987c, 51). "[I]t is my belief, and active hypothesis of this work, that our Western-philosophical concept of a material individual, as explicitly and consciously opposed to a (quantity of a) material stuff, is largely an original formulation – I am tempted to say a deliberate invention – of Aristotle's . . ." (Montgomery Furth, *Substance, Form and Psyche*, 1988, 60).

nation in the *Categories* seems to be that the particular objects he identifies as primary substances have the unity, or oneness, of an individual because these particular objects are somehow the indivisible, or atomic, parts of general objects. As an example, consider the Aristotelian general object, man. It is not divisible by a general object, but it is divisible by number. When the object man is so divided, the many individual men are the particular objects into which man divides. These particular objects, these men, are the indivisible and atomic parts of the general object, man. The indivisibility makes them be individuals.

In the *Metaphysics*, on the other hand, since general objects do not exist, none of the particular objects of the *Categories* can be individuals by being the indivisible and atomic parts of general objects. There are no general objects. A different understanding of the unity and oneness of individuals is now necessary, and in the *Metaphysics*, in thinking once again about the particular objects he had identified as primary substances in the *Categories*, Aristotle discovers that these objects are not primary substances. Since the particular men and horses cannot exist apart from their properties, they do not appear to meet the requirement he imposes on primary substance. There is no clear sense in which these objects are prior to the rest of existence.

In the central books of the *Metaphysics*, Aristotle tries to resolve this problem by conceiving of the substances of things as forms. He has come to think that forms, not the ordinary natural bodies he had identified, meet the conditions for existence as a substance:

> For separability and this[5] seem to belong above all to substance. And so form and the compound of form and matter would be thought to be substance. The substance out of the two, of matter and form, may be dismissed since it is posterior and its nature is clear. And matter also is obvious in a way. But the third must be examined, for it is most perplexing. (*Metaphysics* VII.3.1029a)

Aristotle sets aside the "substance out of the two," by which he seems to mean not the concrete natural body from the *Categories*, but the form in matter that somehow underlies this body. Instead, he decides to investigate whether the form itself is substance most of all.

Aristotle considers the case for forms because he wants to identify something that can unite the complex of properties into an object. The thing that unifies must itself be separable from the properties and underlie them as a substance, but it is not immediately apparent what, if anything, this unifying thing could be. Consider a human being, Socrates. It is natural to think of him as a single thing that persists through time but which may have different features at different times. It is not initially clear, however, just what persists. It does not seem to be a property. Neither Socrates nor any other human being needs any particular property to exist. Of course a human being does need some properties. A human being must have some weight or other, but no particular weight is necessary. It seems that the only thing a human being needs is the particular organization that unifies and makes the material exist as an object of the kind, human being. Aristotle seems to think that this organization of the material is itself a particular object. He seems to think that this organization, this particular object, is the form of the human being. Socrates is a human being because he is material with a certain form. This form in matter persists. It stays unchanged, but the various properties come and go as Socrates changes in various ways over time.[6]

Now even if one were willing to grant that the organization (in the complex of properties that constitute Socrates) is a particular object, as Aristotle maintains, one might initially wonder whether this object under-lies all the properties. Since Socrates is a human being throughout his existence, there is a temptation to think that his form is not separable from the property of being a man and thus cannot underlie this property. For Aristotle, however, this argument poses no problem because he does not think that man is a property. In the *Categories*, he supposes that man exists and is a general object. In the *Metaphysics*, he has changed his mind. He thinks either that nothing is general or that no object is general. Moreover, in the *Metaphysics*, Aristotle appears to think that man does not exist at all. Since man is a universal, man is not a substance. Consequently, since the general objects of the *Categories* do not belong in any of the other categories of existence, it follows that they do not exist and hence are no part of Aristotle's ontology in the *Metaphysics*.

It still might be objected that the form of Socrates is not separable, because although it may need no given property to exist, it needs some properties or other to exist. Aristotle, however, apparently thinks that this objection only proves that the form is not separable without qualification, not that the form is not a substance. The form cannot exist without properties, but, according to Aristotle, the form is *separable* because it is *separable with qualification*. In the *Physics*, he says the student of nature should confine himself to things which are "separable in form, but which are in matter" and that the separable without qualification is "the work of first philosophy to determine" (II.2.194b12–15), not second philosophy. More-over, just prior to this, he claims that the nature of the natural body is "not separable except according to the account" (II.1.193b).

This conception of separateness is an instance of a general idea that manifests itself in the way that Aristotle structures his inquiry into substance in the *Metaphysics*. He begins by considering ordinary sensible objects, such as "animals and plants," and he suggests that each such object is a substance in a way and thus a substance with qualification. The study of these objects is preliminary to a consideration of what is substance most of all. Aristotle thinks that since it "is agreed that there are some substances among the sensible things," the attempt to identify the substances without qualification should begin by investigating what is substantial among the natural bodies because these bodies are the most familiar (VII.2.1028b, VII.3.1029a–1029b, VII.17.1041a).

This investigation is extremely difficult to understand in any detail, as the texts in the central books of *Metaphysics* are certainly some of most vexed in the entire Aristotelian corpus,[7] but the underlying idea seems to consist in the identification of forms as the only objects that are substances without qualification. And so the unmovable first mover is a form. It is "separable and immovable" without qualification, and it ultimately underlies changes in natural bodies. Specific behavior is for the sake of becoming like the unmovable first mover, to the extent that is possible. The unmovable first mover is the reality that underlies change, and this reality is a form.

This ontology is consistent with the fact that the substances of natural bodies are forms in matter. It is true that form, strictly speaking, is completely separable, according to Aristotle. It is also true, as he himself realizes, that the forms in matter he identifies as the substances of natural bodies are not completely separable. They are only separable in account. One might conclude, in this case, that the substances of natural bodies are not forms after all. Instead, however, Aristotle seems to conclude that just as these substances are not substances most of all, so also forms in matter are not forms most of all. They are forms because they are separable and immovable, but they are separable and immovable with qualification. It follows, in turn, that although the forms of natural bodies are forms, they are forms with qualification. They are forms in matter.[8]

8.3   No Universal is a Substance

Aristotle's ontology and theory of substance seems to have been extremely hard-won. He began, in the *Categories*, with a much more Platonic view. He thought that man and other general objects exist. He thought that these general objects are secondary substances because they are with qualification what the particular objects and primary substances are without qualification

(5.2b–3b). This position is much more Platonic in spirit than the one Aristotle adopts in the *Metaphysics*. Although the general objects man and animal are not primary substances in the *Categories*, at least they are substances. In the *Metaphysics*, Aristotle is no longer willing to grant even this much. Now, not only are man and other such objects not substances, they do not exist.[9]

To understand why Aristotle abandoned his view from the *Categories*, it is helpful to place him in historical context. He spent many years as a student in the Academy and hence came to the question of substance with the Platonic ontology in mind. In this ontology, each natural kind exists itself according to itself. Particular natural bodies have a less fundamental existence. They are somehow the various ways the kind appears in the receptacle of becoming. In the *Timaeus*, with respect to "that which always we see coming into being at different times and in different places," Timaeus says "we are not to say that this is fire, but rather we are to say that it is the thing such as fire" (49d).[10] Furthermore, he says that since "intellect and true opinion" are distinct, it is a mistake to suppose that "the things we perceive through the body must be placed as most firm" (51d). Instead of "the things we perceive through the body," Timaeus concludes that the natural kinds themselves "must be placed most firm." These kinds exist according to themselves.

Aristotle does not explicitly direct himself to Timaeus' remarks, but the position he reaches in the *Metaphysics* shows that he would have thought that these remarks do not amount to a valid argument. Aristotle, like Plato, does not place the natural bodies "as most firm," but neither does he try to understand these bodies as the ways general objects appear in the receptacle. Indeed, to the contrary, and in a fundamentally important change of view in the history of philosophy, Aristotle rejects a central platform in the Platonic metaphysics. Aristotle denies that the natural kinds and universals generally are among what there is. They do not exist.[11] He thought that if the natural kind fire were to exist, as is supposed in the *Timaeus*, its existence could only consist in its being the account of fire. It would be by existing as what is said of each of the many portions of fire when each of them is said to be fire, but Aristotle is convinced that substances are particular:

> It is evident that nothing belonging as a universal is a substance and that nothing predicated in common signifies a this. (*Metaphysics* VII.13.1038b–1039a)

Moreover, since the universals do not fall under any of the other categories of being, Aristotle is committed to thinking that natural kinds and universals do not exist. They are not part of reality. Natural bodies fall into natural kinds, but the natural kinds themselves do not exist.

In this way, in the argument for general objects, Aristotle rejects the crucial step. To think that the form of a natural body must be separable without qualification, as Plato seems to suppose in the *Timaeus*, is to think that general facts require the existence of general objects. For Aristotle, the specification of the form of a natural body of a given kind is exactly the same for every natural body of the same kind. This implies that there are general facts, but general facts are not themselves objects. Plato seems to worry that if general facts about the natural bodies are not grounded in the existence of general objects that are themselves immune from change, then instead of general facts there would be the various subjective and different viewpoints of human beings.

Aristotle takes this worry seriously, but he offers a fundamentally different solution. He supposes that what it is to be the species of a given natural body is not subject to change, even if there are no general objects, because the forms of natural bodies, although in matter, are separable in account. To ensure that the account of what the body is in species is not subject to change, and hence has the appropriate "firmness," Aristotle does not separate forms from matter and thereby make their existence consist in what is said of each natural body of a given species. The separateness in account of the forms of natural bodies is separateness enough. Aristotle summarizes his position against Plato and his followers this way: "those who speak of the forms in one way speak rightly, that they are separate if they are substances, but in another way wrongly, in that they say the form is one over many" (*Metaphysics* VII.16.1040b).

Notes

1. Aristotle's discussion is extremely complex and remains the subject of an intense scholarly debate that shows little sign of reaching consensus. Christopher Shields makes the point: "In the middle books of his *Metaphysics*, [Aristotle] embarks upon an intricately woven series of investigations concerning the nature of substance. Although they have proven endlessly fascinating to scholars, little consensus has emerged about Aristotle's conclusions. Debate continues concerning what Aristotle actually decides about primary substance . . ." (*Aristotle*, 2007, 255–256).

2. In "Metasubstance: Critical notice of Frede-Patzig and Furth," Jennifer E. Whiting provides a concise statement of the two main interpretations that appear as viable possibilities: "Although subject to some variation, the traditional view is, roughly, (1) that Aristotle recognizes only one substantial form

for each *infima species*, (2) that these species-forms are the primary substances of *Metaphysics Z*, (3) that species-forms, being common to each individual member of their respective species, are universals, and (4) that matter is the principle of individuation (or pluralization) in the sense that it is what distinguishes co-specific individuals (sharing one and the same form) from one another" (1991, 608). I accept the interpretation Whiting describes as "alternative," an interpretation she associates with Michael Frede and Gunther Patzig: "Frede and Patzig make no pretense that their alternative to the traditional view originated with them. Their alternative – variations of which date back to Alexander of Aphrodisias and have recently been proposed by Lloyd, Sellers, Heinaman and Irwin – is, roughly, (1′) that Aristotle recognizes within each species a plurality of numerically distinct individual forms, each peculiar to the compound to which it belongs, (2′) that these individual forms are the primary substances of *Metaphysics Z*, (3′) that Z rejects the existence of substantial universals common to each and every member of their respective species, and (4′) that the (individual) forms of natural substances, though themselves immaterial in the sense that they do not have any material parts, are nevertheless necessarily enmattered. Frede and Patzig take (3′) to represent a nominalist departure from the realism about substance universals expressed in the early *Categories*. So they see Aristotle in the *Metaphysics* as finally escaping the grip of the Platonic picture" (1991, 609–610).

3. David Ross describes some of what Aristotle may have had in mind about the unmovable first mover: "He moves directly the 'first heaven'; i.e., He causes the daily rotation of the stars around the earth. Since He moves by inspiring love and desire, it seems to be implied that the 'first heaven' has soul. . . . The motions of the sun, moon, and planets are explained by the hypothesis of a 'nest' of concentric spheres each with its poles fixed in the shell of the sphere next outside it. Thus each sphere imparts its own motion to the sphere next inside it, and the prime mover, by moving the outermost sphere, moves all the others. It causes the sun to move round the earth once in twenty-four hours. . . . But the rhythm of the seasons . . . is due to the sun's yearly movement in the ecliptic. . . . And this movement, like other special movements of sun, moon, and planets, is due to the 'intelligences.' These too move 'as ends'; i.e. they move by being desired and loved. Their relation to the first mover is not specified, but since the first mover is the single ruler of the universe, that on which 'the heaven and the whole of nature depend,' we must suppose that it moves the intelligences as the object of their desire and love. The detail of the system is left somewhat obscure, but we must probably think of each heavenly sphere as a unity of soul and body desiring and loving its corresponding 'intelligence'" (*Aristotle*, 1949, 181).

4. "In the traditional ordering of Aristotle's works the logical treatises (the *Organon*) come first. Among the logical treatises the *Categories* and *De Interpretatione* come first, followed by the *Analytics*. This is because the *Categories* deals with terms, the constituents of propositions, the *De Interpretatione* deals with propositions, the constituents of syllogisms, and the *Analytics* deals with

syllogism. This traditional ordering is systematic and is therefore not a guide to the actual chronology of the writings. It is, however, probable that the *Categories* and *De Interpretatione* are in fact early works of Aristotle" (Ackrill, *Aristotle's* Categories *and* De Interpretatione, 1963, 69).

5. As David Ross translates the passage, Aristotle says that "substance must be capable of separate existence and be a 'this' . . .." In his commentary, Ross shows himself to think that being "a 'this'" is being an "individual" (*Aristotle's* Metaphysics, II, 1924, 164–165). This identification in Ross's commentary moves directly into the translation in Jonathan Barnes's revision of Ross's translation for *The Complete Works of Aristotle* (1984). Barnes drops the phrase "a 'this'" and has Aristotle say that "both separability and individuality are thought to belong chiefly to substance."

6. The form in matter is not, or at least not obviously, the same as the concrete particular natural body. Michael Frede makes this point: "It is true that traditionally the composite has been identified with the concrete, particular object. But the concrete, particular object, as we are familiar with it, actually is a composite of not just matter and form, but also of a large number of accidents; it is an object of a certain size, weight, color, and the like, i.e., a complex of entities. Hence, one should not assume without further argument that the composite of matter and form is to be identified without qualification with the concrete particular" ("Substance in Aristotle's *Metaphysics*," 1987d, 74). Aristotle seems to think that the concrete particular natural body is an accidental unity, or "kooky object," to use a term Gareth Matthews introduces. The thing which appears as a persisting concrete natural body is really, it seems, a series of accidental unities of form in matter together with particular properties. The form in matter endures and hence gives the concrete body its reality. "Aristotle's picture of an accidental unity is that of an ephemeral object – an object whose very existence rests on the accidental presence, or compresence, of some feature, or features, in a substance. Accidental unities exist, he supposes, but not in their own right; indeed it is, Aristotle says, only in an accidental sense of the verb 'to be' that they can be said to be (*Metaph.* vi 2)" ("Accidental unities," 1982, 224). "[I]f Socrates is seated, then there exists such a thing as *seated Socrates*. And if the dog is tired, then there exists such a thing as *the tired dog*. What, then, is an accidental compound, or kooky object? Simply put, it is an individual substance plus at least one accident. The compound is to be understood as existing as long as, but only as long as, the substance exists and has that particular accident, or those particular accidents. Thus seated Socrates goes out of existence when Socrates stands up. And the blind man ceases to exist when the man in question regains his sight" ("On knowing how to take Aristotle's kooky objects seriously," 4).

7. For a helpful general discussion of the *Metaphysics* and the primary scholarly disputes over the proper interpretation of Aristotle's thought, see S. Marc Cohen's "Aristotle's metaphysics," 2008.

8. Michael Frede makes the point: "Although he retains the primary substances of the *Categories*, namely objects, these must now yield their status as primary substances to their substantial forms which now come to be called primary substances. The substantiality of concrete particulars is thus now only secondary. The idea of the *Categories* that substances are that which underlies everything else is retained, as we see from Z 1 and Z 3. However, the answer to the question what is it that underlies everything else has changed: now it is the substantial form. Aristotle also adds two new conditions for substancehood quite generally, conditions which, in the *Categories*, applied only to primary substances. They must be τόδε τι, and they must exist independently, i.e., not depend for their existence on any other entities." ("The title, unity, and authenticity of the Aristotelian *Categories*," 1987b, 26). "Aristotle thinks that substances are not as such composite. There are substances that are pure forms, as e.g., the unmoved mover. And it is clear ... that Aristotle thinks that the discussion of composite substances in Z [and] H is only preliminary to the discussion of separate substances. We start by considering composite substances because they are better known to us, we are familiar with them, and they are generally agreed to be substances. But what is better known by nature are the pure forms. Aristotle's remarks suggest that we shall have a full understanding of what substances are only if we understand the way in which pure forms are substances. This, in turn, suggests that he thinks there is a primary use of 'substance' in which 'substance' applies to forms. Particularly clear cases of substance in this first use of 'substance' are pure forms or separate substances. It is for this reason that composite substances are substances only secondarily" ("Substance in Aristotle's *Metaphysics*," 1987d, 79).

9. This position is controversial. The view I have taken is Michael Frede's: "Traditionally it has been assumed that forms are universal. But it is of the very nature of ultimate subjects that they cannot be predicated and, hence, cannot be universal. Therefore, if substantial forms are the ultimate subjects, they must be particular. A moment's reflection, though, shows that this is a view that Aristotle is committed to anyway. For in Z 13 he argues at length that no universal can be a substance" (Substance in Aristotle's *Metaphysics*," 1987d, 77). For an important defense of the competing view, see Alan Code's "No universal is a substance: an interpretation of *Metaphysics* Z.13, 1038b 8–15," 1978.

10. This translation is controversial. For some discussion of the problems, see Harold Cherniss, "A much misread passage in the *Timaeus* (*Timaeus* 49c7–50b5)," 1954, 116). My understanding follows the broad outline of Edward Lee's interpretation: "With this analysis, we can now also trace some relations between [49d4–e7] and its wider context in the *Timaeus*. Plato had earlier complained that people think they know well enough 'what the elements are' (48B5–7 νῦν...ὡς εἰδόσιν πῦρ ὅτι ποτέ ἐστιν, κτλ.). The view he means, no doubt, was that these elements are just the material stuffs that we perceive ... On that view, anyone who seeks a λὸγος of the elements –by asking, for

instance, τί ποτ' ἐστι, τὸ πῦρ: – might (in principle, at least) be answered by presenting him with an actual sample of fire, pointing to it, and saying, τοῦτο πῦρ ἐστι" ("On Plato's *Timaeus*, 49D4–E7," 1967, 24–25). "In short, they hold that there can be 'ostensive definition' of the elements' names" (Note 61 on 25). "In 49B–E, Plato repudiates this view on the semantic ground that no proper λόγος can be had in reference to phenomenal substances" (25).

11. "It is a basic nontrivial fact about the world that things come with forms that are exactly alike, and not just sufficiently similar to class them together in one kind. The reality of kinds amounts to no more than this: that the specification of the form of particular objects turns out to be exactly the same for a variety of objects. But for this to be true, there is no need for a universal form or a universal kind, either a species or a genus. And, in fact, the import of Z 13 seems to be that there are no substantial genera or species in the ontology of the *Metaphysics*. As universals they cannot be substances, and since they do not fall under any of the other categories either, they do not have any status in the ontology" (Michael Frede, "Substance in Aristotle's *Metaphysics*," 1987d, 78). Cf. Lynne Spellman, *Substance and Separation in Aristotle*, 1995, 61: "In short, as I understand Aristotle, the crux of his proposal, worked out in his theory of substances as a response to the Theory of Forms, is just this: that the straddling of universal and particular which is a characteristic of Plato's Forms, and indeed is necessary if what is ontologically fundamental is also to be knowable, can be made unproblematic only if Plato's separation of Forms from sensible objects is rejected. However, if Platonic separation is rejected, so Aristotle argues, forms, though particular in virtue of their numerical sameness with different sensible objects, have on account of their indistinguishability the knowability characteristic of universals."

9

Ethics

The good life for a human being

Aristotle believes that the good life is a matter of proper psychological functioning and that a life of theoretical wisdom is the best and happiest life. In these points he stands squarely within the philosophical framework he inherits from Plato, but Aristotle also works to remove the problems he perceives. First of all, as is now evident, his ontology of the soul and its relation to the body is different from Plato's. Secondly, although the issue is not completely clear, Aristotle seems to work to develop a conception of practical wisdom about ethical matters that is not so closely tied to theoretical wisdom. The cognition underlying practical wisdom about ethical matters involves reason, but it does so in a qualified way. The life of practical wisdom, so understood, is a good life. This life, however, according to Aristotle, is happy secondarily and with qualification.

The subject of Aristotle's ethics[a] is the good life. Like Socrates and Plato, Aristotle supposes that human beings are psychological beings and that the good life is a matter of proper psychological functioning.[1] Like Plato, Aristotle thinks that happiness is primarily a matter of the cognition

---

[a] Aristotle wrote several ethical works. Christopher Rowe summarizes the current scholarly consensus: "The corpus of Aristotle's works handed down to us by tradition includes four ethical treatises: the *Nicomachean Ethics* (named, it appears – by whom, and for what reason, we do not know – after his son); the *Eudemian Ethics* (named after a much-loved student of Aristotle's, though again we have no clear evidence about the precise origins of the title); the so-called *Magna Moralia*, or *Great Ethics* (actually much shorter than either the *Nicomachean* or the *Eudemian*); and the diminutive *On Virtues and Vices*. The last is incontrovertibly not by Aristotle, and while some have defended, and continue to defend, the authenticity of the *Magna Moralia*, its special features seem likely to be best explained by treating it as a work of a student who followed Aristotle's lectures. But the *Nicomachean* and *Eudemian Ethics* are indubitably by Aristotle. These two mostly cover the same range of subjects; and indeed they actually appear – on good but not quite certain authority – to share three books in common (*Nicomachean* V–VII, *Eudemian* IV–V1). Now recent scholarly opinion is probably on the side of treating the *Eudemian* as an earlier work, superseded, perhaps, by the *Nicomachean* ... and if this is right, the easiest hypothesis is that Aristotle simply decided not to rewrite the central books for the *Nicomachean*, but instead to transfer *Eudemian* IV–VI to it ..." ("Historical introduction," 2002, 4).

Ancient Greek Philosophy: From The Presocratics to the Hellenistic Philosophers, First Edition.
Thomas A. Blackson.   © 2011 Thomas A. Blackson. Published 2011 by Blackwell Publishing Ltd.

underlying "reason." He thinks that this cognition, when it takes the form of theoretical wisdom, contributes to happiness most of all. Aristotle, however, in a refinement of the Platonic position, allows that the cognition underlying practical wisdom about ethical matters belongs to "reason" in a way and hence contributes to happiness in a secondary or qualified way.

9.1   The Function Argument

Aristotle understands happiness in terms of the "function" of human beings. This is part of the Socratic and Platonic framework in which he works. Human beings are psychological beings, and happiness is a matter of psychological functioning. In itself, however, this says nothing about what happiness is. It remains to identify the particular psychological functioning in which happiness consists. Hence, to advance the issue, Aristotle tries to get a clearer understanding of the "function of man." This is the import of the following well-known passage:

> It appears agreed that happiness is the chief good, and so a clearer account is necessary. This might be given if we find the function of man. (*Nicomachean Ethics* I.7.1097b)

Aristotle considers the kinds of lives available and quickly settles on the one "peculiar to man":

> Life seems common even to plants, but we are seeking what is peculiar. So let us set aside the life of nutrition and growth. Next there would be a life of perception, but it too seems common to the horse, the ox, and every animal. There remains a life of practice holding with reason. (I.7.1097b–1098a)

The life peculiar to man is "a life of practice holding with reason," and Aristotle concludes that excelling in a life of this sort makes a human being the happiest.

Aristotle's conclusion is more surprising than it may first appear. If "a life of practice holding with reason" is a matter of the psychological functioning which characterizes a human being who makes choices in terms of knowledge of what he likes and what is likely to happen, then it would seem obvious that the expectation for happiness is a matter of "holding with reason." No one should expect to find happiness if he chooses a course of action whose value he expects to be worse than the values he expects from other courses of action open to him. Aristotle, however, understands "holding with reason" much more substantively. He understands it to include a very specific commitment to what is enjoyable. He supposes that "holding with reason" itself is what a human being most enjoys. For Aristotle, this contributes to happiness most of all.

Plato provides the example. He thought that the love of wisdom is the activity a human being enjoys most of all, and he understood this activity as a way of "holding with reason." The love of wisdom is a certain exercise of reason, an exercise that involves knowledge of the forms and is a matter of contemplation. The soul, in its natural and incarnate state, is fixed in this blissful contemplation. Upon becoming incarnate, it becomes confused and embarks on courses of action it believes will make its situation better but in which there in fact is little or no happiness to be found. Ethics is the remedy for this problem, according to Plato. In the *Republic*, Socrates argues that the three parts of the soul must become properly organized, and hence just, so that the reasoning part is in control. It knows the good and can direct action in terms of its knowledge.

Although Aristotle rejects this Platonic ontology of the soul, he accepts certain aspects of the general picture. In particular, he understands "holding with reason" itself to be what a human being enjoys most of all. The unmovable first mover is good without qualification, and natural bodies exercise their specific behaviors for the sake of existing in imitation of the existence the unmovable first mover enjoys. For a human being, the existence most like the existence of the unmovable first mover is a life which may be described generically as "holding with reason." Within this genus, Aristotle considers two more specific ways of holding with reason: the life of politics and the life of "contemplation."[b] A human being holds with reason in both of

---

[b] The Greek is θεωρία. It transliterates as *theoria* and is the etymological ancestor of the English word "theory." Originally it meant "a looking at, viewing, beholding." Plato and Aristotle extend this ordinary sense. John Burnet makes the point: "In theoretical science we are . . . in the position of spectators, and this is the original signification of the word θεωρία. The end or good of such a science lies in conformity to reality, and this conformity is truth" (*The Ethics of Aristotle*, 1900, xxiii). Sarah Brodie is more expansive: "We should not reduce [*theoria*] by the translations 'study' or 'speculation' though these may be suitable in some contexts. The first suggests laboriousness, the second the posing of questions and hazarding of hypotheses. These are features of much of what passes as *theoria* on the human level, but they do not easily transfer to a god's activity or capture the measure of what Aristotle means by 'the divine element in us' [in the *Nicomachean Ethics* at X.1177a]. '*Theoria*' covers any sort of detached, intelligent, attentive pondering, especially when not directed to a practical goal. Thus it can denote the intellectual activity or aesthetic exploration of some object, or the absorbed following of structures as they unfold when we look and stay looking more deeply, whether by means of sensory presentation or abstract concepts. The traditional word 'contemplation' would still be preferable if we could overcome its suggestion of a locked gaze" (*Ethics with Aristotle*, 1991, 401).

these lives, but the life of contemplation is the best. This is clear in Aristotle's remarks in the following:

> There are three prominent types of life, the one of pleasure, the political, and thirdly the contemplative life. The mass of mankind appear altogether slavish. They prefer a life suitable to grazing animals, but there is some argument for this, as many in high places share the tastes of Sardanapallus.[c] People of superior refinement and active in politics identify happiness with honor, for this is roughly the end of the political life. But it seems too superficial to be what we are seeking. (*Nicomachean Ethics* I.5.1095b)

> Happiness seems to be in leisure,[d] since we are busy so that we may have leisure, and fight war so that we may live in peace. Now the practical virtues are exhibited in politics or war, and the actions in these seem to be without leisure. This is completely so for war, but the action of the statesman is also without leisure. So although actions exhibiting virtue in politics and war are distinguished by nobility and greatness, they are without leisure, aim at an end, and are not desirable for their own sake. But the activity of intellect, being contemplative, seems superior in worth, to aim at no end beyond itself, and to have its proper pleasure to itself, and this adds to the activity. It is the complete happiness of man, if it is a complete term of life, since nothing incomplete is proper to happiness. But such a life would be too high for man, since it is not in so far as he is man that he will live so, but in so far as something divine is present in him. And by so much as this is superior to our composite nature is its activity superior to that which is the exercise of this other kind of excellence. If intellect is divine, then, in comparison with man, the life according to it is divine in comparison with human life. (X.7.1177b)

> Everyone supposes that the gods are alive and active, since surely they are not asleep like Endymion.[e] But if action is excluded from a living being, and still more production, what is left but contemplation? Therefore the activity of God, which surpasses all others in blessedness, must be contemplative. The human activity most like this will be happiness the most. An indication of this

---

[c] An Assyrian king who lived in legendary luxury. In II.2 of *Bibliotheca Historica*, Diodorus Siculus paints a vivid and unsympathetic picture of the lavish and decadent lifestyle Sardanapallus enjoyed. (Diodorus Siculus was a Greek historian who lived in the first century BC.)

[d] The Greek word translated as "leisure" is the etymological ancestor of the English words "scholar," "scholarly," and "school." The meaning of the Greek word was not restricted to scholarly activity, but such activity is an important instance of the phenomena to which the noun refers ("V. *a work of leisure*, esp. *a learned discussion, disputation*, Lat. *schola*. VI. *the place where such lectures were given*, a school": Liddell and Scott, *Greek-English Lexicon*, 1976).

[e] Endymion is a character of myth. He was of surpassing beauty and the son of Zeus. Zeus allowed him to choose what he would, and he chose to sleep forever so as to remain deathless and ageless. Endymion's eternal sleep was proverbial in the ancient world. See, e.g., Plato's reference to him in the *Phaedo* at 72c.

is that the other animals have no share in happiness, being altogether deprived of this activity. For while the whole life of the gods is blessed, and that of men too in so far as it has some likeness to this activity, none of the other animals is happy, since they do not share in contemplation in any way. Happiness extends, then, just so far as contemplation does, and those to whom contemplation more fully belongs are more truly happy, not accidentally, but according to contemplation; for this is in itself precious. Happiness must be some sort of contemplation. (X.8.1178b)

Aristotle does not mention the unmovable first mover in these remarks, but it is natural to think he has this mover in mind in his analysis of happiness in terms of the "function" of human beings.[2] The unmovable first mover has the perfect existence. Human beings are good to the extent that their existence resembles that of the unmovable first mover. Since goodness is happiness in human beings, human beings are happier to the extent that their existence resembles that of the unmovable first mover, and their existence most of all resembles the existence of the unmovable first mover to the extent that they function properly and hence engage in "contemplation."[f]

9.2   Theoretical Wisdom

To isolate more precisely what it is to hold with reason, Aristotle divides the cognition involved in "reason" according to subject matter. Sometimes, the subject matter consists in "things whose starting points cannot be otherwise." Other times, it consists in "things whose origins admit of being otherwise." This division in subject matter corresponds to a division in the soul:

> Let it be assumed that there are two parts of the soul[3] that have reason, one
> by which we contemplate things whose starting points cannot be otherwise,

---

[f] In the *Phaedo*, the soul in its natural and disincarnate state is free of practical concerns and the need to exercise reason to meet these concerns. Instead, it is somehow fixed in an exercise of reason involving knowledge of the forms. The soul, in this way, is like a god. Aristotle rejects this Platonic ontology of the soul and its relation to the body, but he is in complete agreement with Plato on the fundamental point: that the most divine cognition in human beings is in the cognition involved in the exercise of reason in contemplation. Terence Irwin states the point: "[Aristotle] declares that happiness consists in theoretical 'study' or 'contemplation' (*theoria*), grasping the ultimate universal truths about the universe (1177a12–18). . . . The exercise of theoretical reason in study is the best exercise of human reason; its activities are choiceworthy solely for their own sake, and in them a human being comes closest to the condition of a purely rational being, a god. Contemplation is the highest fulfilment of our nature as rational beings; it is the sort of rational activity that we share with the gods, who are rational beings with no need to apply reason to practice" (*The Development of Ethics*, I: *From Socrates to the Reformation*, 2007, 149).

and one by which we contemplate things whose starting points can be otherwise. Let one of these be called the one which knows and the other the one which calculates, as deliberating and calculating are the same, but no one deliberates about what cannot be otherwise. Therefore the calculative is one part of the soul that has reason. Since virtue in character is a state concerned with decision, and decision is deliberative desire, both the reason must be true and the desire right, if the decision is to be good. This intellect and truth is practical. The intellect that is contemplative and theoretical is neither practical nor productive. The good and bad of it are truth and falsity. This is the function of what thinks, but the function of what thinks about action is truth in agreement with correct desire. (*Nicomachean Ethics* VI.2.1139a)

For the part of reason that is "theoretical," as opposed to "practical," Aristotle says that excellence is not a matter of desire. The requirement for excellence is "truth," and the particular truths he has in mind are the truths about the general structure of reality. The cognition involved in reason concerned with "things whose starting cannot be otherwise," when the exercise is excellent, consists in the knowledge that makes a human being most resemble the unmovable first mover.

Aristotle's view of "reason" is a variation on a Platonic theme, but it is also a development of the ordinary way in which human beings think about themselves and their actions. In their pursuit of ends, human beings can act reasonably as opposed to foolishly. Since the effective pursuit of ends seems to require the ability to know the relevant truths in the situation at hand, it is natural to think that the ability to form and to preserve knowledge is essential for rationality in its most expert form.

This connection between rationality and knowledge began to attract sustained intellectual attention during the Presocratic period. Thales was famous for predicting a solar eclipse, but his achievement was not regarded simply as a solution to a theoretical problem. Herodotus writes about the prediction in connection with a battle in which the eclipse was regarded as an omen.[4] Parmenides too insists on the importance of reason for knowledge of what exists, and although he does not stress the practical aspect of reason, presumably it would be a mistake to think he denied it. The same is true for Democritus in his insistence on reason as opposed to experience.

It is difficult to know what the historical Socrates thought, but he seems to have understood reason and knowledge similarly. His interest in ethical matters was practical. As Plato portrays him, he insists on knowledge of the definitions of the virtues because he wants his actions to comply with the demands of virtue. The way Socrates proceeds in the early Platonic dialogues suggests the historical figure thought that knowledge of these definitions somehow belongs to reason and that people ordinarily are confused about what to do because they mistakenly rely on experience and hence wrongly conflate the universal with its manifestation in familiar situations.

Although the historical Socrates seems to have placed no importance on (and may have been skeptical about the possibility of) the sort of theoretical understanding the inquirers into nature sought, Plato returns to the idea that knowledge of this sort is an important part of reason. He does not think that the inquirers into nature are correct about reality, but he is convinced that theoretical understanding is possible and has great practical importance. In the *Republic*, Plato describes the education that enables a person "to contemplate that which is, and the brightest of beings, which we say is the good" (VII.518c–d). The student who seeks wisdom proceeds through studies of arithmetic, plane and solid geometry, and astronomy, until finally "through dialectic, without help from the senses, but by reason, he sets out to find that which each itself is, and does not give up before grasping the good itself with intellect alone" (VII.532a–b). The knowledge at issue here is not simply theoretical, something whose possession provides no practical guidance. On the contrary, it is has immense practical value because the lover of wisdom employs it to decide what to do in the situations he encounters. His actions are for the good. In this way, Plato takes a momentous step beyond the ordinary idea that knowledge is essential for rationality. The knowledge necessary for rationality is part of a theoretical understanding of things, knowledge which he thinks is the preeminent example of the cognition in "reason."

In part, Aristotle follows in Plato's footsteps. For Aristotle, theoretical understanding is the end of the process of induction. He does not explain in detail how a human being acquires "reason" and its knowledge and thus moves beyond "experience" in the inductive sequence. Aristotle, however, does think that the exercise of "reason" underlies knowledge in theoretical understanding in the sciences of theology, physics, and mathematics. These sciences have the same structure. They are all demonstrative, but Aristotle privileges theology as the first, or unqualified, love of wisdom. In the *Metaphysics*, he explains that theology is first among the theoretical sciences because, among other things, it demonstrates how the modes of existence characteristic of the objects in the domains of the physics and mathematics depend on the existence of the unmovable first mover.[g]

Moreover, Aristotle, like Plato before him, supposes that the cognition involved in such theoretical understanding contributes to happiness most of

---

[g] In accepting the importance of theory, Aristotle shows the influence of his long study with Plato. "Plato, his teacher for two decades, offered an understanding of the cosmos which located in the activities of the pure intellect the highest and most godlike human achievement, outclassing even the exercise of civic virtue. That Aristotle adopted this view as his own and even constructed his own ethics and cosmology around it should not, given the circumstances of his own life, altogether surprise us" (David Sedley, "'Becoming like god' in the *Timaeus* and Aristotle," 1997, 338–339).

all. Aristotle works out his view about expertise in theology and its connection to happiness against the background of the discussion in the *Timaeus*. Plato, in this dialogue, has his character say that the universe is alive, that it is a soul in a body, and that this cosmic soul animates the universe insofar as the bodily workings of the universe are the visible manifestation of the psychological functioning of the cosmic soul (30a–c, 36d–37a). Furthermore, in an even more remarkable passage, Timaeus says that a human being is happy to the extent that the reasoning part of his soul is like the reason, or intelligence, in the cosmic soul. A human being must "redirect the revolutions" in his head so that he will have a good life and be happy to the extent that he comes to think what the cosmic soul thinks. The "revolutions" in need of redirection are mistaken thoughts about the structure of reality. To correct them, it is necessary to learn "the harmonies and revolutions of the universe." Since these "harmonies and revolutions" are what the cosmic soul thinks, a human being who acquires this theoretical understanding transforms himself so that his existence resembles the existence of the cosmic soul (90a–d).

Aristotle stands squarely within the broad framework of this philosophical tradition. He supposes that there is a perfect being who underlies change, that the principles of reality are in the mind of this being, and a human being becomes good and finds happiness by transforming his psychology so that he becomes like this perfect being. For Aristotle, however, the perfect being does not animate the body of the universe. Unlike the cosmic soul in the *Timaeus*, the unmovable first mover is completely fixed. It is somehow fixed in a set of thoughts whose content is the structure of existence, and a human being who manages to transform his psychology so that he has expertise in theology becomes as much like the unmovable first mover as human nature allows.

Hence, for Aristotle, as for Plato, the cognition in the human soul which constitutes the greatest happiness is the cognition involved in "reason." This, however, need not and presumably does not mean that such cognition is the one and only thing a human enjoys. Rather, the idea seems to be that an uninterrupted life of contemplation, were this possible for a human being, would be better and hence happier than any other human life. This is supposed to be a truth about the human soul, and, whether it is a truth or not, it is what Plato and Aristotle believe.

9.3   Practical Wisdom

In addition to reason in theory, in a departure from Plato at least in emphasis and perhaps also in substance, Aristotle recognizes reason in practice. In this exercise of reason, excellence consists in "truth in agreement with correct desire." Aristotle understands desire along Platonic lines. He supposes that desire arises in the human psychology in three ways (*On the Soul* I.3.414b). Furthermore, and again like Plato, Aristotle supposes that the appetitive and spirited desires are not themselves a matter of reason. This becomes clear in the following passage in which Aristotle distinguishes voluntary action from action that stems from decision:

> Decision seems to be voluntary, not the same thing, since the voluntary extends more widely. Children and the other animals have voluntary action in common, but not decision, and acts done all of a sudden we say are voluntary, but not due to decision. Those who say that decision is appetite or spirit or wish or some kind of opinion do not seem to be correct. For decision is not common to things without reason, but both appetite and spirit are. (*Nicomachean Ethics* III.2.1111b)

Some desires are a matter of belief and hence are a matter of reason, but in human beings not all desires are a matter of reason. The desires of the appetite and spirit are not.[5]

In this way, Aristotle follows Plato against Socrates. In the Tripartite Theory of the Soul, not all desire is a matter of reason. A human being can act contrary to what he knows or believes is better. This is irrational, but Plato and Aristotle believe it is possible. In such cases, the human being has a functioning psychology. He has a belief about what would be good to do in the situation at hand, but his psychology does not function properly. He acts against his belief.

Aristotle discusses this kind of irrationality and improper psychological functioning, but he is more interested in proper psychological functioning and in the exercise of practical reason and practical wisdom about ethical matters.[h] He uses the language of "actuality" to describe the cognition

---

[h] Reason concerned with practice is concerned with "action or production" (VI.2.1139a). In the first case, reason is exercised for the sake of "the fine." In the second case, it is exercised for the sake of some sort of product. This exercise of reason, when it is done well, makes a human being a good builder of houses or a good maker of ships, but Aristotle is not much interested in this. His concern is with the exercise of reason that makes a human being a good human being. "Aristotle makes a distinction between what he sees as fundamentally different activities of reason (1139a6–15). On the one hand, there is the kind of cognition involved in grasping eternal, unchanging, immutable truths (1139b19–24). This is the activity that he calls *theoria* and identifies as the ultimate human good.... Aristotle contrasts it with what he calls practical (*praktike*) reason (1139a36), which deliberates about what to do (1139a11–13; cf. 1142b31–3). Excellence of such reasoning, according to Aristotle, falls into two types: *techne* (skill or craft, defined in VI 4) and *phronesis* (practical wisdom, defined in VI 5). Practical wisdom (*phronesis*) is the excellence of reason involved in the ethical excellences (114b21–8)" (Susan Sauvé Meyer, *Ancient Ethics*, 2008b, 73).

involved in this particular expertise and says that a life characterized by this cognition is "happiest secondarily" in comparison to an uninterrupted life of theoretical wisdom:

> The good for man is an actuality of the soul in accordance with virtue, and if more than one virtue exists, then in accordance with the best and most final. (*Nicomachean Ethics* I.7.1098a)

> If happiness is an actuality in accordance with virtue, it is reasonable for it to be in accordance with the most excellent, and this will be of the best thing. Whether intellect or something else is this, and thought to be our natural ruler and leader and to understand the fine and divine, whether divine or only the most divine element in us, the actuality of this best thing in accordance with its proper virtue will be complete happiness. This happiness is contemplative, as we have said. (X.7.1177a)

> That which is proper to each thing is by nature the best and the most pleasant for it. For man, this is the life according to intellect, if the intellect more than anything else is man. This life therefore is also the happiest. But the life according to the other kind of virtue is happiest secondarily because the actualities in accordance with this are human. (X.8.1178a)

Aristotle's point, in saying that "the good for man is an actuality of the soul," is teleological. When the soul organizes material so that a human being has practical wisdom about ethical matters, "in-end-hold" is true of the human being. This end, however, according to Aristotle, is an end with qualification. It is less qualified than the "in-end-hold" which is true of a human being simply in virtue of being alive. This end, nevertheless, is an end with qualification because it is not the way of "holding with reason" in which a human being is most like the unmovable first mover.

This understanding of practical wisdom and its connection to happiness seems to represent a significant departure from the Platonic position, but it is important to see that Aristotle does not break from the Platonic position completely. First of all, he retains a broadly Socratic and Platonic understanding of what the ethical virtues are. Socrates, as Plato portrays him, suggests that piety and the other ethical virtues are defined in terms of what is appropriate and that what is appropriate may and often does vary from one situation to the next. Aristotle shows himself to have this same general conception of the ethical virtues. This is evident in his doctrine that virtue is a "mean":

> Virtue of character is concerned with passions and actions; in these there is excess, deficiency, and the mean. We can be afraid or confident, have appetites, anger and pity and, as a whole, pleasure or pain, too much or too little, and in both not well, but at the right times, about the right things,

towards the right people, for the right end, and the right way, is what is the mean and the best, and this is proper to virtue. Similarly with regard to actions there is excess, defect, and the mean. Virtue is concerned with passions and actions, in which excess and deficiency go wrong, while the mean is right and brings praise, which is proper to virtue. Virtue is a mean. (*Nicomachean Ethics* II.6.1106b)

Aristotle's discussion of courage illustrates the import of this doctrine. A courageous human being knows the fearful things it is appropriate to flee from and to stand firm against. Further, he takes the appropriate action in the situation because he "holds with reason" and because the appropriate action is the one reason proscribes (III.7.1115b, III.7.1116a, III.8,1116b–1117a).

In addition to his general understanding of the definitions of the virtues, Aristotle also seems to be in agreement with Plato on the kinds of cognition involved in the possession of practical wisdom about ethical matters. Like Plato, Aristotle stresses the need for experience. In fact, Aristotle can seem to say that practical wisdom is completely a matter of experience:

The virtues arise in us neither by nature nor against nature, but by nature we acquire them, becoming complete through habit. We take the virtues by first exercising them, just as in the other arts. For when we learn to make we learn by making, e.g., we become builders by building and lyre-players by playing the lyre, and so too we become just by doing just acts, temperate by doing temperate acts, brave by doing brave acts. (*Nicomachean Ethics* II.1.1103a)

Aristotle, however, like Plato, does *not* think experience is sufficient for practical wisdom about ethical matters. They are rationalists.[6] Practical wisdom about ethical matters is an expertise for Plato and Aristotle, and so the cognition involved in an expertise must consist in something more than the cognition in experience. It must include cognition from the domain of reason.

Aristotle's disagreement with Plato is about how the cognition underlying practical wisdom about ethical matters belongs to reason. By the time of the middle dialogues, Plato thinks that the love of wisdom is really first and foremost the love of theoretical knowledge of a certain sort. Furthermore, he believes that knowledge of the appropriate in ethical matters requires knowledge of the theoretical truth that a human being is an immortal soul in a mortal body and that a certain exercise of reason involving knowledge of the forms contributes to human happiness most of all. Justice in a human being is the psychological organization among the parts of the soul that underlies knowledge of the appropriate in ethical matters. The part of the soul with reason, in a just human being, is not confused about what a human being is and what its interests are, and this knowledge is involved in deciding what is appropriate in the current situation. In contrast to Plato, Aristotle gives no indication that he thinks that a human being who has practical wisdom about ethical matters must have a theoretical understanding of reality.[7] Aristotle, nevertheless, since he is a rationalist about practical wisdom, must have some alternative understanding of how the cognition in reason is involved in practical wisdom about ethical matters.

There may be some temptation to think that for Aristotle, as opposed to Plato, practical wisdom about ethical matters is like the expertise of a practitioner, but this temptation should be resisted. In the discussion of induction in the *Metaphysics*, although the medical practitioner does not know "the why and the cause," he does have a certain expertise. He makes the correct diagnosis and applies the correct remedy in situations in which the layman is more likely to be confused. Aristotle characterizes the expertise that belongs to such a practitioner as a matter of "experience." He opposes this "experience" to the "reason" involved in knowledge of "the why and the cause." Hence, it seems that the cognition involved in knowledge of empirical generalizations, which marks the expertise of the medical practitioner, cannot be what Aristotle has in mind when he says that practical wisdom about ethical matters is a way of "holding with reason."

Rather, Aristotle has in mind the cognition in deliberation. He calls attention to deliberation when he distinguishes practical from theoretical applications of reason. He says that "deliberating and calculating are the same" and that "the calculative is one part of the soul having reason." Further, in the *Eudemian Ethics*, he says that although animals can have beliefs about what should be done, they do not have "reason." They do not have "reason" because they cannot deliberate. They cannot deliberate because they are unable to think about "a certain cause":

> I call it deliberate when deliberation is the source of the desire. The man desires because of the deliberation. Hence in the other animals there is no decision, nor in every time of life, or in every condition in man, neither is deliberation and opinion about the why. But it seems that nothing prevents many animals from having an opinion whether a thing is to be done or not, but not through reasoning. For the reasoning part of the soul is deliberative and that which contemplates a certain cause. The for the sake of which is one of the causes. That for the sake of which something is or comes to be, this we say is a cause, e.g., the fetching of things is the cause of walking, if he is walking for the sake of this. And so those who do not have an aim are not deliberative. (*Eudemian Ethics* II.10.1226b)

Aristotle's remarks are compressed, but his idea is that deliberation is essentially a matter of having a goal and of considering action "for the sake of" this goal. Therefore, for Aristotle, it follows that the cognition in deliberation is a matter of "reason" in a certain way. Deliberation includes thought about the "for the sake of." Hence, practical wisdom about ethical matters is a qualified way of "holding with reason" because deliberation is a qualified way of having knowledge of "the why and the cause" that constitutes theoretical wisdom.[8]

If the interpretation is correct, although Aristotle does not break from Platonism completely, he introduces a significant improvement in the ethical framework he inherits from his teacher. Aristotle takes steps to extend happiness, understood in terms of "reason," beyond the love of wisdom and into the lives of more ordinary human beings.[9] Plato, in the *Phaedo* and the *Republic*, can easily leave his readers with the impression that the lives of most human beings are not very good at all and that happiness is really only to be found in an extremely refined form of thinking that only a few extraordinarily gifted human beings, such as Socrates, can participate in. Aristotle, with his understanding of practical wisdom, relaxes this understanding of happiness.[i]

---

[i] The issue remains in considerable dispute, but many scholars hold that Aristotle (despite his understanding of practical wisdom and happiness) does not depart from the most striking and characteristic parts of the ethical framework Plato pioneered. "The state exists for the sake of the comparatively few rare souls that are able to lead the highest life, and it is undeniable that the rest are to some extent sacrificed to these. But in reply to this Aristotle would say that in a well-ordered state all the citizens have such happiness as they are capable of, and we cannot ask for more" (John Burnet, *The Ethics of Aristotle*, 1900, xxviii). "[A]lthough humans have, unlike gods, essentially physical, emotional, and social needs, and consequently can participate in the divine activity of contemplation (or their approximation to it) only to a limited extent at best, this is nonetheless what they should strive to do. They must, individually and politically, try to organize human life around attaining this as much as is humanly possible" (Gavin Lawrence, "Aristotle and the ideal life," 1993, 20). "Aristotle does not himself deal with these questions, and I cannot here discuss the attempts that have been made to answer them for him. I will, however, mention one suggestion, designed to connect morality to contemplation, and so to prevent good action and *theoria* from seeming to be just unrelated and rival activities. The suggestion is that the very aim of morality is the promotion of *theoria*, that what makes a type of action count as good is precisely its tendency to promote *theoria*. On this view the ultimate justification for requiring and praising the sorts of acts and attitudes characteristic of the good man is that general adherence to the rules and standards he subscribes to would – in the long run and over all – maximize the amount of *theoria* possible in the community. If this is so, then of course there cannot, at bottom, be any *conflict* between morality and philosophy, morality being in essence the system of conduct that favours and promotes philosophy" (J. L. Ackrill, *Aristotle The Philosopher*, 1981, 140).

Notes

1. Scholars commonly remark on Plato's influence on Aristotle. "Aristotle spent many years with Plato in the Academy, and the *Ethics* and the *Politics* in particular show heavy Platonic influence. Although there are large differences, it is fair to say that Aristotelian ethical theory as a whole is essentially a development of the Platonic. This continuity is of the greatest importance for understanding the arguments" (Christopher Rowe, *An Introduction to Greek Ethics*, 1977, 100). "Despite their marked stylistic difference from Plato's vivid dramatic dialogues, ... [Aristotle's ethical treatises] centre around the same set of practical questions. Aristotle writes for an audience who, like the ambitious seekers after *arete* whom we encounter in Plato, desire to become good (*EN* 1103b27–9). They assume without question, like Plato's Socrates and his interlocutors, that we all want to 'do well' (*eu prattein*) or 'live well' (*eu zen*) – that is, to be *eudaimon* ('happy' – 1095a17–20; cf *Euthd.* 278e). Like Plato, Aristotle recognizes that his contemporaries disagree about what sort of life is the best to live (1095a20–3). While Plato typically construes this issue as a question of which life (*bios*) is best, and addresses it by raising the question, 'What is *arete*?', Aristotle construes it as a dispute about what *eudaimonia* (happiness) is" (Susan Sauvé Meyer, *Ancient Ethics*, 2008b, 50).

2. J. L. Ackrill voices a common complaint about the argument. "Aristotle seeks to discover what is the good for man by determining his specific function. ... [But it] is not self-evident that the best thing for a man is to be the best man possible. This little slide is made easier for Plato and Aristotle by the fact that ... 'living well' and 'doing well' are equivalent in Greek with *eudaimonia* ('happiness'). The danger of the slide is not of course apparent in the case of a knife or an eye, since we do not raise questions about the welfare of a knife or an eye, or regard them as deriving benefit from their performances" (*Aristotle's Ethics*, 1973, 20).

3. Although Aristotle uses the terminology of parts, he does not seem to think that the human soul really has parts. For a recent statement of this sort of interpretation, see Hendrik Lorenz: "Aristotle, as we have seen, accepts Plato's three kinds of desire, but does not accept Platonic tripartition of the soul. His psychological theory, to be sure, appeals to parts or aspects of the soul, but it is somewhat unclear what commitment to such items comes to, and they are in any case not the three parts of Plato's theory. They are conceived of in functional terms, as being responsible for sets of interrelated natural capacities that are distinctive of living things" (*The Brute Within*, 2006, 202).

4. Michael Frede makes the point: "[Herodotus gives] us some idea of how Thales' wisdom was perceived: supposedly Thales managed to predict the solar eclipse of May 585, which happened precisely as the Medes and the Lydians joined battle, and which hence one would be tempted to regard as ominous. ... Wisdom here seems to be seen as something that proves itself in a practical way.... There is little or no emphasis on the theoretical achievement the prediction of an eclipse would involve. If Thales had not supposedly been able to predict the eclipse, and

if it had not ominously coincided with the battle, Herodotus hardly would have seen a reason to refer at least indirectly to Thales' attempts to theoretically understand the world" ("The philosopher," 2000, 5–6).

5. Michael Frede sets out this sort of interpretation of Aristotle: "What Aristotle's position may be is a more complicated and more controversial matter. The traditional interpretation, not surprisingly, has it that for Aristotle the motive force for our action has its source in a non-rational desire. But in general, and more specifically in the *Ethics*, it seems to me Aristotle is better understood on the assumption that he attributes motive force to reason itself and distinguishes desires of reason and desires of the irrational part of the soul. Thus, when in the *Nicomachean Ethics* I.13 he tries to establish the basis for his distinctions between intellectual and moral virtue by distinguishing an irrational part of the soul from a rational part, he seems to rely for the latter distinction on an argument reminiscent of Plato's *Republic*. He refers, for instance, to the inclinations of the weak-willed which go in opposite directions (1102b21). This is supposed to suggest that reason inclines us in one way and then hence there must be something else which inclines us in the opposite direction. But that reason inclines us in a certain way is most naturally understood as meaning that this would be how we would act, unless something else intervened" ("Introduction," in *Rationality in Greek Thought*, 1996a, 7–8).

6. Terence Irwin makes the point as part of his interpretation of Aristotle as a rationalist about practical reason. "[Aristotle's] version of naturalism identifies the human function with a life of action of the rational part, and therefore requires a naturalist account of virtue to be a rationalist account.... He does not take the non-rational components of the virtues to be irrelevant or unimportant. On the contrary, we have seen how his claims about the importance of non-rational impulses, pleasures and pains show how one might develop a strongly anti-rationalist account of the virtues of character and of the formation of ends. But Aristotle does not hold an anti-rationalist account; it would undermine the central role of the Function Argument in the *Ethics*. Non-rational elements are prominent in the account of virtue; for if virtue fulfils human nature, it fulfils the non-rational elements of human nature too. But Aristotle's naturalism places the human function in a life guided by practical reason; hence the fulfilment of the non-rational elements of human nature includes their agreement with, and subordination to, practical reason" (*The Development of Ethics*, I: *From Socrates to the Reformation*, 2007, 176–177).

7. This sort of interpretation seems to go back at least to Werner Jaeger's *Aristotle: Fundamentals of the History of his Development*, which was published in 1923. "Jaeger makes the important suggestion that the most significant ethical difference between the mature work of Aristotle and the work of Plato, as well as the earlier Aristotle, is that Aristotle eventually comes to separate *phronesis* from theoretical or philosophical understanding and to establish the independence of each" (Christopher Bobonich, "Aristotle's ethical treatises," 2006, 19). The general point is now common in the secondary literature. "What, according

to Aristotle, *is* the right end at which the *phronimos* aims? To say *'eudaimonia'* is no help, insofar as virtuous action just is (a form of) *eudaimonia*. To settle what is in a given situation the right thing to do, Aristotle appeals to the judgment of the *phronimos*. With what aim in mind does he judge it right? Not the aim of doing what a *phronimos* would think right: that would be a futile circle. Does the *phronimos* aim at promoting theoretical thought? Though Aristotle gives this the highest value, he makes no attempt to show that the rules of conduct of ordinary life are to be justified (ultimately, if not immediately) by their tendency to promote that activity" (J. L. Ackrill, *Aristotle's Ethics*, 1973, 29). "In approaching his discussion we must bear in mind that [Aristotle] is drawing distinctions that had not been made systematically before in Western Philosophy. It would not have been obvious to his audience at the outset that technical expertise is not the right paradigm for understanding practical wisdom. Socrates, after all, had constantly argued as if it were. And Plato in the *Republic* had confused matters still further. Not only did he take it for granted that wisdom is identical with the art of government, which he represented as an expertise requiring specialist training. He also insisted that the training include mastery of pure mathematics and astronomy, as well as 'dialectic,' a science which, according to the *Republic*, excels mathematics in clarity and intelligibility no less than mathematics excels experiential judgments about the everyday world. The implication is that a mind trained in the most abstract and exact theoretical disciplines is essential for practical wisdom. Aristotle seems to have been the first to teach that abstract theoretical understanding does not confer practical wisdom, is not a precondition of that sort of wisdom . . ." (Sarah Broadie, "Philosophical introduction," 2002, 46–47). "In striking contrast with Plato, who portrays the knowledge one needs for living well as a philosopher's grasp of other-worldly eternal truths (*Phd.* 65d–66a; *Rep.* 479e), Aristotle insists that the knowledge expressed in the ethical excellences is practical rather than theoretical" (Susan Sauvé Meyer, *Ancient Ethics*, 2008b, 76).

8. This is controversial. Gabriel Lear suggests that, for Aristotle, practical wisdom about ethical matters "approximates" contemplation because both involve holding certain truths in mind: "Given that the human contemplator cannot engage continuously in the activity he values above all others, he must find some way to approximate it (so as to extend a kind of contemplation and godlikeness into his practical life) and a way to show in his practical life where his heart is. This he does by acting in accordance with the most perfect practical truthfulness of morally virtuous activity" (*Happy Lives and the Highest Good. An Essay on Aristotle's* Nicomachean Ethics, Lear, 2004, 205). "For instance, if a philosopher is at a party, he will not leave early in a way that might offend his hosts and make him seem a spoilsport to the other guests. He cannot, in his practical life, approximate perfect theoretical truthfulness unless he recognizes the truth of himself as not only rational, but also political and animal" (206). "When we protect those we love courageously, dine with them temperately, give to them generously, and accept their honors with greatness of soul, we grasp the practical

truth – we are embodied, political animals who find our rational happiness only in common with others. Grasping this practical truth approximates contemplation and is worth choosing for its sake. . . . As an approximation of the highest good, it embodies the intrinsically valuable character of wise contemplation and can, in its own right, extend *theoria tis* into that practical part of our lives where theoretical contemplation cannot reach" (207).

9. "It is noteworthy that Aristotle hardly ever talks of ethics or practical philosophy as 'philosophy.' One place in which he does so is at the very end of *E.N.* X.9 1181b15, where he speaks of 'the philosophy concerning human affairs' (τὰ ἀνθρώπεια). Thus he implicitly contrasts it with first philosophy which is concerned with wisdom which is divine and of matters divine, for instance God. It is wisdom which affords us the contemplation of truth, which Aristotle earlier in *E. N.* X tells us that it makes our life like that of gods, to the extent that this is humanly possible. But first philosophy is concerned with the good or with what is best, and its concern is a theoretical concern, a concern aimed at satisfying our need to know and understand what is the most important thing to understand, namely God, a principle of all things. By contrast, ethics is just concerned with the human good, and this concern is not theoretical, but a practical concern. It is aimed at being good and living well" (Michael Frede, "Aristotle's account of the origins of philosophy," 2004, 24).

Further Reading for Part IV

1. *Aristotle the Philosopher*, J. L. Ackrill, 1981
   This is probably the most insightful of the general introductions to Aristotle. It is "a guide-book to Aristotle's philosophy," but the aim is "not just to impart information, but to arouse interest in the philosophical problems Aristotle tackles, and in his arguments and ideas" (i, 1).
2. *Aristotle*, Jonathan Barnes, 1982
   This is a survey of the main points of Aristotle's scientific and philosophical thought. Aristotle's thought is difficult, and the texts are confusing. This cannot be denied, but Barnes tries to help the reader see that "the moments of vexation are far outnumbered by the moments of excitement and elation" (4).
3. "Aristotle's metaphysics," S. Marc Cohen (http://plato.stanford.edu/entries/aristotle–metaphysics/), 2008
   This is probably the best short introduction to Aristotle's metaphysics. Aristotle's *Metaphysics* is notorious for being one of the most difficult works in ancient philosophy. Cohen's discussion, however, is remarkably clear and sensible.
4. *The Development of Ethics*, I: *From Socrates to the Reformation*, Terence Irwin, 2007
   Irwin says that had he given his book an ampler title, it would have included the clause "with special attention to Aristotelian naturalism, its formulation, elaboration, criticism, and defense" (1). The title would have been apt. Irwin devotes four chapters to Aristotle and considers issues related to Aristotle in many of the other chapters in the book. The discussion in the chapters on Aristotle is penetrating and historically grounded. It is also extremely interesting philosophically.
5. "Aristotle's Ethics," Richard Kraut (http://plato.stanford.edu/entries/aristotle–ethics/), 2010
   This is the probably the best short introduction to Aristotle's ethics.
6. *Aristotle. The Desire to Understand*, Jonathan Lear.Cambridge University Press, 1988
   This is a philosophical introduction to Aristotle. Lear says that "the undergraduates at Cambridge and Yale to whom I have lectured about Aristotle ... persuaded me that material at this level of difficulty is interesting to them and that a book of this sort would be a help to them" (xi). The discussion is wide-ranging.
7. *Aristotle*, David Ross, 1961
   This is a much more detailed and encyclopedic introduction to Aristotle. It is a very useful reference work. The bibliography contains references to some of the now older but still valuable secondary literature.
8. *Aristotle*, Christopher Shields, 2007
   This is a very good general introduction to Aristotle. Shields says that his "chief objective is ... to *motivate* the principal features of Aristotle's philosophy at least to the degree that it is necessary for his newest readers to approach his writings with facility and understanding ..." (1). The discussion is straightforward, and the

interpretations are sensible. Shields provides a condensed discussion in "Aristotle" (http://plato.stanford.edu/entries/aristotle/), 2008.

9. "Aristotle's psychology," Christopher Shields (http://plato.stanford.edu/entries/aristotle–psychology/), 2010

   This is probably the best short introduction to Aristotle's work in psychology.

Part V

Hellenistic Philosophers

Three schools

The Hellenistic philosophers (the Epicureans, the Stoics, and the Academic Skeptics) react against what they perceive as the excesses of the classical tradition of Plato and Aristotle.

Epicureanism

Epicurus rejects the rationalism that was so central to the classical tradition. He tries to work out an epistemology according to which knowledge of the structure of reality is a matter of memory and the senses, and hence of experience. In addition, he tries to work out a conception of the good life as a matter of enlightened moderation, not reason.

Stoicism

The Stoics also react against the classical tradition. They return to the Socratic conception of the soul according to which all desire is a matter of judgment and hence of reason. Further, they work out a conception of the good life in terms of living in agreement with nature, not the contemplation of reality.

Skepticism

The Academic Skeptics return the Academy to a more skeptical perspective which they take Socrates to exemplify. This puts them on a collision course with the Stoics, who claim that assent is permitted only if no rational means can force its withdrawal. The Skeptics argue that this criterion cannot be met and that impressions need only be convincing or probable.

Time Line

350	300	250	200	150	100	50

Aristotle (384–322)

Epicurus founds the Garden (306)

Zeno founds the Stoic school (301)

Arcesilaus heads the Academy and turns the focus to Skepticism (266)

Chrysippus

Carneades

Clitomachus

Philo

10

Reaction to the Classical Tradition

Aristotle's death in 322 occurred in a tumultuous time. Athens had lost its position of political privilege to Macedonian rule which, under Alexander the Great, was extended over much of the ancient world. Many academic subjects left Athens to relocate in Alexandria, in Egypt, under the patronage of the Ptolemies.[a] Philosophy was an exception. It remained in its ancestral home in Athens, but new schools came into existence and old ones came under new leadership.

The philosophers who flourished during this time are known as the Hellenistic philosophers. This name stems from the time in which they worked, the Hellenistic Age, which is the period from the death of Alexander in 323 to the end of the Roman Republic in 31 BC. These dates mark a period in political history. Hellenistic philosophy, as a period in the history of philosophy, ends somewhat earlier. The commonality that unifies the Hellenistic philosophers is their critical reaction to what they supposed were the excesses of the prior classical tradition. This unity disintegrated sometime around 100 BC as non-skeptical forms of Platonism underwent a resurgence.

10.1 Epicureanism

Epicurus set up his school, the Garden, in Athens in 306. He was an extremely prolific writer, but most of this work has disappeared.[1] The full explanation for this loss is not clear, but the resurgence of Platonism in late antiquity and the subsequent rise and domination of Christianity

---

[a] In 322, Alexander the Great conquered Egypt and installed Ptolemy as ruler. Ptolemy's family ruled Egypt until the Roman conquest in 30 BC.

Ancient Greek Philosophy: From The Presocratics to the Hellenistic Philosophers, First Edition.
Thomas A. Blackson.   © 2011 Thomas A. Blackson. Published 2011 by Blackwell Publishing Ltd.

are part of the explanation. Epicureanism was unappealing in this new intellectual climate.

Against rationalism

Diogenes Laertius says that the Epicureans "reject dialectic as a perversion" (X.31). He does not identify the specific problem with dialectic, but it is clear that the Epicureans, who are atomists, are not skeptics about the structure of reality. Instead, Epicurus and the Epicureans seem to reject dialectic because they understand it in terms of its classical interpretation in Plato and Aristotle. According to Plato, and Aristotle after him, the cognition underlying knowledge of the structure of reality is a matter of "reason," not "experience." By rejecting "dialectic as a perversion," it seems that Epicurus and the Epicureans rejected this Platonic and Aristotelian rationalism.[2]

Diogenes says, in the same paragraph, that the Epicureans hold that "it is sufficient for the inquiry into nature to proceed according to the utterances made by the things." This description of the Epicurean epistemology is obscure, but the fundamental idea is that possessing the right beliefs is not a matter of "reason" but rather of memory and the senses, which are paradigms of the cognitive states and processes traditionally thought to belong to "experience." According to the Epicureans, this epistemology is evident in the ordinary methods of belief formation. Someone who sees something from afar should not assent to the impression straight away. Rather, he should put himself in a position to get a more reliable impression by taking a second look once he is closer:

> Opinion they also call supposition, and they say that it is true and false. If it is attested or uncontested, it is true; if it is unattested or is contested, it comes out false. Hence their introduction of that which is awaited – for example, waiting and getting near the tower and learning how it appears from nearby. (Diogenes Laertius, *Lives and Opinions of the Philosophers* X.34; LS 18 B[3])

In addition, the Epicureans suppose that this familiar procedure for belief formation extends to phenomena not open to immediate inspection. Their idea is that knowledge in this case is not a matter of dialectic, as this was classically understood. Rather, the inquirer naturally assents to impressions whose propositional content is "uniquely consistent" with his prior beliefs. If these prior beliefs are themselves formed by proper reaction to impressions given in experience, then this procedure produces expertise about matters not open to immediate inspection:

> We should not think that any other end is served by knowledge of celestial events, whether they be discussed in a context or in isolation, than freedom from disturbance and firm confidence, just as in the other areas of discourse. And neither should we force through what is impossible, nor should we in all areas keep our study similar either to discourses on the conduct of life or to those belonging to the solution of the other problems of physics, for example that the totality of things is body and intangible substance, or that there are atomic elements, and all the theses of this kind which are uniquely consistent with things evident. In the case of celestial events this is not the case: both the causes of their coming to be and the accounts of their essence are multiple. For physics should not be studied by means of empty judgments and arbitrary fiat, but in the way that things that are evident require. What our life needs is not private theorizing and empty opinion, but an untroubled existence. Now in respect of all things which have a multiplicity of explanations consistent with things evident, complete freedom from trepidation results when someone in the proper way lets stand whatever is plausibly suggested about them. But when someone allows one explanation while rejecting another equally consistent with what is evident, he is clearly abandoning the study of nature altogether and descending into myth. Signs relating to events in the celestial region are provided by certain of the things familiar and evident – things whose mode of existence is open to view – and not by things evident in the celestial region. For these latter are capable of coming to be in multiple ways. We must, nevertheless, observe our impression of each one; and we must distinguish the events which are connected with it, events whose happening in multiple ways is uncontested by familiar events. (Epicurus, *Letter to Pythocles* X.85–88; LS 18 C)

Epicurus says that, unlike in the case of celestial phenomena, which admit multiple explanations, the truth of the atomism is "uniquely consistent with things evident."[4] He does not provide the argument for this surprising claim,[5] but this worry aside, it is pretty clear that Epicurus places no emphasis on "reason" as this was understood by Plato and Aristotle. The view is not worked out in detail, but the idea seems to be that unless one has formed beliefs that are not attested or are contested, sense perceptions, together with the memory of these perceptions, naturally produce the belief in atomism and make all other possibilities about reality appear false. This Epicurean understanding of expertise is undeveloped, but it is important in the history of philosophy because it interrupts the rationalist tradition that goes back through Plato and Aristotle to Parmenides. It is unfortunate that the evidence for this reaction to rationalism is so fragmentary.[b]

Against the classical conception of happiness

Epicurus and the Epicureans do not deny that knowledge of the structure of reality is connected to the good life and hence to happiness. Their interest in such knowledge, however, is completely instrumental. The idea seems to be that this knowledge is important not in itself, but only because it displaces the disturbing opinions to which human beings are naturally prone. Epicurus says that physics dispels the "fears based on mythology" that undermine happiness:

> Were we not upset by the worries that celestial phenomena and death might matter to us, and also by failure to appreciate the limits of pains

---

[b] The connections are not easy to trace, given the existing evidence, but Epicurus and the Epicureans seem to be part of an epistemological tradition that has its fullest expression in antiquity in the medical tradition in a debate between rationalist and empiricist doctors. "The terms 'empiricist' and 'rationalist' go back to antiquity. They have their origin in a particular debate among the ancient doctors concerning the nature and origin of medical knowledge, indeed the nature and origin of technical or expert knowledge quite generally (see Galen, *Subfiguratio Empirica* (*Outline of Empiricism*) p. 87, 2–3; Celsus, *Proemium* 31–2; Galen, *de Sectis Ingredientibus*, p. 10, 26; 11, 6). To mark their opposing views these doctors introduced the terms 'empiricist' (*empeirikos*) and 'rationalist' (*logikos*), and hence themselves came to be known as 'empiricists' and 'rationalists' respectively (Galen, *de Sectis Ingredientibus* p. 2, 7–11). Very roughly speaking, the empiricists were called 'empiricists' since they took the view that knowledge is just a matter of a certain kind of experience (in Greek *empeiria*), whereas the rationalists were so called because they assumed that mere experience, however complex, does not amount to knowledge, that knowledge crucially involves the use of reason (*logos* in Greek, *ratio* in Latin), for example to provide the appropriate kind of justification" (Michael Frede, "An empiricist view of knowledge: Memorism," 1990, 225). The history here is extremely unclear, but the following intellectuals figure prominently in it. Diocles of Carystus (middle fourth century BC) was the most distinguished doctor of his day. He was a critic of excessive theorizing about causes. Herophilus (late fourth, early third century BC) was the first great Alexandrian doctor. He was a proponent of cautious, empiricist epistemology. Erasistratus (middle third century BC) was a younger contemporary of Herophilus. Serapion (late third, early second century BC) was a pupil of Herophilus and probable founder of the Empiricist school. Heraclides of Tarentum (first century BC) was the most distinguished Empiricist doctor of his day and a teacher of Aenesidemus, the late Academic Skeptic who broke away from Academic Skepticism to found Pyrrhonian Skepticism. Menodotus (second century AD) was the leading Empiricist doctor of his day. Sextus Empiricus (second to third century AD) was an empiricist doctor, and sympathizer with and compiler of Pyrrhonian Skepticism.

and desires, we would have no need for the study of nature. There is no way to dispel the fear about matters of supreme importance, for someone who does not know what the nature of the universe is but retains some of the fears based on mythology. Hence without the study of nature there is no way of securing the purity of our pleasures. (Epicurus, *Principal Doctrines*, 11–12; LS 25 B)

Human beings, if they do not understand the nature of reality, are naturally subject to fear of events of the sort displayed in mythology. They tend to make up threatening stories about natural phenomena they do not understand. They tend to think that these phenomena are indications of divine mood, and they think that storms and other such phenomena are punishment from the gods. In this way, Epicurus picks up a theme from the inquirers into nature. He thinks that the purpose of knowledge of physics is to dispel the fears enshrined in the mythological tradition.

This instrumental interest in physics is part of a more general reconsideration of which human lives are the happiest. In Plato, happiness seems to consist in a certain exercise of reason, an exercise he identifies with the love of wisdom and understands to involve knowledge of the forms, which are supposed to be the realities of things. Aristotle relaxes this position somewhat. In the *Nicomachean Ethics*, although he seems to understand the exercise of reason in theology to make the greatest contribution to happiness, he is willing to allow that the exercise of reason in connection with ethical matters also makes a contribution. Epicurus, by contrast, has the more ordinary thought that the good life is most likely a life of enlightened moderation.

The argument for this conception of the good life depends on a certain conception of "pleasure" and on a view about what is most pleasurable in a human life. The argument proceeds against the background assumption, which itself is extremely plausible, that a good life is one in which the subject living the life takes more pleasure than pain in his circumstances:

We are investigating what is the final and ultimate good, which all philosophers agree must be of such a kind that it is the end to which everything is the means, but it is not itself the means to anything. Epicurus situates this in pleasure, which he wants to be the greatest good with pain as the greatest bad. His doctrine begins this way: as soon as every animal is born, it seeks after pleasure and rejoices in it as the greatest good, while it rejects pain as the greatest bad and, as far as possible, avoids it. (Cicero, *On Ends* I.29; LS 21 A)

According to Epicurus and the Epicureans, the pleasure and the pain in a life fall into two categories. The first is the most familiar. It is pleasure and pain in sensations. As Cicero[c] describes this pleasure, on behalf of the Epicureans, it "moves our actual nature with some gratification and is perceived by the senses in company with a certain delight":

> Now I will explain what pleasure is and what it is like, to remove any misunderstandings which inexperienced people may have and to help them to understand how serious, self-controlled, and stern our doctrine is, though it is commonly held to be hedonistic, slack and soft. The pleasure we pursue is not just that which moves our actual nature with some gratification and is perceived by the senses in company with a certain delight; we hold that to be the greatest pleasure which is perceived once all pain is removed. For when we are freed from pain, we rejoice in the actual freedom and absence of all distress. (Cicero, *On Ends* I.37–38; LS 21 A)

> [One should] refer every choice and avoidance to the health of the body and the freedom of the soul from disturbance, since this is the goal of the blessed life. For we do everything for the sake of being neither in pain nor in terror. As soon as we achieve this state every storm in the soul is dispelled . . . (Epicurus, *Letter to Menoeceus* X.128; IG I–4.128)

Not all pleasure and pain, however, essentially involves sensations. Just what the Epicureans have in mind is not obvious, but they seem to think some pleasure and pain is taken in states of affairs which do not involves sensations. The example Cicero cites concerns being "freed from pain" and existing in "the absence of all distress." A human being who understands that he is

---

[c] After Caesar was assassinated in 44 BC, Cicero tried to oppose Antony but was unsuccessful. Not long afterwards Cicero himself was murdered. During the last years of his life, during the dictatorship of Caesar, which had forced him out of public life, Cicero turned to philosophical writing. He decided that since he was unable to serve the public through politics, he would serve through education by writing philosophy in Latin. (He had studied philosophy in the Academy and writes from an Academic point of view.) Charles Brittain describes Cicero's motivation: "The problem was not so much that educated Romans were not interested in philosophy, but that the intellectual elite was effectively bilingual in Latin and Greek, and philosophy was regarded as something best done in Greek ... But Cicero believed ... that Latin could be put to use as a medium for philosophical thought, and so set out to naturalize Hellenistic philosophy into his native culture" (*Cicero. On Academic Skepticism*, 2006, x). Cicero's philosophical writings are the most extensive and important record of the philosophy of the first century BC. In addition, much of the philosophical vocabulary in English is connected to the Greek through the choices Cicero made in casting Greek philosophy into Latin idiom.

"freed from all pain" and "distress" is said to take immense pleasure in this state of affairs.

According to Epicurus and the Epicureans, certain common but nevertheless false beliefs about what is good and bad are an especially noxious source of pain and distress. Human beings, due in part to their failure to acquire knowledge about nature, typically form mistaken beliefs about gods, death, the availability of good things, and the likelihood of experiencing bad things. The truth about these matters, according to Epicureans, is summarized in the "fourfold remedy":

> For who do you believe is better than a man who has pious opinions about the gods, is fearless about death, has reasoned out the natural goal of life and understands that the limit of good things is easy to achieve completely and easy to provide, and that the limit of bad things either has a short duration or causes little trouble? (Epicurus, *Letter to Menoeceus* X.133; IG I–4.133)

> The fourfold remedy: "God presents no fears, death no worries. And while good is readily attainable, bad is readily endurable." (Philodemus,[d]*Against the Sophists*; LS 25 J)

According to the Epicureans, given the facts of human existence, facts they suppose are revealed in experience, not reason, a human being who does not want rare and exotic things and who has the right beliefs about nature has the best chance for the most pleasure and hence for the most happiness in life. In particular, the self-sufficient and right-thinking human being is likely to have fewer worries than the superstitious and to have more satisfaction than the profligate:

> We believe that self-sufficiency is a great good, not in order that we might make do with few things under all circumstances, but so that if we do not have a lot we can make do with few, being genuinely convinced that those who least need extravagance enjoy it the most; and that everything natural is easy to obtain and whatever is groundless is hard to obtain; and that simple flavors provide a pleasure equal to that of an extravagant lifestyle when all pain from want is removed, and barley cakes and water provide the highest pleasure when someone in want

---

[d] Philodemus of Gadara (first century BC) is an Epicurean philosopher. Remains of his works were found at Herculaneum, an ancient Roman town on the Gulf of Naples that was destroyed (along with Pompeii and other towns) in the eruption of Mount Vesuvius in AD 79. One of the more magnificent villas in Herculaneum was a seaside retreat owned by Julius Caesar's father-in-law. In it was an extensive library. The scrolls were carbonized but preserved in the ash fall. This library of scrolls is the only known library to survive intact from antiquity.

takes them. Therefore, becoming accustomed to simple, not extravagant, ways of life makes one completely healthy, makes man unhesitant in the face of life's necessary duties, puts us in a better condition for times of extravagance which occasionally come along, and makes us fearless in the face of chance. So when we say that pleasure is the goal we do not mean the pleasures of the profligate or the pleasures of consumption, as some believe, either from ignorance and disagreement or from deliberate misinterpretation, but rather the lack of pain in the body and distur- bance in the soul. For it is not drinking bouts and continuous partying and enjoying boys and women, or consuming fish and the other delicacies of an extravagant table, which produce the pleasant life, but sober calculation which searches out the reasons for every choice and avoidance, and drives out the opinions which are the source of the greatest turmoil for men's souls. (Epicurus, *Letter to Menoeceus* X.130–132; IG I–4.130–132)

With the right beliefs (as opposed to "opinions which are the source of the greatest turmoil for men's souls"), Epicurus claims that a human being has a certain peace of mind. He no longer worries about the future. He now understands that in the future he is likely to experience many more good things than bad. Moreover, he takes immense pleasure and satisfaction in this knowledge.

Whether or not this conception of the good life is plausible in itself, it is clear that it is not the same as the one in Plato and Aristotle. According to Epicurus and the Epicureans, what a human being likes and rationally pursues as his end is not restricted to the knowledge involved in a certain exercise of reason. Epicurus and the Epicureans reject the epistemology and psychology that underwrites this classical conception of the good life. They believe that knowledge of the structure of reality is a matter of "experience," not "reason." Furthermore, the possession of this knowl- edge is not itself what provides a human being with the most happiness. Indeed, according to the Epicureans, this knowledge is valuable only for what it causes. It frees a human being from the fears associated with myth and superstition. This, in turn, is part of a process in which a human being begins to realize that life's most difficult problem has a solution: namely, that there is an easy-to-execute and effective plan for living in a way that is overwhelmingly likely to result in a life in which the pleasure taken in one's circumstances vastly outweighs the pain. This realization itself, according to Epicurus, is a source of immense relief and tremendous satisfaction. Furthermore, the pleasure taken in this realization continues into the future as one lives out one's life, and thus helps to ensure that the few bad things that do happen do not cause there to be more pain than pleasure. This conception of the good life is very different than one in the classical tradition of Plato and Aristotle.

10.2 Stoicism

Zeno of Citium founded the Stoic school.[e] Cleanthes[f] succeeded him, and Chrysippus[g] succeeded Cleanthes. The Stoics were prolific writers, especially Chrysippus, but their writings have been lost almost completely and must be reconstructed from discussions in subsequent authors.[h]

---

[e] The Stoics take their name from the Στοὰ Ποικίλη. A στοά is a walkway covered by a roof and supported with columns on at least one side. There were various such structures in Athens. Often they were attached to temples or public buildings and served to provide protection from the elements. As Athens became rich, and public works were no longer utilitarian, these roofed structures became more lavish. The Στοὰ Ποικίλη derived its name from its beautiful murals. It was located at the north-west corner of the *agora*, the central square in Athens.

[f] "[Zeno] was succeeded in 262 BC by one of the odder characters in antiquity, an ex-boxer and ditch digger named Cleanthes. The opinion of all ancient reports is unanimous: Cleanthes was not a genius. But he won admirers through the simplicity of his life, his capacity for hard work, and his gentle decency. He wrote over fifty treatises, but all that is left are a few scraps of verse, most notable for their religious fervor. Ancient sources seem puzzled that Zeno chose him to carry on the school, but we are also told that he compared himself to a writing-tablet made of bronze: difficult to make an impression on, but very retentive of whatever it receives. Zeno may have felt that his teachings were safe in Cleanthes' unimaginative hands ..." (Tad Brennan, *The Stoic Life*, 2005, 12–13).

[g] "Chrysippus (c. 280–208 BC) did not start the Stoic school, but his far-reaching logical and philosophical abilities elevated it from the second rank of philosophical systems to the first rank. The philosophy that comes down to us as Stoicism is generally the work of Chrysippus, even when it is attributed merely to 'the Stoics.' Very little of his writing is left – not one of his seven-hundred-plus books survives complete" (Tad Brennan, *The Stoic life*, 2005, 10–11).

[h] As in the case of the work of the Epicureans, the loss of the works of the Stoics is due to the resurgence of Platonism and the emergence of Christianity. In the case of the Stoics, however, the reason is not so much that their views were unappealing in the new intellectual climate. Rather, the explanation turns on the fact that the resurgence of Platonism was not an attempt to identify the historical facts about what Plato believed. Instead, it was an attempt to identify the true philosophy that Plato had glimpsed and that his texts indicate. Since Stoicism was thought to be an attempt to develop Platonism, as Zeno was a student of Polemo, who was the fourth head of the Academy, it was thought that Stoic philosophy could be incorporated in the resurgence of Platonism and that the Stoic texts themselves need not be preserved. The texts which were preserved, primarily those of Seneca, Epictetus, and Marcus Aurelius, were preserved because they seemed to serve a practical moral need consistent with the dominant world view.

Against the classical theory of the soul

The Stoics reject the classical theory of human motivation and desire. Plato and Aristotle thought that some desires are not a matter of belief and hence that not all action is a function of the cognition in reason. The Stoics, by contrast, try to work out a more Socratic understanding of human desire and motivation. They argue that all desire in the adult is really a matter of a certain sort of belief or knowledge and therefore that all action is a matter of reason.

In their return to a more Socratic position, the Stoics offer a new understanding of human maturation. First of all, the Stoics do not think that an adult human being, in so far as he is rational, controls his actions by controlling the "affections" in the non-reasoning parts of his soul. Instead, they think that such affections cease to exist once the human being becomes an adult:

> Whereas the ancients claimed that the commotions are natural and have nothing to do with reason, and whereas they located desire in one part of the soul, and reason in another, Zeno would not even agree with that. For he thought that these commotions were equally voluntary and arose from a judgment which was a matter of mere opinion ... (Cicero, *Academica* I.39[6])

They suppose that the underlying mistake, in the classical tradition of Plato and Aristotle, was in the failure to realize that the reasoning soul replaces rather than coexists with the animal soul. The Stoics do not deny that out of fear, for example, a human being might act contrary to his interests. This happens, but they believe that the failure in such cases is not a failure to control desires that stem from parts of the soul without reason. They deny the existence of such parts.[7]

The Stoics think that in the transition to human adult a new psychology emerges. The child, according to the Stoics, naturally has what they call "impulsive impressions." These impressions are conducive to his or her preservation. Certain facts about the environment, such as the presence of food or a dangerous animal, naturally impress themselves on the child. Some of these impressions are impulsive or motivating. They straightaway move the child toward or away from the object of the impression, and it is a fact about human beings, as they are naturally constituted, that these impulsive impressions help the child move through their environment in ways conducive to their survival.

As the child acquires reason, a significant change is supposed to occur. Nature now operates in a more complicated way. The adult does not move instinctually in terms of impulsive impressions. On the contrary, they act as a result of their *assent* to impulsive impressions. Moreover, these impulsive impressions are a part of reason. They are structured by concepts and hence can figure in inference. In the child, impulsive impressions – and impressions generally – lack propositional structure and instead somehow represent things in terms of images. It is true that impulsive impressions are motivating in both the child and the adult, but in the adult this motivation occurs against a background of beliefs about the good and does not issue in action in the absence of assent. In the adult, the presence of the impression is not sufficient for action. Impulses to action are now judgments. The adult must decide that the propositional content of the impression is true, and this decision is motivating only against a background of certain beliefs about what is good and bad.

An example helps put this theory of motivation into sharper focus. Consider someone who believes that illness is bad and who has the impression that taking the medicine in front of him will cure him of his illness. According to the Stoics, this impression is impulsive. The impression alone, however, does not issue in action and hence does not cause the human being to take the medicine, but if he assents to the impression, and thus forms the belief that the propositional content of the impression is true, then he is motivated to take the medicine. Unless he believes something else is better for him, or is prevented from acting, he will act to take the medicine. Hence, according to the Stoics, Socrates was right about motivation in the human adult: there are no actions that stem from desires which are not themselves a matter of belief or knowledge and hence a matter of reason.[8]

Living in agreement with nature

The Stoics believe that happiness is a matter of having the right psychology and that this psychology includes knowledge of the good. Furthermore, and more strikingly, the Stoics believe that unless a human being is maimed or otherwise defective, he will acquire knowledge of the good in the natural course of acquiring reason. The problem is that, in addition to the knowledge acquired in acquiring reason, human beings almost invariably acquire a host of false beliefs about what is good. These beliefs undermine proper psychological functioning and hence happiness.

To understand this view, it is necessary to understand in more detail how the Stoics conceive of the acquisition of reason and its knowledge in the transition from child to human adult. The texts are second-hand and not especially clear or detailed, but the leading idea seems to be that human beings acquire reason, and thereby leave their animal souls behind, in something like the inductive process Aristotle had described in the *Posterior Analytics* and the *Metaphysics*:

> When a man is born, the Stoics say, he has the commanding-part of his soul like a sheet of paper ready for writing upon. On this he inscribes each one of his conceptions. The first method of inscription is through the senses. For by perceiving something, e.g., white, they have a memory of it when it has departed. And when many memories of a similar kind have occurred, we then say we have experience. For the plurality of similar impressions is experience. Some conceptions arise naturally in the aforesaid ways and undesignedly, others through our own instruction and attention. The latter are called conceptions only, the former are called preconceptions as well. Reason, for which we are called rational, is said to be completed from our preconceptions during our first seven years. (Aetius[i] 4.11.1–4; LS 39 E)

Human beings are subject to a process whose end is a set of conceptions adequate for understanding certain aspects of the world. This information is necessary for them to orient themselves properly, and nature arranges for human beings to acquire this information, since the information itself is too important to allow human beings to acquire entirely of their own accord.

The conceptions human beings acquire are of two kinds. Some come to human beings in just the way children get their adult teeth. The process happens naturally, and there is nothing the child needs to do to help it along. In the case of other conceptions, human beings must themselves contribute to the process. These conceptions require "instruction and attention," and the good seems to be among this set of conceptions. Cicero makes an effort to explain the way this works:

> The first proper function (this is my term for καθῆκον) is to preserve oneself in one's natural constitution; the second is to seize hold of the things that accord with nature and to banish their opposites. Once this procedure of selection and rejection has been discovered, the next consequence is selection exercised with proper functioning; then such selection performed continuously; finally, selection which is absolutely

---

[i] Aetius was a Greek doxographer in the first or second century BC. His work was reconstructed out of later material transmitted under the names of Plutarch, Stobaeus, and others. (For a general discussion of doxography, see Jaap Mansfeld, "Doxography of ancient philosophy," 2008.)

consistent with nature. At this point, for the first time, that which can be truly called good begins to be present in a man, and understood. For a man's first affiliation is towards those things which are in accordance with nature. But as soon as he has acquired understanding, or rather, the conception which the Stoics call ἔννοιαν, and as he has seen the regularity and, so to speak, the harmony of conduct, he comes to value this far higher than all those objects of his initial affection; and thus by insight and reasoning he comes to the conclusion that this constitutes the highest human good which is worthy of praise and desirable for its own sake. It rests in what the Stoics call ὁμολογίαν, but which we may call agreement ... (*On Ends* III.20–21; LS 59 D)

The conception of the good is not acquired in the way children get their adult teeth as they mature. The process is natural, but human beings must contribute to the process. As Cicero describes the process, a person must notice something about his behavior. He must notice that he acts to preserve himself. Noticing this fact results in a certain "insight" into reality. It causes him to realize that the good is not as it is so often conceived, for example, that he gets food and drink when he is hungry and thirsty. Rather, he comes to see and understand that the good is something else altogether: what Cicero describes as the "harmony of conduct" and "agreement."

In supposing that the good consists in "agreement," the Stoics think that the good is a matter of making decisions and acting in a way that somehow "fits" or "agrees" with nature. Diogenes Laertius provides the primary evidence for this interpretation:

Zeno first, in his book *On the Nature of Man*, said that the goal was to live in agreement with nature, which is to live according to virtue.[9] For nature leads us to virtue. ... Again, to live in accordance with virtue is equivalent to living according to the experience of events which occur by nature, as Chrysippus says in book one of his *On Goals*. For our own natures are parts of the universe. Therefore, the goal becomes to live consistently with nature, i.e., according to one's own nature and that of the universe, doing nothing that is forbidden by the common law, which is right reason, penetrating all things, being the same as Zeus who is the leader of the administration of things. And this itself is the virtue of the happy man and a smooth flow of life, whenever all things are done according to the harmony of the spirit dwelling in each of us with the will of the administrator of the universe. So Diogenes[j] says explicitly

---

[j] Diogenes of Babylon was the fifth head of the Stoic school. Along with Carneades and Critolaos, he was one of the philosophers sent to Rome in 155 BC to represent Athens in a petition before the senate. Otherwise, little is known about him. (Rome had imposed a fine on Athens for the sack of Oropus. Athens hoped to have the fine reduced.)

> that the goal is to act with good reason in the selection of things according to
> nature. (*Lives and Opinions of the Philosophers* VII.87–88; IG II–94.87–88)

Human beings, of their own accord, if they are wise and hence not confused
about the good, act in "agreement" with the order in the universe. Human
beings have a part to play in nature. They play this part by making decisions
and acting on the basis of these decisions, since they are by nature
psychological beings. When they choose to live in "agreement with nature,"
and thus make decisions and act in "accordance with nature," they live lives
of complete happiness.

An example helps to clarify the idea. Consider, again, a human being
who has the ordinary beliefs that health and life are good and that death
and illness are bad. He will be disturbed by certain thoughts, say, that
the new year is likely to bring a virulent flu virus. This disturbance,
according to the Stoics, is caused by confusion about the good. Really,
illness and death have no value in themselves. Once this is understood,
the thought about the flu virus is no longer so disturbing. A human
being who understands that illness and death have no value will act
appropriately given his partial understanding of the order in nature. It is
appropriate and reasonable for him to take precaution against illness,
given the imperfect state of his knowledge of nature, but if the flu strikes
him, this experience can contribute negatively to how much he likes
his present circumstances only if he is confused about the good. In the
absence of such false beliefs, he is not upset when he fails to obtain or
avoid what he sets out to obtain or avoid. He understands that the
good is to "live in agreement with nature," not to obtain or avoid
certain things.[10]

In this way, a human being who knows the good, and does not attribute to
anything else a value it does not possess, is wise. He has no independent
motivation that could be frustrated if he does not obtain or avoid the objects
of his impulses. His state of mind is very different from the ordinary human
being who laments his choices or their outcomes. Rather than think that,
other things being equal, it is appropriate and reasonable for him to obtain
or avoid various things, the confused human being attributes values to the
objects of his impulses that they do not possess. He believes that it is good or
bad to satisfy these impulses, when in fact it is neither.[k]

---

[k] Cf. Tad Brennan, "Stoic moral psychology," 2003, 271: "If you really see that it is indifferent,
then you feel indifference to it – and that is not a recommendation of psychological hygiene,
but rather a general law of psychology."

This Stoic conception of happiness and the good life is significantly different from the classical conception in Plato and Aristotle. Socrates seems to have thought that the human psychology is somehow just reason and that knowledge of the structure of reality, at least of the sort the inquirers into nature pursued, was not necessary for the good life (and may not even be humanly possible). Plato rejected both views. He introduced a tripartite conception of the soul and reasserted the supreme importance of theoretical knowledge for happiness and the good life. He thought that the incarnate soul must take control of its life in the body so that it can return to its real interest, which is to have a theoretical understanding of things generally. The Stoics return to a more Socratic conception according to which the adult soul is not tripartite, and a theoretical understanding of things is not the end. The Stoic sage has some theoretical knowledge. He is not confused about the good. Such knowledge, however, is not the end of rational action. The end is that he "lives in agreement with nature" and hence that his psychology functions properly. If his motivational structure is correct, and he forms and maintains beliefs properly, this is all that matters.

10.3 Skepticism

Academic Skepticism begins in 268 with Arcesilaus. He reinterprets Plato and the Academy in terms of the Socratic practice of exposing the pretense to wisdom in those who put themselves forward as experts.[11] After Arcesilaus, the history of the Academy seems to have been relatively undistinguished until Carneades became head in about 155. Carnaedes seems to have invigorated the Academy by working out the main principles of Academic Skepticism. After he retired in 137, a controversy seems to have erupted over how he should be understood and hence how Academic Skepticism itself should be understood. This dispute was resolved in different ways by the subsequent most important heads of the Academy: Clitomachus and Philo.[1]

---

[1] Arcesilaus and Carneades wrote nothing, presumably in emulation of Socrates. Clitomachus wrote several books in connection with the dispute over how Carneades should be understood. Philo wrote two books in Rome near the end of his life as part of this same dispute. These books are called the "Roman Books," in the absence of their title and in reference to their place of origin. Philo sought refuge in Rome because of the Mithridatic War. (In about 121, Mithridates VI of Pontus had come to power in the Hellenized region of Asia Minor. He tried to extend his rule at the expense of Rome, which had been the main power in the region.) Philo's "Roman Books," unfortunately, have been lost. What is now known about Academic Skepticism depends primarily on Cicero's *Academica* and on the much later discussion by Sextus Empiricus in *Against the Professors* VII.

Withholding assent

The skepticism that took hold in the Academy can appear to consist in a simple-minded inconsistency. Cicero says that Arcesilaus argued "against the opinions of all men, so that when equally weighty reasons were found on opposite sides on the same subject, it was easier to withhold assent from either side" (*Academica* I.45–46).[m] The historical Socrates had done something similar in his conversations, but Cicero also reports that Arcesilaus said that "there is nothing that can be known" and that "no one must make any positive statement or affirmation or give the approval of his assent to any proposition" (I.45). This is not the same as exposing the pretense to expertise by asking questions to get the pretender to advance his own beliefs and to conclude by his own standards that the beliefs he advances in response to questioning conflict with his original assertions. Consequently, contrary to the Socratic practice of simply exposing pretense to expertise, Arcesilaus can appear to assent to the proposition that no one should ever assent to any proposition.

Since this cannot be the right interpretation of Academic Skepticism (which, given its long history, is unlikely to consist in a simple-minded confusion), the prohibition against assent must have been a prohibition against a particular *kind* of assent, not all assent. To appreciate this point, the important first step is to realize that the prohibition is directed against the Stoics.

Arcesilaus, in emulation of Socrates, seems to have tried to get Zeno and the Stoics to conclude, by their own standards, that they themselves are committed to the proposition that even the wise should withhold assent and hence that there is no rational method of forming and maintaining beliefs that is guaranteed to avoid falsehood. Cicero imagines the argument to take place as follows:

> We may take him to have asked Zeno, what would happen if the wise man could not cognize anything, but it was the mark of the wise man not to opine.

---

[m] *Academica* I and II are formed from parts of two prior works that Cicero wrote. The first of these prior works consisted in the now lost *Catulus* and the extant *Lucullus*. (Catulus (Quintus Lutatius Catulus) and Lucullus (Lucius Licinius Lucullus) were Roman generals. The other participants are Hortensius (Quntus Hortensisus Hortalus) and Cicero. Hortensius was an orator.) *Academica* II is *Lucullus*. At some point, Cicero recast the *Catulus* and *Lucullus* into a set of four books with new characters. (Varro (Marcus Terentius Varro) and Atticus (Titus Pomponius Atticus) replace Lucullus, Hortensius, and Catulus. Varro was a prolific scholar with wide-ranging interests. Atticus was an Epicurean). Only a portion of the first of this set of four books has survived. It is *Academica* I.

Zeno, I imagine, replied that the wise man would not opine since there was something cognitive. What then was this? Zeno, I suppose, said it was an impression. What kind of impression? Zeno then defined it as an impression stamped and reproduced from something which is, exactly as it is. Arcesilaus asked whether this was still valid if a true impression was just like a false one. At this point Zeno was sharp enough to see that if an impression from what is were such that an impression from what is not could be most like it, there was no cognitive impression. (*Academica* II.77–78; LS 40 D)

Arcesilaus invites Zeno to draw the conclusion that the wise should withhold assent because no one is ever in a position to see his way through all current and future impressions whose propositional content is contrary to the content of the impression to which he has assented. Zeno, however, does not accept the invitation. He maintains that there are "cognitive" impressions.[n]

The "cognitive" impression is central to the Stoic epistemology, and this epistemology is also the key to understanding how, without immediate absurdity, the Academic Skeptic may be understood to assent to the impression that assent is prohibited. For the Stoics, "cognition" is the name of the propositional attitude which results from assent to a "cognitive impression." A cognitive impression correctly represents the world, and so a cognition is true because the propositional content of the cognitive impression to which assent is given is true. Not every cognition, however, is knowledge. According to the Stoics, knowledge results from a certain sort of assent to cognitive impressions. If the assent is to result in knowledge, it must somehow be firm:

Zeno did not attach reliability to all impressions but only to those which have a peculiar power of revealing their objects. Since this impression is discerned just by itself, he called it cognitive.... But once it has been received and accepted, he called it a cognition, resembling objects gripped in the hand, and

---

[n]   Cicero uses *comprehensio, perceptio,* and *cognitio* to render the Greek term κατάληψις. The use of the English terms "cognitive" and "cognition" in the translation is intended to convey the general idea that, in Stoic epistemology, cognitive impressions and cognitions are a natural part of the cognitive process involved in acquiring knowledge. "Cicero also renders '*katalepsis*' by '*cognito*,' and this seems to be a particularly apt term to refer to the kind of grasp which goes beyond mere belief, and which already would amount to knowledge, if the Stoics did not further require of knowledge that one cannot be argued out of what one knows to be the case. Later times which were not particularly interested in this further requirement did in fact treat cognition as the basic form of knowledge, as we can see, for instance, in Augustine's *Contra Academicos*" (Michael Frede, "Stoic epistemology," 1999a, 299).

in fact he had derived the actual term from manual prehension, nobody
before having used the word in such a sense . . . (*Academica* I.41; LS 40 B)

Zeno would spread out the fingers of one hand and display its open palm,
saying an impression is like this. Next he clenched his fingers a little and said
assent is like this. Then, pressing his fingers quite together, he made a fist, and
said that this was cognition. . . . Then he brought his left hand against his right
fist and gripped it tightly and forcefully, and said that knowledge was like this
and possessed by none except the wise man . . . (*Academica* II.145; LS 41 A)

The assent to a cognitive impression that results in cognition (but not
knowledge) consists in a "one-handed grip" on reality. This grip is weak and
may be overcome. To make it steadfast, the free hand must grip the first
hand. This metaphor of the two-handed grip conveys the idea that the assent
to an impression that results in knowledge is strong: no rational means can
show that the assent is unwarranted.

Given this understanding of what knowledge is, the question is
whether anyone actually has knowledge. The Stoics, in answer to this
question, seem to hold that although human beings *can* have knowledge,
it is not clear that any human being *has* knowledge. In particular, it is not
clear that any human being has the proper understanding of the good.
Human beings are naturally constructed so that they get cognitive
impressions and cognitions in something like the inductive process
Aristotle sketched, but they also form all kinds of false beliefs. These
false beliefs leave them susceptible to chains of reasoning that end in the
contradiction of what they already believe is true. In this way, according
to the Stoics, their assent does not consist in a "two-handed grip." It is
not firm enough to be knowledge. It is weak, and hence all their beliefs are
mere opinions. Only the wise can do what Arcesilaus, in the argument
with Zeno, suggested that no human being can do: assent to an
impression with the assurance that no rational means can demonstrate
that his assent is unwarranted.

This Stoic epistemology helps bring the Skepticism of the Academy into
sharper focus. The Academic Skeptics, to hold their ground, must show that
they can endorse the position that defines the school without at the same
time undermining this position. The position they endorse is that

(S) the condition for assent the Stoics require for knowledge cannot be met.

In order both to accept (S) and to hold their ground, the Academic
Skeptics must show that their acceptance is not an instance of the
assent which they claim is not possible. Otherwise, the Academic Skeptic

commits himself to the absurdity that he knows that no one knows anything.

The surviving texts do not reveal very clearly what the Academic Skeptics had in mind, but these texts do show that they made a concerted effort to show that their skepticism was not self-defeating. In the passage that follows the interchange between Arcesilaus and Zeno, Cicero indicates that it was controversial among Carneades' successors whether assent was permitted:

> The indiscernibility of true from false impressions is the one controversial issue that has lasted up to the present time. For the thesis that the wise man will assent to nothing had nothing to do with this dispute; for he might grasp nothing and yet opine – a thesis Carneades is said to have accepted, although for my part, trusting Clitomachus more than Philo or Metrodorus, I think that this was put forward in debate by him rather than accepted. (*Academica* II.78; LS 69 H)

Clitomachus and Philo, as Cicero says, were divided on how best to understand Carneades' apparent commitment to the proposition that it was permitted for the wise man to grasp nothing cognitively but yet to hold an opinion.° Given that Carneades did not, in the manner of a Socrates, simply advance this proposition in a dialectical argument, the question for the school is how Carneades' assent should be understand so that it is consistent with Academic Skepticism.

Carneades' discussion of the "convincing impression" provides some indication of how he himself seems to have understood the assent permitted to the Academic Skeptic. Carneades wrote nothing, presumably in emulation of Socrates, but Clitomachus wrote about what Carneades had in mind. On the basis of what Clitomachus wrote, works which themselves unfortunately no longer survive, Cicero reports that Carneades allowed for assent in the case of the "probable":

> I will say nothing such that anyone might suspect me of making it up. I shall take it from Clitomachus who was with Carneades until his old age –

° Carneades here may build on prior work by Arcesialus. "Arcesilaus says that one who suspends judgment about everything will regulate choice and avoidance and actions in general by 'the reasonable'; and that by proceeding in accordance with this criterion he will act rightly; for happiness is acquired through prudence, and prudence resides in right action, and right action is whatever, once it has been done, has a reasonable justification; therefore one who attends to the reasonable will act rightly and be happy" (Sextus Empiricus, *Against the Professors* VII.158; LS 69 B).

Clitomachus was a sharp man, a Carthaginian, and exceedingly studious and hard-working. There are four books of his on withholding assent, and the things I am about to say are taken from Book One. According to Carneades [as his follower Clitomachus understood him], there are . . . impressions that are probable[P] and those that are not. . . . For it is contrary to nature for nothing to be probable; the entire subversion of life follows [if nothing is probable]. . . . Thus, many impressions are probable. . . . And so the wise man will employ whatever apparently probable impressions he encounters, provided there is nothing which opposes its probability, and thus will every plan of life be governed. (*Academica* II.98–99; IG III–20.98–99.)

Much later in the tradition, Sextus Empiricus provides an example from medicine:

Just as some doctors do not conclude from one symptom that someone is really feverish . . . but from a concurrence . . . so also the Academic makes the judgment about the truth on the basis of a concurrence of impressions, and when none of these impressions provokes in him a suspicion of its falsity, he asserts that the impression is true. (*Against the Professors* VII.179; IG III-18.179)

This example suggests that Carneades conceives of following the convincing impression as the way people in ordinary life form and retain their beliefs. The doctor, for example, depending on what is at stake in the circumstances, tests his impression to decide whether to rely on it. He examines the patient a second time, and so on, and if the impression still seems right after having been given the appropriate consideration, he assents to it because he has found it convincing.

In the Academy, it seems to have been thought that this way of understanding assent in terms of the convincing impression admits of different interpretations. Clitomachus, according to Cicero, thought that to follow the probable is a matter of saying "yes" and "no" to certain impressions:

[Clitomachus] added that the wise man is said to suspend assent in two senses: one, when it means that he assents to nothing at all; the other, when he

---

[P] In this and other passages, Cicero seems to have tried to reproduce the logical and etymological connection in Greek between the adjective πιθανός and the verb πείθεσθαι by the using the Latin adjective and verb *probabilis* and *probare* to describe Carneades' position. The basic senses of these words are "persuasive": "be persuaded," "worthy of approval," and "approve" respectively. Just as the convincing or persuasive impression invites one to be persuaded by it, so also the probable impression invites one to approve it as a basis for practice and theory.

checks himself from responding in such a way to accept or reject.... This being so, he adopts the former, so that he never assents; but retains the latter [kind of assent], with the result that by following convincingness he can respond "yes" whenever it is present or "no" whatever it is missing. (*Academica* II.104; LS 69 I)

Catulus, in the conversation, invokes the opposing Philonian position:

> I return to the view of my father, who said it was also Carneades' view: although I hold that nothing can be perceived, I also think that the wise man will assent to something which is not perceived, i.e., will opine and hold a [mere] opinion, but in such a way that he realizes that he is opining and that there is nothing which can be grasped and perceived. Hence, while I † . . . †[12] approve the suspension of judgment over all things, I vehemently assent to that other position, that there is nothing which can be perceived. (II.148; LS 69 K, IG III–15)

Philo seems to hold that to follow the probable is to say "yes" or "no" to certain impressions against the background awareness that no one has knowledge. Philo's interpretation is supposed to be different from Clitomachus' interpretation,[13] but because these passages in Cicero's *Academica* are the primary evidence for this extremely important debate within the Academy, it is very difficult if not impossible to understand the details of these competing interpretations.

It is clear, however, as a matter of historical fact, that Philo won the dispute within the Academy about how Carneades should be understood. Furthermore, it is clear that Philo consolidated his position in a way that seemed to narrow the ground between the Skeptics and their opponents. In his "Roman Books," Philo argues that although there is no "knowledge," as the Stoics conceive of it, some assent does result in knowledge. Sextus Empiricus makes the point:

> Philo says that, so far as the Stoic criterion is concerned, i.e., the cognitive impression, things are unknowable, but, so far as the nature of things themselves is concerned, knowable. (*Outlines of Pyrrhonism* I.235; LS 68 T)

Philo argues that assent in terms of the probable may issue in knowledge because assent need not meet the Stoic requirement to issue in knowledge. This had not been sufficiently realized, according to Philo, because the Stoics had been allowed to frame the terms of the debate.

These developments caused considerable internal strife within the Academy, and they eventually prompted Aenesidemus (first century BC) to found a breakaway Skeptical movement under the name of "Pyrrhonian Skepticism."[14] To Aenesidemus, the Academy had lost its way under the leadership of Philo. Instead of resisting dogmatism in the manner of Socrates, the Academy lapsed into a family dispute with the Stoics. To his dismay, the Academy had become "Stoics fighting with Stoics" because its members were wrongly content to "determine many things firmly."[q]

The development of Pyrrhonian Skepticism is extremely important in the history of ancient philosophy and in the history of philosophy generally,[r] but it falls outside the Period of Schools. In about 100 BC, the critical attitude to the prior classical tradition began to give way to a resurgence of interest in non-skeptical forms of Platonism. This interest grew stronger over time, and after Philo's death in 83 BC, the Academy itself ceased to function.[s] There was less and less interest in the conception of rationality that the Skeptics were trying to articulate and defend. Eventually, in the third century, the Pyrrhonian school itself closed. The surviving strand of the Skeptical movement had come to an end, and Skepticism soon was rejected as a mistake from the past.[t]

---

[q] Aenesidemus' works have not survived, but some of what he wrote was summarized by Photius in his *Bibliotheca*. Photius was the Christian patriarch of Constantinople in the ninth century. His *Bibliotheca* is a collection of extracts from and abridgments of classical authors that he read. *Bibliotheca* 212 is entitled "Aenesidemus, *Pyrrhonian Writings*." Long and Sedley (1987) translate the relevant passages in 71 C and 72 L.

[r] Among other things, the development is important for the way it incorporates an empiricist tradition from medicine. "One of the more intriguing facts in the history of ancient Greek medicine and philosophy concerns the close relation between the Empirical school and Pyrrhonian skepticism. According to the list preserved by Diogenes Laertius, apart from Sextus Empricus himself, a further five of the eight heads of the Pyrrhonian school after Aenesdemus, its probable founder, were also Empirical physicians (D.L. 9.115)" (James Allen, *Inference from Signs*, 2001, 89).

[s] In the Mithridatic War, Athens and other Greek cities revolted against their Roman masters. In 86, as punishment, Rome had the general Sula lay siege to Athens. Sula looted and destroyed much of the city, including the Academy and the Lyceum. Much later, in 410 AD, the Academy was re-established as the home of Neoplatonism. The school persisted until 529, when the Christian Emperor Justinian forbade pagans to teach in the schools.

[t] Michael Frede provides an elegant statement of the historical situation and the pressures responsible for the closure of the Pyrrhonian school: "[The Skeptical understanding of human reason] was a view that quickly lost ground during the second and third centuries. We know of only one successor of Sextus in the third century, Saturninus (D L IX 116). The temptation had become too great: if mere reason could not lead us to the truth we need for our salvation and beatitude, it would require cleansed, purified, and illuminated reason, perhaps even reason in the light of some revelation; but whatever it takes, we must have the real truth if our lives are not to fail" ("The Skeptic's beliefs," 1987f, 199). cf. "The Skeptic's two kinds of assent," 1987g, 218: "[L]ater antiquity found some form of Platonism or other, in Christian or pagan garb, more congenial, and thus skepticism, with some odd exceptions like Uranius in the sixth century (cf. Agathias, *Historiarum libri quinque* II, 29, 7), came to be a historical position to be vehemently rejected. . . ."

Notes

1. Diogenes Laertius lists the 41 titles of Epicurus' "best" books, and the work *Of nature* itself was composed of thirty-seven books (*Lives and Opinions of the Philosophers* X27). This has all disappeared. What is now known about Epicurus and his philosophy depends primarily on three letters Diogenes quotes in Book X of his *Lives and Opinions of the Philosophers*: *Letter to Herodotus* (which outlines the Epicurean philosophy of nature), *Letter to Pythocles* (which discusses natural phenomena in the sky), and *Letter to Menoeceus* (which outlines the Epicurean position on happiness). In addition to the letters, Diogenes includes a set of short remarks known as the *Principal Doctrines*. Finally, there is a collection of sayings preserved in the Vatican Library known as the *Gnomologium Vaticanum Epicureum*.

2. Michael Frede provides this sort of explanation and interpretation of the Epicurean rejection of dialectic: "Epicurus' *Letter to Herodotus*, for instance, is replete with references to memory. He tells us to remember firmly the basic principles of Epicureanism, in fact to memorise them. What is behind these admonitions does not seem to be just the trivial view that if one wants to be an Epicurean one had better remember the basic tenets of Epircureanism, but rather the view that our whole way of thinking is determined by our memory, by what we remember having experienced and what we have committed to memory in the, perhaps wrong, belief that it is the case. It is tempting to think that Epicurus' rejection of dialectic or logic is related to this (see D.L. x.31). As understood by Platonists, Peripatetics or Stoics, dialectic or logic, as we noted earlier, is based on the assumption that there are certain relations between terms or propositions, or rather their counterparts in the world, such that in virtue of these relations certain things follow from, or are excluded by, other things. Dialectic teaches us to see these sometimes complex relations and to reason accordingly. In fact, this is what it is to reason, to argue on the basis of one's adequate or inadequate grasp of, or insight into, these relations. So when Epicurus rejects dialectic, one is inclined to assume that he is rejecting this rationalist view of thought and inference . . ." ("An empiricist view of knowledge: Memorism," 1990, 240–241).

3. The abbreviation 'LS' refers to the texts in *The Hellenistic Philosophers* by A. A. Long and D. N. Sedley (1987). This is the standard set of English translations of the principal sources for the Hellenistic philosophers. Long and Sedley arrange the sources according to subject matter. Within numbered chapters, they assign each source a letter and subdivide it into numbered sentences. My translations are based closely on those in *The Hellenistic Philosophers* and on those in *Hellenistic Philosophy. Introductory Readings*, by Brad Inwood and L. P. Gerson (1997).

4. Epicurus seems to have thought that autonomous human action is not compatible with atomism unless the atoms sometimes "swerve" without themselves having been caused to swerve. He does not make this claim in the

surviving fragments, but he is clearly aware of the problem. In the *Letter to Menoeceus*, Epicurus says the "fate of the natural philosophers" carries an "inexorable necessity" and therefore is incompatible with human autonomy: "Whom do you consider superior to the man who ... would deride the fate which some introduce as overlord of everything, but sees that some things are necessitated, others are due to fortune, and others depend on us, since necessity is accountable to no one, and fortune is an unstable thing to watch, while that which depends on us, with which culpability and its opposite are naturally associated, is free of an overlord? For it would be better to follow the mythology about gods than be a slave to the fate (εἱμαρμένη) of the naturalists: the former at least hints at the hope of begging the gods off by means of worship, whereas the latter involves an inexorable necessity" (X.133–134; LS 20 A). Cicero provides related texts that help fill in the details in the interpretation. See, for example, *On Divination* I.125–6; LS 55 L and *On Fate*, 22–23; LS 20 E.

5. Many scholars have expressed a negative assessment of Epicurus' argument for the "unique consistency of atomism." Terence Irwin is an influential example: "[Epicurus'] arguments . . . seem to show only that [atomism] is consistent with observation; he hardly shows that it is the only theory of this sort. It seems easy to imagine a non-atomist account of the world that is consistent with the senses" (*Classical Thought*, 1989, 153).

6. This is Michael Frede's translation: "The Stoic doctrine of the affections of the soul," 1986, 97.

7. The point is common in the secondary literature. "The absence of the Stoic account of any faculty of the soul corresponding to the Platonic or Aristotelian desire or appetite is significant. For Chrysippus all functioning of the human ruling principle is rational – not of course in the sense that it is in accordance with right reason, but in the sense that it involves an exercise of judgment" (R. W. Sharples, *Stoics, Epicureans and Skeptics*, 1996, 68). "The views of the Hellenistic philosophical schools on the nature of the human soul mark one more very important point of contrast to those of Plato and Aristotle. And if we may dare one more -ism, let us label this belief the Socraticism of Epicurus and the Stoics. In the earliest dialogues of Plato, those in which we conventionally assume that Socrates' own views are expressed most clearly, there is, fairly obviously, an assumption that the human soul is fundamentally and exclusively a rational entity. For ethical purposes, it is assumed throughout the early dialogues that reason dominates the life of the soul to such a degree that rational decisions about the best life fully determine the behavior of the human being. That view was eventually rejected by Plato and Aristotle, both of whom argued for the existence in the soul of fundamentally non-rational desiderative powers, which were, to be sure, amenable to control by reason, but which nevertheless were quasi-autonomous in their function. . . . The Epicureans and the orthodox Stoics returned to the view of Socrates, that the entire human soul was dominated by reason, that all of its desiderative states and powers were

in some way expressions of a man's beliefs and decisions" (Brad Inwood and L. P. Gerson, *Hellenstic Philosophy. Introductory Readings*, 1997, xviii).

8. Michael Frede makes the general point, and I have followed his interpretation: "The Stoics revert to Socrates' extreme intellectualism. They deny an irrational part of the soul. The soul is a mind or reason. Its contents are impressions or thoughts, to which the mind gives assent or prefers to give assent. In giving assent to an impression, we espouse a belief. Desires are just beliefs of a certain kind, the product of our assent to a so-called impulsive impression" ("The philosopher," 2000, 10). "[T]he emotional character of the emotion has its source in the distinctive feature of impulsive impressions as being disturbing or being tempting, as opposed to other impressions, as the case may be. But this is a genuine integral feature of rational impressions, that is to say of impressions produced by reason. And this feature, in turn, has its source in certain beliefs of reason. If I did not believe that death was a bad thing, or money a good thing, the mere thought that I was going to die next year would not be disturbing, and the mere thought that I might have a lot of money if I just robbed a bank would not be tempting" ("The Stoic conception of reason," 1993–1994, 60).

9. Since, according to the Stoics, everything that happens is a matter of the providence and immanent reason in the universe, everything that happens is in accordance with nature. Hence, it would seem that all actions are "appropriate," or "fitting," but not necessarily "correct" and hence virtuous. Gisela Striker describes the distinction: "An action may be objectively appropriate without being done for the right sort of reason. For example, people will eat and drink, or avoid precipices, without considering whether such practices conform to nature's general rule to keep oneself alive and well. Here the action will be merely appropriate, but not perfectly right, not what the Stoics called a *katorhoma*, since what makes an action perfect or good in the strict sense is that it be done with the intention of following nature, and from a stable disposition so to act. Only thus will one act in agreement with nature, as opposed to merely leading a natural life (*kata phusin bios*). Virtue, according to the Stoics, is achieved when one's every action is both appropriate and done for the right reason. Since such a stable disposition is only reached at the stage of complete wisdom, perfectly right actions are reserved to the wise" ("Following nature: A study in Stoic ethics," 1996, 252). In just what the "right reason" consists is not completely clear, but the correct understanding of the good seems to be an essential part of it.

10. Here, as so often in other cases, I have followed Michael Frede's interpretation: "[T]he Stoic sage does not gain his equanimity by shedding human concerns, but by coming to realise what these concerns are meant to be, and hence what they ought to be, namely the means by which nature maintains its natural, rational order. And we have to realize that in this order our concerns play a very, very subordinate role, and are easily overridden by more important considerations, though we may find it difficult to accept this. But it does not follow from the fact that they play a very subordinate role, that they play no role whatsoever.

Nature is provident down to the smallest detail. Hence it must be a caricature of the wise man to think that he has become insensitive to human concerns and only thus manages to achieve his equanimity. Things do move him, but not in such a way as to disturb his balanced judgment and make him attribute an importance to them which they do not have" ("The Stoic doctrine of the affections of the soul," 1986, 110). "Claims sometimes made to the contrary notwithstanding, even the Stoic sage is not omniscient. He disposes of a general body of knowledge in virtue of which he has a general understanding of the world. But this knowledge does not put him into a position to know what he is supposed to do in a concrete situation. It does not even allow him to know all the facts which are relevant to a decision in a particular situation. He, for instance, does not know whether the ship he considers embarking on will reach its destination. The Stoic emphasis on intention, as opposed to the outcome or the consequences of an action, in part is due to the assumption that the outcome, as opposed to the intention, is a matter of fate and hence not only not, or at least not completely, under our control, but also, as a rule, unknown to us. Therefore, even the perfect rationality of the sage is a rationality which relies on experience and conjecture, and involves following what is reasonable or probable. It is crucially a perfect rationality under partial ignorance" ("Introduction," in *Rationality in Greek Thought*, 1996a, 16–17).

11. This is the standard interpretation of the transition within the Academy. A. A. Long and D. N. Sedley put the point as follows: "If, as seems likely, Polemo and his contemporaries had already begun to react against the efforts of their predecessors, Speusippus and Xenocrates, to create a hard-and-fast system of Plato's dialogues, this will have encouraged Arcesilaus to challenge the whole enterprise of reading Plato as a doctrinaire philosopher" (*The Hellenistic Philosophers*, I: *Translations of the Principal Sources with Philosophical Commentary*, 1987, 445).

12. The text here is corrupt. It can be read as asserting either the rejection or the affirmation of the commitment to the suspension of judgment. For discussion, see Charles Brittain's *Philo of Larissa. The Last of the Academic Skeptics*, 2001, 80.

13. Charles Brittain offers this interpretation: "On the Clitomachean view of Carneades, however, while the Academics will 'follow' persuasive impressions, or 'approve' them, they will not *assent* to them: that is, the Academics will act on such impressions without taking them to be *true*. . . . The crucial difference [is between] the purely subjective Clitomachian interpretation of the pithanon under which there is no inference from what is persuasive to what is true . . . [and] the Philonian/Metrodorians' quasi-objective use of it as evidence for truth. . . . [T]he Philonian/Metrodorians took over the Clitomachean version of Carneades' schema, but understood the persuasiveness of their impressions to have objective grounds, and thus to produce (in some cases) provisional or 'probable' results" (*Philo of Larissa. The Last of the Academic Skeptics*, 2001, 16). Brittain makes similar remarks in *Cicero. On Academic Skepticism*: "Hence,

Clitomachus argued, we should distinguish between 'assenting' to an impression in the Stoic sense and 'approving' it in one of these latter ways, i.e., acting on it *as if* we took it to be true. The Academic thus gives his approval to the impression he acts on – he 'follows' persuasive impressions – but does not assent to them (*Ac.* 2.104)" (2006, xxvii). "[T]he mitigated skeptics will assent to persuasive impression or claims when the evidence supporting them is sufficiently strong – and they assume that persuasiveness under the appropriate conditions does provide *evidence* for the truth (cf. Sextus M.7.435–38)" (2006, xxix). For more discussion, and a different interpretation of the Clitomachean and Philonian positions, see Michael Frede, "The skeptic's two kinds of assent and the question of the possibility of knowledge" (1987g).

14. This is a standard interpretation of the birth of Pyrrhonian Skepticism. "[As the Academy] under the headship of Philo of Larissa in the early first century BC drifted away from its skeptical stance, one disillusioned member, Aenesidemus, founded a breakaway movement, under the title 'Pyrrhonists.' This was the group which in time – probably not before the mid-first century AD – became known as the 'Skeptics,' literally 'searchers.' Another title was *ephektikoi*, 'suspenders of judgment.' The eventual outlook of the school is well presented in the surviving works of Sextus Empiricus, who wrote in the second century AD" (A. A. Long and D. N. Sedley, *The Hellenistic Philosophers*, I: *Translations of the Principal Sources with Philosophical Commentary*, 1987, 470).

Further Reading for Part V

1. *The Stoic Life. Emotions, Duties, and Fate*, Tad Brennan, 2005
   This is a good introduction to certain issues in Stoicism. The questions Brennan seeks to answers are these: "What is it to be a Stoic, that is, to live as the Stoic philosophers told us we should live? And why would one want to live like that – why be a Stoic?" The discussion is more philosophical than historical.
2. *The Development of Ethics*, Volume 1. *From Socrates to the Reformation*, Terence Irwin, 2007
   In chapters 10–14, Irwin discusses the Skeptics, Epicurus, and the Stoics. The discussion is detailed and interesting. As with the other parts of the book, there is "philosophical discussion as well as description and exegesis" (1).
3. *Hellenistic Philosophy. Stoics, Epicureans, Skeptics*, A. A. Long, 2nd edn., 1986
   This may be the best general introduction to Hellenistic philosophy. It is both scholarly and readable. The "purpose of this book is to trace the main developments in Greek philosophy during the period which runs from the death of Alexander the Great in 323 BC to the end of the Roman Republic (31 BC)" (vii).
4. *Ancient Ethics. A Critical Introduction*. Susan Sauvé Meyer, 2008b
   This is a very nice history of ancient ethics, and the final chapters on Epicurus and the Stoics are especially valuable. Throughout the work Meyer combines historical sensitivity with philosophical insight.
5. *Epicureanism*, Tim O'Keefe, 2010
   This is a general introduction to Epicureanism. The discussion is both historical and philosophical.
6. *Epicurus: An Introduction*, J. M. Rist, 1972.
   In this book, Rist "present[s] an elementary account of what we know about the philosophy of Epicurus" (x). The discussion is more historical than philosophical.
7. *Stoics, Epicureans and Skeptics. An introduction to Hellenistic philosophy*, R. W. Sharples, 1996
   This is another good introduction to Hellenistic philosophy. The book has the "following aims: to introduce the subject in a way which requires no previous knowledge of either the ancient world or of contemporary philosophy, but which will be of interest to students who already have knowledge of either or both of these; and to bring out the interest of this period of philosophical thought not only in the historical context of the ancient culture which it influenced, but also for us now" (ix). It is somewhat more accessible than Long's *Hellenistic Philosophy*.
8. *Ancient Skepticism*, Harald Thorsrud, 2009
   This is a general introduction to Academic and Pyrrhonian Skepticism. The discussion is more historical than philosophical. Thorsrud says he tries "first and foremost to provide historically accurate accounts of the development of Academic and Pyrrhonian Skepticism" (15). The bibliography is especially valuable.

References

Ackrill, J. L. (1963) Aristotle's Categories *and* De Interpretatione. Oxford University Press.

Ackrill, J. L. (1973) *Aristotle's Ethics*. Humanities Press.

Ackrill, J. L. (1981) *Aristotle The Philosopher*. Oxford University Press.

Adam, J. (1905) *The Republic of Plato*. Cambridge University Press.

Allen, James (2001) *Inference from Signs*. Oxford University Press.

Allen, R. E. (1984) Euthyphro, Apology, Crito, Meno, Gorgias, Menexenus. *The Dialogues of Plato*. Yale University Press.

Annas, Julia (1981) *An Introduction to Plato's* Republic. Oxford University Press.

Annas, Julia (1988) Classical Greek philosophy. *The Oxford History of Greece and the Hellenistic World* (ed. J. Boardman, J. Griffin and O. Murrary), 277–305. Oxford University Press.

Annas, Julia (2000) *Ancient Philosophy. A Very Short Introduction*. Oxford University Press.

Annas, Julia (2001) *Voices of Ancient Philosophy. An Introductory Reader*. Oxford University Press.

Barnes, Jonathan (1979) *The Presocratic Philosophers*. Vol. 1: *Thales to Zeno*. Vol. 2: *Empedocles to Democritus*. Routledge & Kegan Paul.

Barnes, Jonathan (1982) *Aristotle*. Oxford University Press.

Barnes, Jonathan (1984) *The Complete Works of Aristotle. A Revised Oxford Translation*. 2 vols. Princeton University Press.

Barnes, Jonathan (1987) *Early Greek Philosophy*. Penguin.

Barnes, Jonathan (2006) Bagpipe music. *Topoi* 25, 17–20.

Bluck, R. S. (1961) *Plato's Meno*. Cambridge University Press.

Bobonich, Christopher (2006) Aristotle's ethical treatises. *The Blackwell Guide to Aristotle's Nicomachean Ethics* (ed. Richard Kraut), 12–36. Blackwell.

Brennan, Tad (2003) Stoic Moral Psychology. *The Cambridge Companion to the Stoics* (ed. Brad Inwood), 257–294. Cambridge University Press.

Brennan, Tad (2005) *The Stoic Life*. Oxford University Press.

Brickhouse, Thomas and Nicholas Smith (2000) *The Philosophy of Socrates*. Westview Press.

Brittain, Charles (2001) *Philo of Larissa. The Last of the Academic Sceptics*. Oxford University Press.

Ancient Greek Philosophy: From The Presocratics to the Hellenistic Philosophers, First Edition.
Thomas A. Blackson. © 2011 Thomas A. Blackson. Published 2011 by Blackwell Publishing Ltd.

Brittain, Charles (2006) *Cicero. On Academic Scepticism.* Hackett Publishing Company.

Broadie, Sarah (1991) *Ethics with Aristotle.* Oxford University Press.

Broadie, Sarah (2002) Philosophical introduction. *Aristotle.* Nicomachean Ethics (Sarah Broadie and Christopher Rowe), 9–91. Oxford University Press.

Burnet, John (1900–7) *Platonis Opera.* 5 vols. Oxford University Press.

Burnet, John (1900) *The Ethics of Aristotle.* Methuen & Co.

Burnet, John (1911) *Plato's Phaedo.* Oxford University Press.

Burnet, John (1920) *Early Greek Philosophy,* 3rd edn. Adam & Charles Black.

Burnet, John (1968) The Socratic doctrine of the soul. Second Annual Philosophical Lecture. Read to the British Academy, January 26, 1916. Reprinted in *Essays and Addresses,* 126–162. Books for Libraries Press.

Caston, Victor (2006) Aristotle's psychology. *A Companion to Ancient Philosophy* (ed. Mary Louise Gill and Pierre Pellegrin), 316–346. Blackwell.

Charlton, W. (1970) *Aristotle's* Physics I, II. Oxford University Press.

Cherniss, Harold (1954) A much misread passage in the *Timaeus* (*Timaeus* 49c7–50b5). *American Journal of Philology* 75, 113–130.

Code, Alan (1978) No universal is a substance: an interpretation of *Metaphysics* Z.13, 1038b 8–15. *Paideia: Special Aristotle Issue,* 65–74.

Cohen, S. Marc (2000) *Readings in Ancient Greek Philosophy: From Thales to Aristotle* (ed. S. Marc Cohen, Patricia Curd, and C. D. C. Reeve). Hackett Publishing Company.

Cohen, S. Marc (2008) Aristotle's metaphysics. *Stanford Encyclopedia of Philosophy.*

Cooper, John M. (1997) *Plato, Complete Works.* Hackett Publishing Company.

Cooper, John M. (1997) Introduction. *Plato, Complete Works.* Hackett Publishing Company, 1997.

Cooper, John M. (1999) Plato's theory of human motivation. *Reason and Emotion. Essays on Ancient Moral Psychology and Ethical Theory* (ed. John Cooper), 118–137. Princeton University Press.

Cooper, John M. (1999) The psychology of justice in Plato. *Reason and Emotion. Essays on Ancient Moral Psychology and Ethical Theory* (ed. John Cooper), 138–149. Princeton University Press.

Cornford, F. M. (1932) *Before and After Socrates.* Cambridge University Press.

Cornford, F. M. (1937) *Plato's Cosmology.* Routledge & Kegan Paul.

DeLacy, Philip. (1939) The problem of causation in Plato's philosophy. *Classical Philology* 34, 97–115.

Diels, H. and Kranz, W. (1952) *Die Fragmente der Vorsokratiker,* 6th edn. Berlin: Weidmann.

Ferejohn, Michael (1991) *The Origins of Aristotelian Science.* Yale University Press.

Ferejohn, Michael (2007) Empiricism and first principles of Aristotelian science. *A Companion To Aristotle* (ed. G. Anagnostopoulis), 66–80. Blackwell.

Frede, Michael (1985) Introduction. *Galen. Three Treatises on the Nature of Science* (trans. Richard Walzer and Michael Frede), ix–xxxvi. Hackett Publishing Company.

Frede, Michael (1986) The Stoic doctrine of the affections of the soul. *The Norms of Nature* (ed. Malcolm Schofield and Gisela Striker), 93–110. Cambridge University Press.

Frede, Michael (1987a) Introduction: The study of ancient philosophy. *Essays in Ancient Philosophy* (ed. Michael Frede), ix–xxvii. University of Minnesota Press.

Frede, Michael (1987b) The title, unity, and authenticity of the Aristotelian *Categories*. *Essays in Ancient Philosophy* (ed. Michael Frede), 11–28. University of Minnesota Press.

Frede, Michael (1987c) Individuals in Aristotle. *Essays in Ancient Philosophy* (ed. Michael Frede), 49–71. University of Minnesota Press.

Frede, Michael (1987d) Substance in Aristotle's *Metaphysics*. *Essays in Ancient Philosophy* (ed. Michael Frede), 72–80. University of Minnesota Press.

Frede, Michael (1987e) The unity of general and special metaphysics: Aristotle's conception of metaphysics. *Essays in Ancient Philosophy* (ed. Michael Frede), 81–95. University of Minnesota Press.

Frede, Michael (1987f) The Sceptic's beliefs. *Essays in Ancient Philosophy* (ed. Michael Frede), 179–200. University of Minnesota Press.

Frede, Michael (1987g) The Sceptic's two kinds of assent and the question of the possibility of knowledge. *Essays in Ancient Philosophy* (ed. Michael Frede), 201–222. University of Minnesota Press.

Frede, Michael (1987h) Philosophy and medicine in antiquity. *Essays in Ancient Philosophy* (ed. Michael Frede), 225–242. University of Minnesota Press.

Frede, Michael (1988) Being and becoming in Plato. *Oxford Studies in Ancient Philosophy. Supplementary Volume*, 37–52.

Frede, Michael (1990) An empiricist view of knowledge: Memorism. *Companions to Ancient Thought*. Vol. I: *Epistemology* (ed. Stephen Everson), 225–250. Cambridge University Press.

Frede, Michael (1992a) On Aristotle's conception of the soul. Modern thinkers and ancient thinkers: the Stanley Victor Keeling memorial lectures, 1981–1991 (ed. Robert W. Sharples), 138–156. Westview Press, 1993. Revised in *Essays on Aristotle's De Anima* (ed. Martha Nussbaum and Amelie Rorty), 93–107. Oxford University Press.

Frede, Michael (1992b) Introduction. *Plato*. Protagoras (trans., with notes, by Stanley Lombardo and Karen Bell), vii–xxxii. Hackett Publishing Company.

Frede, Michael (1993–4) The Stoic conception of reason. *Hellenistic Philosophy* (ed. K. Boudouris), 50–60. Athens: International Society for Greek Philosophy and Culture.

Frede, Michael (1996a) Introduction. *Rationality in Greek Thought* (ed. Michael Frede and Gisela Striker), 1–28. Oxford University Press.

Frede, Michael (1996b) Aristotle's rationalism. *Rationality in Greek Thought* (ed. Michael Frede and Gisela Striker), 157–173. Oxford University Press.

Frede, Michael (1999a) Stoic epistemology. *The Cambridge History of Hellenistic Philosophy* (ed. Keimpe Algra, Jonathan Barnes, Jaap Mansfeld, and Malcolm Schofield), 295–322. Cambridge University Press.

Frede, Michael (1999b) Epilogue. *The Cambridge History of Hellenistic Philosophy* (ed. Keimpe Algra, Jonathan Barnes, Jaap Mansfeld, and Malcolm Schofield), 771–797. Cambridge University Press.

Frede, Michael (1999c) On the Stoic conception of the good. *Topics in Stoic Philosophy* (ed. Katerina Ierodiakonou), 71–94. Oxford University Press.

Frede, Michael (2000) The philosopher. *Greek Thought. A Guide to Classical Knowledge* (ed. Jacques Brunschwig and Geoffrey E. R. Lloyd), 1–18. Harvard University Press.

Frede, Michael (2004) Aristotle's account of the origins of philosophy. *Rhizai: Journal for Ancient Philosophy and Science* 1, 9–44.

Furth, Montgomery (1985) *Aristotle*, Metaphysics. *Books Zeta, Eta, Theta, Iota (VII–X)*. Hackett Publishing Company.

Furth, Montgomery (1988) *Substance, Form and Psyche: An Aristotelian Metaphysics*. Cambridge University Press.

Gallop, David (1986) *Plato, Phaedo*. Oxford University Press.

Gill, M. L. and Pellegrin, Pierre (2006) Introduction. *A Companion to Ancient Philosophy* (ed. Mary Louise Gill and Pierre Pellegrin), xxix–xxxvi. Blackwell.

Guthrie, W. K. C. (1962) *A History of Greek Philosophy*. Vol. I: *The Earlier Presocratics and Pythagoreans*. Cambridge University Press.

Guthrie, W. K. C. (1965) *A History of Greek Philosophy*. Vol. II: *The Presocratic Tradition from Parmenides to Democritus*. Cambridge University Press.

Guthrie, W. K. C. (1971) *A History of Greek Philosophy*. Vol. III: *The Fifth-Century Enlightenment*. Part 1: *The Sophists*; Part 2: *Socrates*. Cambridge University Press.

Hackforth, R. (1959) Plato's cosmogony (*Timaeus* 27dff.). *Classical Quarterly* 9, 17–22.

Hadot, Pierre (2002) *What is Ancient Philosophy?* (trans. Michael Chase). Harvard University Press.

Hardie, W. F. R. (1936) *A Study in Plato*. Oxford University Press.

Heidel, William (1933) *The Heroic Age of Science*. Williams & Wilkins.

Hicks, R. D. (1972) *Diogenes Laertius. Lives of Eminent Philosophers*, Vol. 1. Harvard University Press.

Hussey, Edward (1972) *The Presocratics*. Duckworth.

Hussey, Edward (2006) The beginnings of science and philosophy. *A Companion to Ancient Philosophy* (ed. Mary Louise Gill and Pierre Pellegrin), 3–19. Blackwell.

Hussey, Edward (1999) Heraclitus. *The Cambridge Companion to Early Greek Philosophy* (ed. A. A. Long), 88–112. Cambridge University Press.

Inwood, Brad (2001) *The Poem of Empedocles*. University of Toronto Press.

Inwood, Brad and Gerson, L. P. (1997) *Hellenistic Philosophy. Introductory Readings*, 2nd edn. Hackett Publishing Company.

Irwin, Terence (1977) Plato's Heracleiteanism. *Philosophical Quarterly* 27, 1–13.

Irwin, Terence (1989) *Classical Thought*. Oxford University Press.

Irwin, Terence (1995) *Plato's Ethics*. Oxford University Press.

Irwin, Terence (1999) *Classical Philosophy*. Oxford University Press.

Irwin, Terence (2007) *The Development of Ethics. A Historical and Critical Study*. Vol. 1: *From Socrates to the Reformation*. Oxford University Press.

Kahn, Charles (1968) The thesis of Parmenides. *The Review of Metaphysics* 22, 700–724.

Kahn, Charles (1973) Language and ontology in Plato's *Cratylus*. *Exegesis and Argument* (ed. E. Lee et al.), 152–176. Van Gorcum.

Kahn, Charles (1979) *The Art and Thought of Heraclitus*. Cambridge University Press.

Kahn, Charles (1985) Democritus and the origins of moral psychology. *The American Journal of Philology* 106, 1–31.

Kahn, Charles (1991) The origins of Greek science and philosophy. *Science and Philosophy in Classical Greece* (ed. A. C. Bowen), 1–10. Garland.

Kahn, Charles (1996) *Plato and the Socratic dialogue*. Cambridge University Press.

Kahn, Charles (1998) Pre-Platonic ethics. *Companions to Ancient Thought*. Vol. 4: *Ethics* (ed. Stephen Everson), 27–48. Cambridge University Press.

Kahn, Charles (2004) From *Republic* to *Laws*. A discussion of Christopher Bobonich, *Plato's* Utopia Recast. *Oxford Studies in Ancient Philosophy*, 25, 337–362.

Kahn, Charles (2001) *Pythagoras and the Pythagoreans*. Hackett Publishing Company.

Kerferd, G. B. (1981) *The Sophistic Movement*. Cambridge University Press.

Kirk, G. S., Raven, J. E., and Schofield, M. (1983) *The Presocratic Philosophers. A Critical History with a Selection of Texts*, 2nd edition. Cambridge University Press.

Kraut, Richard (1992) The defense of justice in Plato's *Republic*. *A Cambridge Companion to Plato* (ed. Richard Kraut), 311–337 Cambridge University Press.

Kraut, Richard (2010) Aristotle's Ethics. *Stanford Encyclopedia of Philosophy*.

Lawrence, Gavin (1993) Aristotle and the ideal life. *The Philosophical Review* 102, 1–34.

Lear, Gabriel (2004) *Happy Lives and the Highest Good. An Essay on Aristotle's Nicomachean Ethics*. Princeton University Press.

Lear, Jonathan (1988) *Aristotle. The Desire to Understand*. Cambridge University Press.

Lee, Edward (1967) On Plato's *Timaeus*, 49D4–E7. *American Journal of Philology* 88, 1–28.

Lennox, James G. (2006) Aristotle's biology and Aristotle's philosophy. *A Companion to Ancient Philosophy* (ed. Mary Louise Gill and Pierre Pellegrin), 292–315. Blackwell.

Liddell, H. G. and Scott, R. (1976) *A Lexicon. Abridged from Liddell and Scott's Greek-English Lexicon*. Oxford University Press.

Long, A. A. (1986) *Hellenistic Philosophy. Stoics, Epicureans, Skeptics*. 2nd edn. University of California Press.

Long, A. A. (1999a) Lives and writings of the early Greek philosophers. *The Cambridge Companion to Early Greek Philosophy* (ed. A. A. Long), xvii–xxviii. Cambridge University Press.

Long, A. A. (1999b) The scope of early Greek philosophy. *The Cambridge Companion to Early Greek Philosophy* (ed. A. A. Long), 1–21. Cambridge University Press.

Long, A. A. and Sedley, D. N. (1987) *The Hellenistic Philosophers*. Vol. I: *Translations of the Principal Sources, with Philosophical Commentary*. Vol. II: *Greek and Latin Texts, with Notes and Bibliography*. Cambridge University Press.

Long, Herbert S. (1972) Introduction *Diogenes Laertius. Lives of Eminent Philosophers*, iv–xxx. Loeb Classical Library. Harvard University Press.

Lonie, I. (1981) *The Hippocratic Treatises On Generation, On the Nature of the Child, Disease IV: A Commentary*. Walter de Gruyter.

Lord, Carnes (1981) The character and composition of Aristotle's *Politics. Political Theory* 9, 459–478.

Lorenz, Hendrik (2006) *The Brute Within. Appetitive Desire in Plato and Aristotle*. Oxford University Press.

Mann, Wolfgang-Rainer (2000) *The Discovery of Things. Aristotle's Categories and their Context*. Princeton University Press.

Mansfeld, J. (1999) Sources. *The Cambridge Companion to Early Greek Philosophy* (ed. A. A. Long), 22–44. Cambridge University Press.

Mansfeld, J. (2008) Doxography of ancient philosophy. *Stanford Encyclopedia of Philosophy*.

Matthews, Gareth B. (1982) Accidental unities. *Language and Logos* (ed. M. Schofield and M.C. Nussbaum), 223–40. Cambridge University Press.

Matthews, Gareth B. (2009) Whatever became of the Socratic Elenchus? Philosophical analysis in Plato. *Philosophy Compass* 4/3, 439–450.

Matthews, Gareth B. (1999) *Socratic Perplexity and the Nature of Philosophy*. Oxford University Press.

Matthews, Gareth B. On knowing how to take Aristotle's kooky objects seriously. Unpublished manuscript.

McKirahan, Jr., Richard (1994) *Philosophy Before Socrates. An Introduction with Texts and Commentary*. Hackett Publishing Company.

McPherran, Mark L. (1996) *The Religion of Socrates*. The Pennsylvania State University Press.

Mejer, Jorgen (2006) Ancient philosophy and the doxographical tradition. *A Companion to Ancient Philosophy* (ed. Mary Louise Gill and Pierre Pellegrin), 20–33. Blackwell.

Meyer, Susan Sauvé (2008a) Aristotle, teleology, and reduction. *Philosophical Review* 101(1992), 791–825.

Meyer, Susan Sauvé (2008b) *Ancient Ethics. A Critical Introduction*. Routledge.

Morrison, Donald (2003) Happiness, rationality, and egoism in Plato's Socrates, in *Rationality and Happiness: From the Ancients to the Early Medievals* (ed. Jiyuan Yu and Jorge J. E. Gracia), 17–34. The University of Rochester Press.

Mourelatos, Alexander (2006) The concept of the universal in some later pre-Platonic cosmologists. *A Companion to Ancient Philosophy* (ed. Mary Louise Gill and Pierre Pellegrin), 56–76. Blackwell.

Nagel, Thomas (1986) *The View from Nowhere.* Oxford University Press.

O'Keefe, Tim (2010) *Epicureanism.* Acumen.

Pellegrin, Pierre (2006) The Aristotelian way. *A Companion to Ancient Philosophy* (ed. Mary Louise Gill and Pierre Pellegrin), 235–244. Blackwell.

Penner, Terry (1991) Desire and power in Socrates: the argument of *Gorgias* 466a–468e that orators and tyrants have no power in the city. *Aperion* 24, 147–202.

Penner, Terry (2007) What is the form of the good the form *of*? A question about the plot of the *Republic. Pursuing the Good. Ethics and Metaphysics in Plato's* Republic (ed. Douglas Cairns, Fritz-Gregor Herrmann, and Terry Penner), 15–41. University of Edinburgh Press.

Penner, Terry and Rowe, Christopher (1994) The desire for good: Is the *Meno* consistent with the *Gorgias? Phronesis* 39, 1–25.

Prior, William J. (1985) *Unity and Development in Plato's Metaphysics.* Croom Helm.

Pritchard, H. A. (1949) Moral obligation, in *Moral Obligation: Essays and Lectures by H. A. Pritchard* (ed. David Ross), 87–163. Oxford University Press.

Ring, Merrill (2000) *Beginning with the pre-Socratics,* 2nd edn. Mayfield Publishing Company.

Rist, J. M. (1972) *Epicurus: An Introduction.* Cambridge University Press.

Roochnik, David (2004) *Retrieving the Ancients. An Introduction to Greek Philosophy.* Blackwell.

Ross, David (1924) Aristotle's Metaphysics. *A Revised Text with Introduction and Commentary.* Oxford University Press.

Ross, David (1949) *Aristotle,* 5th edn. Methuen.

Ross, David (1961) *Aristotle,* De Anima. Oxford University Press.

Rowe, Christopher (1977) *An Introduction to Greek Ethics.* Harper & Row.

Rowe, Christopher (2002) Historical Introduction. *Aristotle. Nicomachean Ethics* (Sarah Broadie and Christopher Rowe), 3–8. Oxford University Press.

Rowe, Christopher (2003) *Plato,* 2nd edn. Bristol Classical Press.

Sedley, D. N. (1997) "Becoming like god" in the *Timaeus* and Aristotle. *Interpreting the* Timaeus-Critias. *Proceedings of the IV Symposium Platonicum* (ed. Tomas Calvo and Luc Brisson.), 327–339. Academica Verlag.

Sedley, D. N. (2004) *The Midwife of Platonism. Text and Subtext of Plato's* Theaetetus. Oxford University Press.

Sharples, R. W. (1985) *Plato:* Meno. Bolchazy Carducci.

Sharples, R. W. (1996) *Stoics, Epicureans, and Sceptics. An Introduction to Hellenistic Philosophy.* Routledge.

Shields, Christopher (2003) *Classical Philosophy. A Contemporary Introduction.* Routledge.

Shields, Christopher (2007) *Aristotle.* Routledge.

Shields, Christopher (2008) Aristotle. *Stanford Encyclopedia of Philosophy.*

Shields, Christopher (2010) Aristotle's psychology. *Stanford Encyclopedia of Philosophy.*

Smith, Martin Ferguson (1993) *Diogenes of Oenoanda: The Epicurean Inscription.* Bibliopolis, Naples.

Spellman, Lynne (1995) *Substance and Separation in Aristotle.* Cambridge University Press.

Striker, G. (1996) Following nature: A study in Stoic ethics. *Essays on Hellenistic Epistemology and Ethics* (ed. Gisela Striker), 221–280. Cambridge University Press.

Taylor, C. C. W. (1998a) Platonic ethics, in *Companions to Ancient Thought.* Vol. 4: *Ethics* (ed. Stephen Everson), 49–76. Cambridge University Press.

Taylor, C. C. W. (1998b) *Socrates. A Very Short Introduction.* Oxford University Press.

Thorsrud, Harald (2009) *Ancient Scepticism.* Acumen.

Vlastos, Gregory (1996) The Socratic *Elenchus. Oxford Studies in Ancient Philosophy,* Vol. 1 (1983), 27–58. Reprinted in *Socrates. Critical Assessments.* Vol. III: *Socratic Method* (ed. William J. Prior), 29–55. Routledge.

Vlastos, Gregory (1983) Afterthoughts on the Socratic *Elenchus.* Oxford Studies in Ancient Philosophy, Vol. 1 (1983), 71–74. Reprinted in *Socrates. Critical Assessments.* Vol. III: *Socratic Method* (ed. William J. Prior), 30–59. Routledge.

White, Nicholas (1979) *A Companion to Plato's* Republic. Hackett Publishing Company.

Whiting, Jennifer E. (1991) Metasubstance: Critical notice of Frede-Patzig and Furth. *The Philosophical Review* 100, 607–639.

Zeyl, Donald (1987) *Plato. Gorgias.* Translated with Introduction and Notes. Hackett Publishing Company.

Index of Passages

Ancient Greek Philosophy: From The Presocratics to the Hellenistic Philosophers, First Edition.
Thomas A. Blackson.   © 2011 Thomas A. Blackson. Published 2011 by Blackwell Publishing Ltd.

General Index

Ancient Greek Philosophy: From The Presocratics to the Hellenistic Philosophers, First Edition.
Thomas A. Blackson. © 2011 Thomas A. Blackson. Published 2011 by Blackwell Publishing Ltd.

information can be obtained
CGtesting.com
the USA
312260317
LV00007B/153/P